D0160291

BROKENNESS

SURRENDER

HOLINESS

NANCY LEIGH DeMOSS

BROKENNESS

SURRENDER

HOLINESS

A REVIVE OUR HEARTS TRILOGY

MOODY PUBLISHERS
CHICAGO

Editor: Cheryl Dunlop
Interior Design: Smartt Guys
Cover Design: Smartt Guys
Cover Photos: Daryl Benson, Douglas Walker, David Mendelsohn/Masterfile

ISBN-10: 0-8024-1282-3
ISBN-13: 978-0-8024-1282-9

We hope you enjoy this book from Moody Publishers. Our goal is to provide high-
quality, thought-provoking books and products that connect truth to your real needs
and challenges. For more information on other books and products written and produced from a biblical perspective, go to www.moodypublishers.com or write to:

Moody Publishers
820 N. LaSalle Boulevard
Chicago, IL 60610

5 7 9 10 8 6 4

Printed in the United States of America

CONTENTS

BROKENNESS

SURRENDER

HOLINESS

BROKENNESS
The Heart God Revives

Editor: Cheryl Dunlop
Interior Design: BlueFrog Design
Cover Design: Smartt Guys
Cover Photo: Daryl Benson/Masterfile

Library of Congress Cataloging-in-Publication Data

DeMoss, Nancy Leigh.
    Brokenness : the heart God revives.
        p. cm.
    Includes bibliographical references.
    ISBN-13: 978-0-8024-1281-2
    ISBN-10: 0-8024-1281-5
    1. Humility—Religious aspects—Christianity. 2. Christian life.
3. Revivals. I. Title.

BV4647.H8D46 2005
248.4—dc22
2005007375

Lord, High and Holy, meek and lowly,
Thou hast brought me to the valley of vision,
 where I live in the depths but see thee in the heights;
 hemmed in by mountains of sin I behold thy glory.

Let me learn by paradox
 that the way down is the way up,
 that to be low is to be high,
 that the broken heart is the healed heart,
 that the contrite spirit is the rejoicing spirit,
 that the repenting soul is the victorious soul,
 that to have nothing is to possess all,
 that to bear the cross is to wear the crown,
 that to give is to receive,
 that the valley is the place of vision.
Lord, in the daytime stars can be seen from deepest wells,
 and the deeper the wells the brighter thy stars shine;
Let me find thy light in my darkness,
  thy life in my death,
  thy joy in my sorrow,
  thy grace in my sin,
  thy riches in my poverty,
  thy glory in my valley.

   —from *The Valley of Vision: A Collection of Puritan*
   Prayers and Devotions

CONTENTS

FOREWORD

IN NOVEMBER 2001, I witnessed an incredible moving of God upon more than five hundred pastors and other leaders in Korea. God's presence came suddenly, and with profound and thorough conviction of sin, bringing deep repentance and personal and corporate brokenness. Some were before the Lord all night before He would let them go. They were convinced that God was inviting them to see their sin as He saw it, to quickly and thoroughly forsake their sins, and to be ready as clean vessels of the Lord to guide His people in a fresh time of revival in their land (Acts 3:19).

It was an awesome sight and sound to hear and see the wailing before the Lord in genuine repentance, cleansing, and brokenness and to hear the expectant cries for revival among God's people and for spiritual awakening in their nation. They were especially grieved over the lost condition of their countrymen in North Korea.

Utter brokenness in God's holy presence is a prerequisite to any mighty moving of God in revival. I was with Nancy Leigh DeMoss in Fort Collins, Colorado, in July 1995, when utter brokenness occurred, an event she so adequately relates in this book. Nancy describes her own response to God's touch on His people and on our lives also. Truly, neither of us will ever be the same again.

May this be repeated all across our nation as we take seriously what God is saying to His pastors, leaders, and people. It remains absolutely true today that:

IF God permits crises, as spoken by God:

When I shut up heaven and there is no rain, or command the locusts to devour the land, or send pestilence among My people . . . (2 Chronicles 7:13).

THEN

if My people who are called by My name will humble themselves, and pray and seek My face, and turn from their wicked ways, then I will hear from heaven, and will forgive their sin and heal their land (2 Chronicles 7:14).

I believe God is saying one more time:

Now My eyes will be open and My ears attentive . . . (2 Chronicles 7:15).

I am making clear and strong changes in my life for these days, praying that a much-needed revival may come to our nation and our world. I am especially seeking opportunities for personal revival and prayer.

I want to challenge you to heed the call that God has so clearly given to Nancy: a call to brokenness. Give careful attention to her helpful guidance in practically implementing this message in your life, your family, and your church. Make the adjustments in your life to God immediately and thoroughly.

Much of our world is making major adjustments to the new realities we now face as a result of September 11, 2001. Will God's leaders and

God's people continue with business as usual? We must not! Since many do not know how to identify spiritual crises, and therefore do not know clearly what to do before God, this book will be both a very timely word from God and a practical guide to returning to God, so He can work once again through His people toward revival and spiritual awakening.

—Henry T. Blackaby

ACKNOWLEDGMENTS

MORE THAN ANY OTHER message I have written or shared from the platform, the "credit" for this particular message should rightly be shared with others. Many of the components of this book—including specific scriptural insights, applications, and, in a few cases, actual wording—were developed over several years in collaboration with the staff of Life Action Ministries, particularly *Del Fehsenfeld Jr.* (now with the Lord) and *Tim St. Clair,* as we served together in revival ministry.

Over the years, Tim, Del, and I have exchanged insights and notes and delivered similar messages, making it difficult to know with certainty at points "who first said what." The heart of these men is such that they have never sought credit for their work, desiring only that the message be proclaimed and heeded by the people of God. Even more than the content of their messages, their lives have shown me the meaning of true brokenness. This book is the fruit of our combined labors and partnership in ministry.

Others have also made a significant contribution to this work. Special appreciation is due to:

Lela Gilbert and *Cheryl Dunlop* for their editorial efforts that have helped me to communicate my heart more effectively. And Carolyn McCulley, for her assistance in developing the discussion guide.

Greg Thornton, Bill Thrasher, Elsa Mazon, and my other friends at Moody Publishers, without whose vision, support, and partnership this book would not have been birthed.

The men and women who serve on the staff of Revive Our Hearts, and whose faithful, diligent efforts make it possible for me to focus on developing and presenting the message of revival.

My team of Praying Friends, whose intercession before the Throne has been the means of great grace in my life, and whose encouragement has often helped me press on when I felt I had nothing left to give.

Far surpassing all other contributors is *my precious Lord Jesus,* whose brokenness continues to call me to brokenness, and whose sacrifice at Calvary makes the offering of my heart and of this book acceptable to the Father.

Come as the fire,
and purge our hearts

With sacrificial flame;

Let our whole soul an offering be

To our Redeemer's Name.

———————

ANDREW REED

INTRODUCTION

IN JULY 1995, anticipation was unusually high as four thousand staff members of Campus Crusade for Christ converged on Moby Gym at Colorado State University in Fort Collins, Colorado, from all across the United States. Throughout the preceding spring, spiritual stirrings had been spontaneously ignited at a number of college campuses—some Christian, some secular. A number of Campus Crusade staff members had witnessed these events firsthand and were eager to see God do more.

Desiring a fresh work of God among their staff, the ministry leadership had been prompted to make revival the focus of their biannual staff conference. The seriousness of their intent was seen when they agreed to depart from their normal schedule and to set apart extended times each morning during the weeklong conference for the staff to seek the Lord. Only one or two speakers were scheduled for each of these extended sessions. No time limitations were placed on the speakers. Significant blocks of time were simply left open to see how God would lead.

The conference began on Friday with a day of worship, prayer, and fasting. The corporate sense of longing for God to move was palpable at points. The prayers and longing intensified over the next few days as the staff heard messages from men such as Dr. Bill Bright about "first love" for Jesus, and Dennis Rainey about the need to honor parents. There were also a number of firsthand reports from some who had witnessed what God had done on college campuses that spring.

Several months earlier, knowing of my burden for revival, the leadership had asked if I would address the staff at this particular gathering. Feeling keenly the responsibility of this assignment, I had been waiting on the Lord for direction for my message. Not until two weeks before the conference did I finally sense what I was to address—the subject of brokenness and humility. The burden emerged out of study and meditation I had been doing in the book of Isaiah for several months. It also came out of a work that God had been doing in my own heart. He had recently brought me to a new level of repentance and brokenness in a particular issue in my life.

God wants to reveal His presence and glory to His people.

On Monday morning, I stood to speak to a group of Christian workers whom God had been preparing for this moment. I spoke with the staff about what God had been teaching me about the meaning of true brokenness. About ten minutes before the end of the message, out of the corner of my eye I noticed two men who had slipped out of their seats somewhere in that vast room and had walked to the front of the gym. They quietly knelt on the floor in front of the platform where I was speaking. To this day, I have no idea who those men were or exactly why they came. But in retrospect, I believe their humility set the stage and paved the way for the brokenness and humility of others.

At the close of the message, I referred to an old gospel song that had been sung in many of the student revivals of the past spring:

Pass me not, O gentle Savior,
Hear my humble cry;

While on others Thou art calling,
Do not pass me by.

I suggested that we sing that song and encouraged those present to take any step of humility and brokenness that God was putting on their hearts. As I recall, that was at about 10:30 in the morning. What happened over the next hours and days is almost too sacred and precious to describe. In fact, this is the first time I have attempted to write about that week—I did not even record it in my personal journal.

I have struggled with whether or not I should write even this brief account. I tremble at the thought that I might in any way deflect any credit or glory for that divine visitation away from God. I know all too well that I had nothing to do with what took place —that I was (and am) more a candidate for revival than in any way responsible for it. I know, and will tell in the pages that follow, some of the battles of my own heart with the deadly sin of pride—the very thing I felt led to address and expose that day.

What has compelled me to proceed is the conviction that what God did in Moby Gym that week was just a glimpse of what He longs to do throughout Christendom. He wants to reveal His presence and glory to His people. He wants to fill our hearts and homes, our churches and ministries with His love and His Spirit. He wants to pour out His grace on the dry, thirsty ground of our lives.

He wants to restore our "first love" for Jesus, rekindle the fire of devotion that once burned brightly in our hearts, reconcile broken relationships, and rebuild the parts of our lives that are in a state of disrepair. In short, He wants to revive our hearts. *And it all begins with brokenness and humility.* No exceptions. No shortcuts. No substitutes.

No human fully knows or could possibly capture what took place that hot July day in Colorado. But I believe most who were present would agree that God was there and that His presence was manifest in an extraordinary way. As He began to move in the hearts of His people, all scheduled events for the rest of the day were canceled; the same thing happened the next day and half of the following day. There were no official breaks during the service that began at 9:00 Monday morning and continued until midnight that night. Most of those in attendance had no desire to leave, though some slipped in and out as necessary for physical nourishment or to tend to needs of children. Throughout the day, hour after hour, people stayed glued to their seats on the main floor or in the bleachers as we waited, listened, repented, prayed, and worshiped.

Pretense and masks were stripped off in His presence.

Moby Gym is just that—a gym—home of the Colorado State Rams. It is not the kind of setting where one would ordinarily expect to encounter God. But that week it became a sanctuary—a holy place where the presence of God was experienced in an unusual way among His people. The entire room became an altar where men and women made a living sacrifice of their lives to the Lord. Throughout that vast auditorium, hundreds of men and women humbled themselves before God and before one another. Husbands and wives, parents and young people, colleagues, supervisors, and subordinates—people got serious about being honest with God and with each other. Over the next few days, long-standing grievances were confessed and breaches were reconciled—some of them going back for decades.

Under the Spirit's conviction, scores and scores of men and women came to the microphone to confess specific sins before God and their fellow workers. Pretense and masks were stripped off in His presence. Spiritual needs and failures were confessed openly. At midnight on Monday night, when the decision was made to break for sleep and resume the next day, staff members were still standing in line waiting to reach the microphone.

One of the most vivid memories I have of that week is a scene that took place again and again: As each person finished his or her confession, ten, twenty, thirty, or even fifty or more people would leave their seats, rushing to encircle the person and pray for him or her. At any given time there were several of these groups praying near the platform. Earnest intercession poured forth on behalf of broken believers who were repenting of every conceivable sin and bondage.

The brokenness that flowed in that room was both intensely per-

sonal and profoundly corporate. What a fragrance must have wafted up
to the throne of God as this family of believers repented and humbled
themselves before Him.

Not everything that took place during those days was neat, clean,
and easy to explain. Revival can be messy. It was as if a large rock had
been overturned and a floodlight turned on, exposing all kinds of worms
and insects. Not everyone was comfortable with the public nature of
the confessions. But there was a widespread sense that what was happening was not man-initiated, and that trying to control it would have
been like standing in front of a fast-moving freight train and telling it to
stop.

The leaders of the ministry were united in their concern not to
quench or grieve the Holy Spirit in any way. From hour to hour, they
sought the Lord as to "what next?" Should they let this continue? (To
do so meant dispensing with other scheduled speakers and training
sessions.) How and to what extent should it be steered? (In a group
that size there were also practical considerations—what about the fifteen hundred children in child care?) In the midst of a stirring of God's
Spirit, there are no "experts." Nothing anyone had read or experienced
had prepared them to know how to "manage" this moment. That, too,
was humbling.

In God's providence, Dr. Henry Blackaby, author of *Experiencing
God*, had been invited to speak to the staff. When he arrived that first
evening, he sat and listened and prayed as person after person unbur-
dened his heart and expressed his need for a fresh cleansing and filling
of the Spirit. The next morning, he preached an anointed message on
the nature of true repentance. Then for the next seven or eight hours,
he stood by the side of others who came to the microphone to confess
the issues over which God had convicted their hearts. His pastoral, biblical input helped people move into thorough, genuine repentance.

The truth that God used to bring His children into a new level of
freedom and fruitfulness that week is intended to be a way of life for
every believer. Yet, by and large, it is a missing element in evangelicalism today. With all our talk of worship, unity, reconciliation, love, and
the power of God, we have bypassed the essential ingredient that makes

these things possible. I believe a return to this truth—the need for brokenness and humility—is the starting place for experiencing the revival we so desperately need in our lives, our homes, and our churches.

This is not a new truth. As you will see, it is a timeless principle that runs as a thread through all the Word of God. It is the only way you and I can draw near to a holy God. It is God's prescription for nearly every condition that ails human hearts and relationships. Loneliness, fear, sinful bondages, fragmented relationships, communication barriers, generation gaps, unresolved conflicts, guilt, shame, self-absorption, addictions, hypocrisy, and at times even shyness—all these issues and more have their root in pride; but they can crumble through genuine brokenness and humility.

Do you need a fresh infusion of the grace of God in your life?

Do you need a fresh infusion of the grace of God in your life? Do you long to experience the abundant life, to live in the realm of the supernatural, and to enjoy the free flow of God's Spirit in your life? Do you want to be set free from those selfish, sinful patterns that plague your walk and poison your relationships? Do you want to find fullness of joy? Does your heart need to be revived?

This book is an invitation to encounter God in a whole new way. It is a call to discover His heart and His ways; a challenge to embrace a radically new way of thinking and living, in which the way up is down, death brings life, and brokenness is the pathway to wholeness.

*It is a wonder what
God can do with a broken heart,
if He gets all the pieces.*

SAMUEL CHADWICK

THE HEART
of the MATTER

IF YOU WERE TO MEET Wayne and Gwyn Stanford today, you would find a tenderhearted, warm, compassionate, humble couple. If you conversed with them for any length of time, they would undoubtedly tell you something fresh that God was teaching them or doing in their lives.

It wasn't always that way. When I first met this couple more than twenty years ago, they were in their early fifties. By the world's standards, they had it made. Wayne was a successful businessman; he and Gwyn had a lovely home in the Midwest and a vacation home in Florida. They were respected leaders in their community and were active in their local church and their denomination. But, as they later said publicly, they were both afflicted with a deadly heart condition that they didn't realize they had—a malady known as *pride*.

Today they are able to see what they were blind to at the time. Gwyn admits,

> I was proud of my reputation and my position. I was known at the country club where I was an officer, known among the elite of the

community, and known as a leader at my church. I was at the church every time the doors were open. It was important to me to have everyone notice me and what I was doing. I was extremely self-righteous and thought I was more spiritual than others. Others had needs, but not Gwyn Stanford. Others needed revival, but not I!

Though they both appeared to be spiritually prosperous, the truth was that their hearts were hollow, hard, and spiritually starved. "Right in the middle of religion, I was so very far away from God," Gwyn says with regret.

Though Wayne was oblivious to his own spiritual need, it was readily apparent to those around him. His pastor at the time remembers the Wayne Stanford of those days as "a cold, calculating, highly opinionated man. He almost demanded that I follow his ideas for leading the church. He was extremely judgmental and critical. Our attempted fellowships together generally ended in frustrated anger. There was a deep chasm between us."

Gwyn's heart condition manifested itself in more subtle ways:

I was unteachable; although I was a leader, I wasn't in the Word; I lived, acted, and operated based on the world's way of thinking. I didn't know what it meant to be honest, open, and transparent before God and others. The one thing I did know was how to play church—I knew how to pretend.

Wayne and Gwyn might well have lived the rest of their lives in that condition—spiritually deceived, hardened, and unusable—had not the Lord graciously intervened to show them their need and rescue them from their pride.

In 1982 I was part of a team that was invited to minister in Wayne and Gwyn's church for a concentrated two-week period of seeking the Lord.[1] During that time, church members were challenged to face the reality of their spiritual condition. The Stanfords' lives would never be the same again as a result of that honest look.

The second Sunday morning of that series of meetings is indelibly etched on Wayne's mind. The message was based on the Old Testament story of Naaman (2 Kings 5). As the respected, capable commander in chief of the Syrian army, Naaman appeared to have it all together—except for the fact that he had leprosy. Naaman wanted to be healed, but not at the expense of his pride. Wayne was stopped short as he saw himself in this proud general:

> He did what I probably would have done: he loaded up six thousand shekels of gold and ten talents of silver, and he went down to buy his way out of his problem. Right in the middle of that message, God said to me, *You're just like Naaman! You've got spiritual leprosy and you need to be healed. You can be restored, but you're going to have to do it My way.*

That morning, in the middle of the service, Wayne made his way to a room that had been designated for those who needed prayer—that in itself was a big step of humility, as he had previously determined he would not go to that room. As he arrived at the prayer room, this respected leader fell on his knees and cried out to God to have mercy on him; he confessed his sin of pride and pretense, and surrendered himself to do whatever God wanted him to do.

That same week, Gwyn attended a special prayer meeting for the women of the church. It was there that she had a life-changing encounter with God. That morning the leader spoke three words that penetrated her heart: "God is alive!" That simple phrase wakened her from her spiritual sleep and transformed her life. She remembers thinking, *Gwyn, you're living as if God is dead.* For the first time, she saw herself as God saw her—and it wasn't the Gwyn who had it all put together. She saw herself as sinful and desperately needy of His grace.

The conviction of God's Spirit was intense. For the first time in her life, she responded to that conviction in humility. In fact, she realized that, in spite of her religious appearance and activity, she had never been truly born again. She cried out to God to save her and received assurance that He had given her a new, clean heart.

31

Issues of the Heart

What took place in Wayne's and Gwyn's lives more than two decades ago was nothing short of major heart surgery. In Gwyn's case, she had been deceived for years into believing that she was a child of God, simply because she was a faithful, active church member. She needed—and received—a heart transplant. In Wayne's case, his spiritual arteries had become hardened—clogged and crusted over with self, pride, religious works, and "keeping up appearances."

The Old Testament prophet Jeremiah understood that the heart was what mattered to God, and that if the heart were sick, the whole body would be in trouble. Relentlessly, persistently, he addressed the matter of the heart. There are more than seventy references to the heart in his writings. God gave him discernment to see beyond the impressive, external religious life of His people. Jeremiah penetrated and probed and held the people's hearts up to the light; he pleaded with them to see what God saw.

From all appearances, the Jews—God's chosen people—were deeply religious; but Jeremiah proclaimed that their hearts had turned away from the God who had redeemed them: "This people has a defiant and rebellious *heart*" (5:23, italics added, and so with all references in this chapter).

The Old Testament Jews dutifully performed countless rituals of ceremonial cleansing. But Jeremiah understood that all those physical washings were merely intended to be a picture of purity of heart, so he urged: "O Jerusalem, wash your *heart* from wickedness" (4:14).

If their hearts weren't right, they weren't right.

Though God had revealed Himself and His law to the His people, their hearts were stubborn and they had become desensitized to His Word: "Each one follows the dictates [walks after the stubbornness; marginal reading NKJV] of his own evil *heart*, so that no one listens to Me" (16:12).

When we open the New Testament, we encounter the Lord Jesus, God's final Prophet, picking up the same theme that reverberates throughout the pages of the Old Testament. During His earthly ministry, He upset the whole religious system of His day because fused to be impressed with the things that men esteem most highly and insisted on exposing the hearts of people as what really mattered.

He looked the most religious men of His day in the face and confronted them with the fact that they were obsessed with putting on a good appearance and a good performance, while their hearts were empty and corrupt:

> *Hypocrites! Well did Isaiah prophesy about you, saying:*
> *"These people draw near to Me with their mouth,*
> *And honor Me with their lips,*
> *But their heart is far from Me.*
> *And in vain they worship Me."*
> —Matthew 15:7–9

When the disciples asked Jesus to explain why He had been so hard on the Pharisees, He pointed out that they were fastidious about washing their hands before eating, so as not to become ceremonially defiled, but were oblivious to the corruption of their hearts: "Out of the heart proceed evil thoughts, murders, adulteries, fornications, thefts, false witness, blasphemies. These are the things which defile a man, but to eat with unwashed hands does not defile a man" (Matthew 15:19–20).

Over and over again, He kept coming back to the issue of the *heart*. It didn't matter if they circumcised their bodies and tithed everything they owned, down to their herbs; it didn't matter if they washed their hands every time they ate and could quote the Law from beginning to end; it didn't matter if they scrupulously observed every feast day, every fast day, and every Sabbath day; it didn't matter if everyone else respected them as devout believers—if their hearts weren't right, *they* weren't right.

The medical profession stresses the importance of regular physical checkups. Anyone with a family history of heart disease is encouraged to get his cholesterol tested. We don't assume that because we look fine outwardly, we have nothing to worry about. If our heart is not functioning properly or there is blockage in our arteries, we want to know about the problem so we can do whatever is necessary to deal with the situation. We know that neglecting our physical heart condition could be fatal.

Should we be any less concerned about our spiritual heart condition? The fact is, when it comes to spiritual matters, we all have a family history of "heart disease." We must be willing to let Him examine our hearts and diagnose that which we may be unable to see for ourselves.

The good news of the gospel is that the Great Physician has made available a cure for our deceived, diseased hearts. Jesus came to do radical heart surgery—to cleanse and transform us from the inside out, by the power of His death and resurrection. "I will cleanse you from all your filthiness and from all your idols. I will give you a new *heart* and put a new spirit within you; I will take the *heart* of stone out of your flesh and give you a *heart* of flesh. I will put My Spirit within you" (Ezekiel 36:25–27).

A Complete Takeover

The transformation that took place in Wayne and Gwyn Stanfords' lives when God gave them new, clean hearts was dramatic. As another friend said after having a similar encounter with God, "Revival is not just an emotional touch; it's a complete takeover!"

Gwyn remembers some of the first evidences that her heart had been changed: "Immediately I became so hungry for His Word that I could hardly wait to get up in the morning to see what He was going to reveal to me. I wanted to spend time with Him. I found myself loving people I'd never loved before."

In Wayne's case, when God changed his heart, his whole demeanor changed. The same pastor who had felt the brunt of Wayne's controlling, critical spirit later wrote: "It is difficult to believe that the Wayne Stanford I first met is the same Spirit-filled, gentle, long-suffering, compassionate, prayer warrior we know today."

God began to deal with Wayne about his business and financial affairs, resulting in a radical change of values. He began to lead his family spiritually—by his example and by his words. As they began to see the reality of Christ in their parents, Wayne and Gwyn's three grown daughters—already professing believers—all came to genuine faith in Christ.

Rather than living for themselves and accumulating things for their own pleasure, Wayne and Gwyn began to look for ways to invest their time and resources to further the kingdom of Christ. A self-centered lifestyle was replaced with a sacrificial lifestyle.

The personal revival Wayne and Gwyn experienced in 1982 was not short-lived. For more than twenty years, they have continued to walk humbly with God and to love and serve Him and others. That initial "breaking point" has become an ongoing process of daily brokenness. Gwyn acknowledges that there have been ups and downs in that process:

> I'm not going to tell you that I have it all together. I will tell you that I have needs and struggles. But I'm learning to acknowledge my need to God and others, and to be open, honest, and transparent. My attitude used to be, "I don't need you, but you very much need me." I was willing to help, but I was not willing to unmask and be helped. Now I know that when I humble and unmask myself, then, and only then, can I truly experience God's grace and be victorious and free.

Wayne and Gwyn discovered a secret that delivered them from religion and released them to enjoy the fullness of life in the Spirit—they learned what kind of heart God revives. They learned that God's values are not the same as man's values. They learned that real life, freedom, and joy are not to be found in climbing up the socioeconomic ladder, but in humbling ourselves; not in being self-sufficient, but in acknowledging need. They were willing to take off their religious masks and get real. And when they did, God met them in a way they had never experienced before.

Heart Check

What about you? What is the condition of your heart? Could it be that you, like Wayne and Gwyn, have been going through the motions, playing church, pretending that all is well, when the truth is that you need major heart surgery—perhaps even a heart transplant?

Would you be willing to make an appointment with the Great Physician, place yourself on His table, and ask Him to examine your heart? If so, pray the prayer of the psalmist: "Search me, O God, and know my heart" (Psalm 139:23).

He wants to revive our hearts. However, there is a condition that must be met if our hearts are to be revived. The truth you will read on the following pages may turn your world and your thinking upside down, as it did to those who heard it in the Bible days. At first, God's way may seem negative, confining, or painful. But, as my friends Wayne and Gwyn discovered, it is actually the pathway to freedom, fullness, victory, fruitfulness, and joy.

Note

1. Since 1971 teams from Life Action Ministries have conducted more than a thousand extended revival meetings in local churches. For more information about this ministry or to inquire about scheduling a team in your church, contact Life Action Ministries, P.O. Box 31, Buchanan, MI 49107; 269/697-8600; e-mail: info@lifeaction.org; www.lifeaction.org.

*To be broken is
the beginning of revival.
It is painful, it is humiliating,
but it is the only way.*

ROY HESSION[1]

WHAT IS BROKENNESS?

WALK THROUGH ANY Christian bookstore today, and you'll find an array of books and products offering to help you be successful in every dimension and season of life:

+ how to find peace, happiness, and fulfillment

+ how to have a more intimate marriage

+ how to have a better relationship with your kids

+ how to feel closer to God

+ how to deal with hurts and wounds in your past

+ how to get along better with people

+ how to succeed at work, at school, and at home

+ how to have an effective ministry

+ how to grow a great church

+ how to get more out of the Bible

We have more tools and resources for our questions and hurts and needs today than any time in the history of the church. Why, then, do so many Christians live frustrated, defeated, empty, barren lives? Deep down, many of us long to experience a greater reality of God's presence and power in our lives. Our hearts need to be revived. But so few voices today are pointing us to the truth that will revive our hearts and set us free.

The Scripture is clear about the kind of heart God revives. The secret that transformed Wayne's and Gwyn's lives is really no secret at all. It is interwoven as a thread all through the Word of God.

> For thus says the High and Lofty One
> Who inhabits eternity,
> whose name is Holy:
> "I dwell in the high and holy place,
> With him who has a contrite and humble spirit,
> To revive the spirit of the humble,
> And to revive the heart of the contrite ones."
> —Isaiah 57:15, emphasis added,
> and so through this chapter

According to this passage, God has two "addresses." The first one comes as no surprise. We are told that the high and exalted God of the universe lives in "eternity, in the high and holy place." Yet, the Scripture says, God has another "address," and I find this one astounding. He lives with those who have a humble and contrite spirit. Generally, we would think of kings as being comfortable with the high and mighty, with the wealthy and the successful. But this King chooses to dwell with those who are contrite and humble.

To what kind of person does God draw near? What kind of person does He rescue and deliver? He is attracted to those who have a broken, contrite spirit.

Psalm 51 is the heartfelt, penitent prayer written by King David after he committed his great sin with Bathsheba. He realized that there was absolutely nothing he could do to earn his way back into God's favor.

"For You do not desire sacrifice, or else I would give it; You do not delight in burnt offering" (verse 16).

David is saying, "Lord, if You wanted ten thousand sheep or oxen or bullocks, I would offer them as a sacrifice." Have you ever noticed how many people feel they need to jump through some sort of spiritual hoop to earn God's favor? David understood that God wasn't looking for religious acts or devout behavior. The only offering God really wanted was a humble, contrite heart.

> *The sacrifices of God are* a broken spirit,
> A broken and a contrite heart—
> *These, O God, You will not despise.*
> —Psalm 51:17

Jesus began the first recorded sermon of His earthly ministry on this same theme: "Blessed are the *poor in spirit* . . ." (Matthew 5:3). Jesus was talking about how to experience true joy—how to be happy. It begins, He explained, by being poor. Now in today's world, if we were asked to suggest ways to be blessed, I'm not sure we would have started in that particular place. We don't generally think of poverty as a blessing. But Jesus came to introduce a whole new economy—a radically different way of thinking about life.

We want the resurrection without going through the grave.

In the Greek language in which the New Testament was originally written, there are two words Jesus could have chosen to speak of someone being "poor." The first word suggests someone who lives just below the poverty line, someone who is always having to scrimp and scrape to survive, someone who makes it, but barely. That is not the word Jesus chose. He used another word that means *a beggar*—a person who is utterly, absolutely destitute. This beggar has no hope of surviving unless somebody reaches out a hand and pulls him up.

What is Jesus saying? Blessed are *the beggars*—those who recognize that they are spiritually destitute and bankrupt. They know that they have no chance of survival apart from God's intervening mercy and grace. Because of their need, they reach out to Him. Because they reach out to Him, He responds by lavishing them with the riches of His kingdom and reviving their hearts.

Our culture is obsessed with being whole and feeling good. That drive affects even the way we view the Christian life. We want a "painless Pentecost"; we want a "laughing" revival. We want gain without pain; we want the resurrection without going through the grave; we want life without experiencing death; we want a crown without going by way of the cross. But in God's economy, the way up is down.

You and I will never meet God in revival until we first meet Him in brokenness. Our families will never be whole until husbands and wives, moms and dads, and young people have been broken. Our churches will never be the vibrant witness God intended them to be in the world until their members—pastors and laypeople alike—have experienced true brokenness.

That is the heart of what we read about in the book of James:

Draw near to God and He will draw near to you. Cleanse your hands, you sinners; and purify your hearts, you double-minded. Lament and mourn and weep! Let your laughter be turned to mourning and your joy to gloom. Humble yourselves in the sight of the Lord, and He will lift you up.
—James 4:8–10

This is a message today's men and women are not eager to hear. Most of us don't walk into a Christian bookstore and say, "Can you help me find a book on how to 'mourn and weep'?" We want to know how to be happy and whole, how to improve our self-esteem, how to feel better about ourselves and our lives. We think our problem is that we are gloomy and depressed and we need someone to make us happy. But God's Word says, "No, before you can get close to God, you have to find the highway of lowliness." We want to lift ourselves up. He says, "No, humble yourself, and I will lift you up."

Misconceptions About Brokenness

I believe one of the reasons many believers are afraid of the idea of brokenness is that they have misconceptions about what brokenness really means. As is true in so many other areas, our idea of brokenness and God's idea of brokenness are usually quite different.

For example, some people think of brokenness as always being sad or gloomy. They assume it means having a downcast countenance. They imagine that broken people never smile or laugh. How could a broken person possibly be happy or at peace? In reality brokenness brings a release, which produces a deep sense of joy and peace.

Others think of brokenness as being morbidly introspective: "Oh, woe is me! I've confessed every sin I can possibly think of; but surely there must be something I've missed. Oh, what a worm I am!" This kind of "confession" can lead to false humility, wherein people are quick to put themselves down and cannot receive genuine affirmation or encouragement. False humility and morbid introspection are, in fact, the opposite of brokenness, as they reveal a preoccupation with self, rather than Christ.

For many, brokenness conjures up the image of the shedding of tears—having a deeply emotional experience. They think of a time when they were deeply stirred by a song, moved by a message, or touched by an experience. Unfortunately, countless people have shed buckets full of tears and yet have never experienced a moment of true brokenness. It is difficult to conceive of being truly broken without our emotions being involved. But it is important to understand that it is possible to shed tears without being broken, and it is possible to experience brokenness without shedding any tears at all.

How is brokenness to be recognized in our lives?

Many people equate brokenness with being deeply hurt by tragic circumstances—by the failure of a child, a financial reversal, or perhaps a debilitating illness or death of a loved one. God often uses tragedy to get people's attention and turn their hearts toward Him. But tragedy doesn't guarantee brokenness. You may have experienced many deep hurts and tragedies and never yet been truly broken.

So what is true brokenness? Someone has said that brokenness, like a fragrance, is easier to detect than to define. How is brokenness to be recognized in our lives?

True Brokenness

Brokenness is not a feeling or an emotion. Rather, it requires a choice, an act of the will. Further, this choice is not primarily a onetime experience, though there may be profound and life-changing spiritual turning points in our lives. True brokenness is an ongoing, constant way of life. True brokenness is a lifestyle—a moment-by-moment lifestyle of agreeing with God about the true condition of my heart and life—not as everyone else thinks it is but as He knows it to be.

Brokenness is the shattering of my self-will—the absolute surrender of my will to the will of God. It is saying "Yes, Lord!"—no resistance, no chafing, no stubbornness—simply submitting myself to His direction and will in my life.

Contrite is one word that is used in the Old Testament to speak of brokenness. That word suggests something that is crushed into small particles or ground into powder, as a rock is pulverized. What is it that God wants to pulverize in us? It is not our spirit He wants to break, nor is it our essential personhood. He wants to break our self-will.

When we speak of a horse being "broken," we don't mean that someone physically breaks its legs; we mean that the horse's *will* has been broken—that it is now compliant and submissive to the wishes of its rider. In the same sense, true brokenness is the breaking of my self-will, so that the life and spirit of the Lord Jesus may be released through me. It is my humble and obedient response to the conviction of God's Word and His Holy Spirit.

> *The broken, contrite heart is easily molded by the hand of God.*

Brokenness is the stripping of self-reliance and independence from God. The broken person has no confidence in his own righteousness or his own works, but he is cast in total dependence upon the grace of God working in and through him.

Brokenness is the softening of the soil of my heart—it is the breaking up of any clods of resistance that could keep the seed from penetrating and taking root. I believe one of the reasons many pastors faithfully preach the Word week after week and see so little fruit in the lives of their listeners is that the soil in many of our hearts has become so hard and fallow that the seed cannot penetrate. Believers with broken, contrite hearts are receptive and responsive to the Word.

As wax or clay must be soft and pliable in order to be molded by the artist's hands, so the broken, contrite heart is easily molded by the hand of God and does not harden itself against the circumstances God chooses to mold it.

Roof Off, Walls Down

In 1 John, the apostle explains that our relationship with God is inseparably linked to our relationship with other believers. He wrote, "If we walk in the light as He is in the light, we have fellowship with one another, and the blood of Jesus Christ His Son cleanses us from all sin" (1 John 1:7). Brokenness in the life of a believer has both a vertical and a horizontal dimension—it goes two ways. First, a broken man or woman walks in transparent honesty and humility before God. That is what it means to "walk in the light." Our lives are open and exposed before the eyes of Him who knows and sees all. Walking in the light means that there is nothing between my soul and my Savior.

However, it is not enough that we be humble and broken before God. Invariably, our relationship with God is reflected in our relationships with others. A person who has been broken before God will also be humble and broken before others. One writer has likened our lives to a house with a roof and walls.[2] For our hearts to be revived, the roof must come off (brokenness toward God) and the walls must come down (brokenness toward man).

I'll never forget listening to one particular man who stood before his fellow staff members as God was moving during the Campus Crusade conference in 1995. As he later recounted in a report to friends and financial supporters, God found this full-time Christian worker in a spiritual drought. During that week, God exposed his heart and took him through a painful process of brokenness that ultimately led to joy and

release. That process first required that he let the roof come off in repentance toward God; the process continued and produced rich fruit
when he became willing to let the walls down before others. This is
what "Jordan" wrote when he looked back on that week:

> I showed up at the beginning of the conference with a cold,
> weary heart. It was difficult for me to sing along with the various
> praise songs sung during the opening sessions. At times I didn't
> even try . . . I just listened to everyone else. Friday, Saturday, and
> Sunday's sessions came and went. Then came Monday.
>
> On Monday morning Nancy addressed the entire staff. In
> her message, she asked the question, "What kind of heart does
> God revive?" She contrasted two types of hearts: one being a bro-
> ken and contrite heart; the other a heart that's full of pride.
>
> What occurred next is something I will remember for the
> rest of my life. From all across the gymnasium, staff began to
> make their way to the stage to confess and repent of their sins.
> A line formed, and for the next thirteen hours there was nonstop
> public confession. The leadership of our ministry let God move
> within the hearts of His people and there was true revival!
>
> I had never experienced anything like this before. As I sat in
> the bleachers, hour after hour, and witnessed fellow staff mem-
> bers weeping in brokenness as they confessed their sin (many
> times being moved to tears myself by their deep grief), I began to
> notice God softening my heart as the Holy Spirit began convict-
> ing me of my own sin and revealing my need for repentance.
>
> Throughout Monday afternoon I remained in the bleachers
> and confessed my sin to God, asking Him to forgive me, cleanse
> me, and create within me a new heart. At first, I didn't believe I
> needed to go to the microphone. However, by Monday evening,
> in addition to the sin the Holy Spirit had revealed to me through-
> out the day, He had revealed to me some sinful attitudes I
> needed to confess to my fellow staff. Later that night, at one in
> the morning, I wrote a four-page letter of confession to God and
> the staff.

The next day, God gave Jordan the courage to humble himself before the staff and leadership of Campus Crusade, as he read that entire letter publicly and asked for their forgiveness. Jordan's letter was no superficial confession. He made no attempt to whitewash his sins but brought them out into the light. With his wife standing by his side, he confessed a whole list of specific sins of which God had convicted him: impure motives, a desire for recognition, comparison, caring more about projects and tasks than people, a critical, judgmental spirit, keeping people at arm's length, and a spirit of jealousy and envy. And there was more; he continued reading to the staff what God had put on his heart:

> I am a man of many addictions. Brought up in a home without much nurturing or expressed love, by two people who had their own pain, I quickly learned how to love myself as a young boy. I loved myself with overeating, then added personal immoral habits, then added spending, and then in college added pornography.
>
> Although I received Christ as a high school student, these addictions followed me into my adult life. Most of my twenties and thirties have been spent in battling these addictive behaviors—each addiction being a form of self-love, each an attempt to mask pain in my life.
>
> Today at the age of thirty-eight, I battle each of these still. I desire victory. I confess each area as sin. Whatever things happened to put these addictions in place don't matter—I'm an adult now and assume full responsibility for their ongoing pull and presence in my life.
>
> I also confess to you and the Lord that I have been loving the world and the things of the world more than Him. I have not been experiencing the joy of a close, intimate relationship with God. As a result, my heart has had an emptiness that bass fishing, jazz, chess, and computers simply cannot fill.
>
> I want these things to change. I want repentance. I want brokenness. Please pray that in the months ahead God will place within me a deep brokenness and create within me a new, clean heart—a heart that loves Him more than my own life.

When he recounted the story later, Jordan told how those around him extended the grace and love of God when he allowed the walls of pride to come down: "Afterward, I was immediately surrounded by over twenty staff members who prayed for me, forgave me, hugged me, and expressed their love for me. There are truly very few moments in my life that have been more meaningful. God is so good. Like the gracious, loving father of the Prodigal Son, He is always ready to restore and welcome His children home."

For Jordan, that initial point of brokenness was accompanied by a fresh sense of release and joy in his spirit:

> Later that evening, we sang many of the same songs that were sung the first night of the conference. This time, however, I was singing! And not just singing, but with a joy in my heart that I haven't felt for years. As we sang one song entitled "White as Snow," I couldn't help weeping as I experienced the joy of sins forgiven. Much like the sinner woman who couldn't stop weeping at the feet of Jesus, I, too, had been touched by His cleansing love.

He signed his report, "Yielded, broken, and grateful before our gracious, gentle Savior . . ."

About a year later, I had an opportunity to meet Jordan and his wife personally. On a number of occasions since then, I have been able to fellowship with this couple. As painful as it was to expose himself in this way, it was part of the process God used to bring Jordan to a place of newfound freedom and victory. Recently I received a letter from his wife:

> Jordan continues to keep his relationship with God fresh and open. He has a goal to read through the Bible this year, and for two years we have faithfully prayed together nightly before we go to sleep. He has kept his commitment to me, to himself, and to the Lord—not flawlessly, but it's our humanness that reminds us both of our never-ending, always present need for the Savior.

When failure has happened (which is rare), confession and forgiveness is quickly sought.

Jordan's pathway has not been easy and he has not walked it without some failures along the way. So it will be with anyone who chooses the pathway of brokenness. But as Jordan testifies, the grace of God in his life and in the life of his family has reached beyond anything he'd ever imagined possible. God's richest blessings come only through brokenness. We learn this from our own experiences and from the stories of people like Jordan. And we learn this from the lives of men and women whose encounters with God animate the pages of Scripture.

Notes
1. Roy Hession, *The Calvary Road* (Fort Washington, Pa.: Christian Literature Crusade, 1990), 21.
2. Norman Grubb, *Continuous Revival* (Fort Washington, Pa.: Christian Literature Crusade, 1997), 15.

God creates out of nothing.

Therefore until a man is nothing,

God can make nothing out of him.

——————————

MARTIN LUTHER

BIBLICAL PORTRAITS:
BROKEN *and*
UNBROKEN

BROKENNESS IS NOT a new idea. From the ancient Hebrew Scriptures to the New Testament, the biblical record provides us with numerous illustrations of people who were broken and humbled before God. Interestingly, these examples are often set in contrast to stories of people who were *not* broken. As we will see, in every case, both individuals sinned. The difference was not so much in the magnitude of their sin but in their response when confronted with their sin.

Two Kings

Nearly a thousand years before the birth of Christ, two kings ruled over the nation of Israel. The first king was guilty of what most would consider a few relatively minor infractions. But they cost him his kingdom, his family, and, ultimately, his life.

By comparison, his successor was guilty of far greater offenses. In a fit of passion, he committed adultery with his neighbor's wife and then plotted to have his neighbor killed. Yet when the story of his life was

told, this man was called "a man after God's own heart" (see 1 Samuel
13:14). What made the difference?

When the first man, King Saul, was confronted with his sin, he defended, justified, and excused himself, blamed others, and tried to cover
up both the sin and its consequences. Although he
finally admitted, "I have sinned," when caught red-
handed by the prophet Samuel, the true condition
of Saul's heart was revealed in his next words:
"Please don't tell the people!" (see 1 Samuel 15:30).
King Saul was more concerned about preserving
his reputation and his position—about *looking* good
—than about being right with God. His response to
God's prophet revealed a proud, unbroken heart.

*Broken men and
women have
nothing to protect
and nothing to lose.*

On the other hand, when King David was faced with his sin, he was
willing to acknowledge his failure, to take personal responsibility for his
wrongdoing, and to confess and repent of his sin. The roof came off as
he repented toward God. The walls came down as he penned two songs
of contrition—Psalm 32 and Psalm 51—humbling himself before
countless future believers who would read his confession and learn of
his failure.

Broken men and women don't care who finds out about their sin;
they have nothing to protect and nothing to lose. They are eager for God
to be vindicated. David's response when confronted with his wrongdoing was that of a humble, broken man. And his was the heart that God
honored. Again and again, God's Word reveals that He is not as concerned about the depth or extent of the sin we commit as He is about
our attitude and response when we are confronted with our sin.

Stories of Pharisees and Other Sinners

In the Gospel of Luke, we find three vivid illustrations of the contrast
between a broken person and a proud, unbroken person. Interestingly,
in each case, proud people are linked with Pharisees. Now when you
and I think of Pharisees, we think of the "bad guys." But in those days,
the Pharisees were considered the "good guys." These were the seminary
graduates, the biblical scholars, the pastors, the spiritual leaders of their

day. Everyone looked up to them; no one questioned their spirituality or their authority. And no one felt that he could possibly measure up to them. It was assumed that the Pharisees were closer to God than anyone else.

When Jesus came along, He stripped away the theological aura the Pharisees had carefully wrapped around themselves. He probed deeply, past their external appearance and acts of apparent devotion, right into the heart where only God can see. Over and over again, He exposed the proud, self-righteous attitudes and motives of the Pharisees and insisted that God rejects that kind of heart. By contrast, He pointed to lowly sinners who had been rejected by everyone else but had repentant hearts. Then and now, broken sinners are the kinds of people God chooses to save, to bless, and to help.

Two Who Prayed

In Luke 18, Jesus told a parable about two men who went into the temple to pray. Both were involved in spiritual activity. But one man's prayer was acceptable to God and the other man's prayer didn't make it past the roof. What made the difference? Once again, it was not the outward actions of the men but the condition of their hearts.

The first man, while making an outward show and pretense of piety, was not a true worshiper of God (though he had everyone fooled, including himself). In reality, he worshiped himself; his world revolved around himself. The Scripture says, "The Pharisee stood and prayed thus *with* [*to*; marginal note NIV] *himself*" (verse 11, italics added). Though his remarks were addressed to God, apparently God wasn't paying much attention as this proud religious leader paraded his spiritual credentials: "God, I thank You that I am not like other men—extortioners, unjust, adulterers, or even as this tax collector. I fast twice a week; I give tithes of all that I possess" (verses 11–12).

Pride led this so-called worshiper to compare himself favorably to other "sinners." It made him utterly blind to his condition and oblivious to the depravity of his own heart.

The other man—a low-down, despised tax collector, who made his living through extortion—apparently had experienced a change of heart.

No one needed to tell him he was a sinner. He knew that he had no right to ask or expect anything from God. He could not even bring himself to lift up his eyes to heaven. His eyes downcast, in brokenness and anguish of soul, he simply cried out, "God, be merciful to me a sinner!" (verse 13). This man did not attempt to justify himself; rather, he justified God and recognized that his only hope was if God would have mercy on him.

There is no question about the audience Jesus was trying to reach with this story: "[Jesus] spoke this parable to some who trusted in themselves that they were righteous, and despised others" (verse 9). Jesus intended to be direct; He intended for His story to penetrate and expose the hearts of the proud and unbroken.

You can imagine how uncomfortable and indignant those self-righteous Pharisees must have felt. Could it be that Jesus thought the tax collectors were more righteous before God than they were? Jesus' conclusion to the parable brought the point home even further: "Everyone who exalts himself will be humbled [put down; marginal note NKJV], and he who humbles himself will be exalted" (verse 14).

The Pharisees had impressed men with their righteous appearance and their public religious acts, but God was not impressed at all. It is in His very nature to be repulsed by pride and to draw near to those who have a humble, broken spirit.

Two People at a Banquet

In the seventh chapter of Luke's gospel, we read about Jesus being invited for dinner at the home of a Pharisee named Simon. The first verse of this passage gives a glimpse into the heart of this Pharisee: "One of the Pharisees *asked* Him to eat with him" (verse 36, italics added). In the original language, the verb translated "asked" is used in a form that would ordinarily be used to make a request of a peer, rather than the form that would be used to ask a favor of a superior. Simon the Pharisee saw himself being of equal stature with Jesus.

We don't know who else was on the list of invited guests for this dinner, but we do know that one woman came to the dinner without being invited. We are not told her name. We know only that she was a "woman in the city who was a sinner" (verse 37). The implication is that she was a woman of ill repute, a woman with a reputation for sexual promiscuity. She certainly would not have been welcomed at this social gathering by anyone other than Jesus, who gladly welcomes sinners who recognize their need for mercy.

As I have studied this passage and those that parallel it in the Synoptic Gospels, I have come to believe that this woman had recently encountered Jesus. Before this occasion, she had responded to His call to repentance, turned from her sin, and embraced Him as the Messiah. He, in turn, had forgiven her and set her free from her sin. Now this newly forgiven woman was returning to Jesus to say "Thank You!" She wanted to express her profound gratitude and love for this One who had transformed her life.

Bearing an alabaster flask of costly perfume, she stood behind the feet of Jesus as He lay reclining at dinner, according to the custom of the day. As she stood quietly in His presence, she began to weep. Now I don't believe this woman came into this dinner intending to be noticed or to make a scene. I don't think she planned to draw attention to herself at all. Instead, she was probably oblivious to the fact that anyone besides Jesus was in that room. She was so overcome with the realization of how Jesus had found her and what He had done for her that she couldn't restrain her spontaneous display of emotion.

Tears of sincere gratitude coursed down her cheeks and onto the Savior's feet. Almost as if she was embarrassed, she stooped and began to wipe the tears off His feet with her hair. This was a picture of the forgiveness she had experienced, for Jesus had wiped her sinful heart clean. Then, presumably stooping even lower, she began to kiss His feet and to anoint them with the perfumed oil she had brought with her. Who better could she lavish this precious substance on than the Son of Man who had delivered her from herself and her sin? Spontaneous and blissfully unself-conscious worship and adoration flowed out of the life of this broken, contrite, forgiven woman.

By contrast, Simon the Pharisee, who had hosted this dinner, was incensed. In his self-righteous state of mind, this woman's behavior and, indeed, her very presence seemed utterly inappropriate to him. But, of course, Simon's real complaint was not with the woman but with Jesus. Muttering to himself, he said, "This man, if He were a prophet, would know who and what manner of woman this is who is touching Him, for she is a sinner" (Luke 7:39).

Not only did Jesus know what kind of woman she was, He also knew what kind of man Simon was. Further, He knew exactly what Simon was thinking. Jesus spoke to him, "Simon, I have something to say to you." Simon responded, "Teacher, say it."

Jesus proceeded to tell a story about two men who owed a debt to a moneylender. One of the men owed an exorbitant amount—more than he could have ever repaid. The other owed just a paltry sum, but he, too, was without the resources to pay even that small amount. The money-lender "freely forgave them both." Now Jesus said, "Tell Me, which of them will love the moneylender more?"

Simon correctly answered, "The one who was forgiven the bigger debt."

"You're right," said Jesus. Then, to help Simon apply the word picture, He reminded him of what had just taken place in Simon's own home. Simon had not treated Jesus with even common courtesy, much less the respect that would normally be shown a guest of honor. He had not provided water to wash His feet, he had not greeted Jesus with a kiss (equal to a handshake in our day), and he had not offered oil to anoint Jesus' head.

The woman, on the other hand, though an outcast and tainted by past failure and shame, had washed Jesus' feet with her tears and wiped them with the hair of her head. She had kissed His feet and anointed them with oil.

According to Jesus, because this woman had been forgiven of such serious sin, she felt herself to be a great debtor and therefore loved Jesus greatly. It wasn't that Simon's need for forgiveness was any less than hers. However, in the blind arrogance of his heart, he simply didn't realize how great a sinner he was, nor how great was his need for forgiveness. Consequently, he was not able to express the kind of worship and love that this woman had lavished on Jesus.

As I reread this passage, I have to acknowledge that my own relationship and responses to the Lord Jesus often resemble Simon's more than that of the "sinner woman." I am grieved by the coldness, indifference, and hardness of my heart toward the Savior; I long to be able to express that spontaneous, extravagant love and devotion that pours forth out of a broken, contrite heart—a heart that recognizes the greatness of my sin and the surpassing greatness of His grace.

Two Sons and Their Father

When the scene opens in Luke chapter 15, we find two kinds of people in the audience: "Then all the *tax collectors and the sinners* drew near to Him to hear Him. And the *Pharisees and scribes* complained, saying, 'This Man receives sinners and eats with them.' So He spoke this parable to them . . ." (verses 1–3, italics added).

As was generally the case, some in the crowd were all too aware that they were sinners, and they were drawn like a magnet to Jesus and His teaching. They hung on Jesus' every word, for His message was their only hope. Meanwhile, there was another group over on the sidelines. Although these religious men were equally sinful, they did not see themselves as such. Instead, they did what proud, unbroken people usually do when confronted with the truth: They criticized and picked apart the message and the messenger: "*Can you believe it*—this man welcomes *sinners*! He even *eats* with them!" They not only failed to see themselves as sinners in need of God's grace, but they also despised others and couldn't bear the thought of guilt by association with those whom they thought of as common, ordinary sinners. These prideful religious characters kept their distance from everybody else.

In an effort to expose their proud, self-righteous hearts, Jesus told three stories. He spoke first of the lost sheep, then of the lost coin, and finally He told the familiar story of the lost son.

Actually, there were two lost sons in this story—two young men whose responses revealed the true condition of their hearts. The younger son, commonly called "the Prodigal Son," abused his family name and squandered his inheritance. Finally, having lost it all, he woke up to what he had done and where it had led him.

Alone and poverty-stricken, he was truly broken. Realizing that he had nowhere else to turn, he made a decision to repent; he chose the pathway of brokenness and humility. He made the tough choice to return to the place where his failure had begun and to be reconciled with those he had wronged.

For this broken, repentant son there was no self-justification, no trivializing of his behavior, no whitewashing of his sin, no making excuses, no blaming others, no expectation of being treated royally. He knew he had nothing to offer but an honest acknowledgment of his failure and a humble plea for mercy.

The response of the boy's father is a powerful and poignant picture of our heavenly Father's welcome toward us when we come to Him in genuine repentance. This called for a celebration—the once-haughty rebel had returned home as a broken and humble repenter.

It's a great story with a great ending.

But remember that there were two types of people in the crowd that day. The tax collectors and sinners had to love this story—it spoke of hope, of forgiveness, of mercy. But what about the Pharisees and scribes? What were they thinking? Did they find it hard to swallow such a generous display of grace for one so undeserving? Did they find themselves looking around to see to whom this story could possibly apply?

Jesus wasn't finished. Just as there were two kinds of people listening, there were also two sons in the story. Where was the prodigal's older brother while all the partying was going on? He was, of course, right where he was supposed to be—out in the field, being faithful, working hard, doing his job. Here we encounter a stereotypical obedient, compliant, respectable firstborn. I should know; I'm one too.

This son had never given his father a moment's grief, especially not when compared with his free-spirited sibling. He had never been rebellious, at least not outwardly. But God is not impressed with outward appearances; He looks into the *heart*. And a celebration surrounding a repentant brother's return was the perfect setting in which to expose the elder brother's motives and attitudes.

As the older son approached his house, he heard, of all things, music and dancing. What in the world was going on? There hadn't been a party around that place since his rebellious younger brother left home. Rather than going to his father (could this suggest that although he was a "model son," he didn't have much of a relationship with his dad?), he found a servant and asked, "What's going on?"

The servant gave him the bottom line, "Your brother has returned home and your dad is throwing a party." The servant, unfortunately, failed to mention the heart of the matter—the younger brother's transformation into a contrite, humble son.

Do we fail to recognize the "elder brother" when he is staring back at us in the mirror?

Now the older boy's real nature began to be exposed: "He was angry and would not go in" (verse 28). How typical this is of proud, unbroken people. They cannot rejoice over repentant sinners. They are consumed with a sense of their own rights and expectations. And if they don't get the treatment they feel they deserve, they throw a pity party for themselves.

In the midst of celebrating the return of his lost son, news of his older son's boycott reached the father. He immediately left the party to deal with another troubled offspring.

I understand that in the ancient Jewish culture, when the head of the home left the party, the music and the dancing stopped until the host returned. Isn't that a picture of what is happening in so many of our churches and ministries today? There's no joy, no celebration, no partying over lost sinners being restored, because the pastor and the leadership are so distracted with having to deal with petty, pouting "Pharisees" ("elder brothers") who are throwing fits because they didn't get their way.

The pride, self-righteousness, and blindness of the older son's heart finally came to the surface in his angry, accusatory speech to his dad: "Lo, these many years I have been serving you [what was his motive for serving?]; I never transgressed your commandment at any time [was he really that perfect?]; and yet you never gave me a young goat, that I might make merry with my friends [what ingratitude—at least half the inheritance was already his]. But as soon as this son of yours came [not *my brother* but *your son*], who has devoured your livelihood with harlots [says who? he assumes the worst], you killed the fatted calf for him" (verses 29–30).

Buried beneath the older son's seemingly perfect exterior lay a dark, cancerous mass of anger, rebellion, and envy, fueled by hidden, unfulfilled expectations. This young man had an inflated sense of his own worth and a secret desire for recognition that surfaced when someone he deemed less worthy than himself became a recipient of lavish grace.

The application of this story to the Pharisees who were seated in the crowd that day seems obvious to us. But I wonder if it was obvious to them. Or were they so blinded by their pride that they couldn't see that Jesus' description of the elder brother fit them perfectly? And could we be so blind to our own need that we fail to recognize the "elder brother" when he is staring back at us in the mirror?

Broken or Unbroken?

We've reflected upon four biblical accounts. We've seen four individuals who were humble and broken, and four people or groups of people who were proud and unbroken. Is it merely coincidental that in all four cases, the proud people were respected individuals who held an elevated position or had some sort of leadership responsibility?

We may be missing the heart of the gospel and the grace of Christ.

The fact is, the higher up we find ourselves in terms of power, influence, and wealth—the more people look up to us—the more vulnerable we are to pride and self-deceit, and the more prone we are to be blind to our spiritual needs and deficiencies. Once we are established in a position of influence, we have a reputation to maintain. We have a lot to lose if we get honest about our real spiritual needs. For most of us, the subtle encroachment of pride is more dangerous, and more likely to render us useless to God and others, than any other kind of failure.

As you consider these four comparisons between proud and broken people, with which of those characters do you most identify? Do you relate to adulterous King David? To the cheating tax collector? To the sexually promiscuous woman? To the lustful, wild-living Prodigal? "No way," you say. "I'd never do anything like that!"

Well, then, do you relate to proud King Saul? To the self-righteous Pharisees? To the angry elder brother?

And, by the way, with which of these kinds of individuals do you think Jesus was most comfortable? Though it seemed scandalous and outrageous to the Pharisees of His day, as it does to modern-day Pharisees, Jesus was always drawn to those whose sin seemed to be more egregious (from a human point of view), but who were repentant over their sin. On the other hand, He was repulsed by those who looked like perfect saints but whose hearts were proud and unbroken.

Could it be that God is more offended by those of us who appear to be respectable and spiritual but who have proud, unteachable spirits, than He is by adulterers, fornicators, sodomites, abortionists, or pornographers who make no pretense of being godly? The sobering reality is that proud, unbroken Christians have done far more damage to the church of Jesus Christ than any sinners outside the church could inflict.

In our focus on the needs and failures of those we consider less spiritual than ourselves, and in our drive to perform and to protect our image, we may be missing the heart of the gospel and the grace of Christ.

You see, the message of repentance is not just for adulterers and prodigals; it is also for elder brothers and Pharisees and respected leaders. The good news is that, regardless of which category we may find ourselves in, the grace of God is always available to those who lay down their pride and offer the sacrifice of a broken, contrite heart.

Pride is the greatest of all evils that beset us, and of all our enemies it is that which dies the slowest and hardest.

———————

J. N. DARBY[1]

AM I *a* PROUD
or a BROKEN PERSON?

YEARS AGO A MISSIONARY served in a region in Africa that had known seasons of true revival. He reported that whenever he would mention the name of any Christian, the national believers would ask him, "Is he a broken Christian?" They did not ask, "Is he a committed Christian?" or "Is he a knowledgeable Christian?" or "Is he a hardworking Christian?" They wanted to know, "Is he a broken Christian?"

Are you a broken Christian? Am I? How can we know?

Over the years I have asked the Lord to show me some of the characteristics of a broken person, and how they compare with a person with a proud spirit. In the form of a "proud versus broken" comparison, I have listed some of the things that have come to my attention as I've allowed the Lord to search my own heart. This is by no means an exhaustive list; the Lord will undoubtedly show you other characteristics as you open your heart to Him.

Let me encourage you to avoid the temptation to skim through this list. Instead, take time to read it prayerfully and ask God to show you, "Am I a proud or a broken person?" You may even want to place a small check mark next to any evidences of pride that you see in your life. That simple act could be an important step toward cultivating the broken, humble heart that God revives.

ATTITUDES TOWARD OTHERS

1. PROUD PEOPLE FOCUS ON THE FAILURES OF OTHERS AND CAN READILY POINT OUT THOSE FAULTS.
❧ *Broken people are more conscious of their own spiritual need than of anyone else's.*

2. PROUD PEOPLE HAVE A CRITICAL, FAULTFINDING SPIRIT. THEY LOOK AT EVERYONE ELSE'S FAULTS WITH A MICROSCOPE BUT VIEW THEIR OWN WITH A TELESCOPE.
❧ *Broken people are compassionate—they have the kind of love that overlooks a multitude of sins; they can forgive much because they know how much they have been forgiven.*

3. PROUD PEOPLE ARE ESPECIALLY PRONE TO CRITICIZE THOSE IN POSITIONS OF AUTHORITY—THEIR PASTOR, THEIR BOSS, THEIR HUSBAND, THEIR PARENTS—AND THEY TALK TO OTHERS ABOUT THE FAULTS THEY SEE.
❧ *Broken people reverence, encourage, and lift up those that God has placed in positions of authority, and they talk to God in intercession, rather than gossiping about the faults they see in others.*

4. PROUD PEOPLE ARE SELF-RIGHTEOUS; THEY THINK HIGHLY OF THEMSELVES AND LOOK DOWN ON OTHERS.
❧ *Broken people think the best of others; they esteem others as better than themselves.*

5. PROUD PEOPLE HAVE AN INDEPENDENT, SELF-SUFFICIENT SPIRIT.

🕊 Broken people have a dependent spirit; they recognize their need for God and for others.

ATTITUDES ABOUT RIGHTS

6. PROUD PEOPLE HAVE TO PROVE THAT THEY ARE RIGHT—THEY HAVE TO GET THE LAST WORD.
🕊 Broken people are willing to yield the right to be right.

7. PROUD PEOPLE CLAIM RIGHTS AND HAVE A DEMANDING SPIRIT.
🕊 Broken people yield their rights and have a meek spirit.

8. PROUD PEOPLE ARE SELF-PROTECTIVE OF THEIR TIME, THEIR RIGHTS, AND THEIR REPUTATION.
🕊 Broken people are self-denying and self-sacrificing.

ATTITUDES ABOUT SERVICE AND MINISTRY

9. PROUD PEOPLE DESIRE TO BE SERVED—THEY WANT LIFE TO REVOLVE AROUND THEM AND THEIR OWN NEEDS.
🕊 Broken people are motivated to serve others and to be sure others' needs are met before their own.

10. PROUD PEOPLE DESIRE TO BE KNOWN AS A SUCCESS.
🕊 Broken people are motivated to be faithful and to make others successful.

11. PROUD PEOPLE HAVE A FEELING—CONSCIOUS OR SUBCONSCIOUS—THAT "THIS MINISTRY (OR THIS

ORGANIZATION) IS PRIVILEGED TO HAVE ME AND MY GIFTS." THEY FOCUS ON WHAT THEY CAN DO FOR GOD.
❧ *Broken people have a heart attitude that says, "I don't deserve to have any part in this ministry"; they know that they have nothing to offer God except the life of Jesus flowing through their broken lives.*

ATTITUDES ABOUT RECOGNITION

12. PROUD PEOPLE CRAVE SELF-ADVANCEMENT.
❧ *Broken people desire to promote others.*

13. PROUD PEOPLE HAVE A DRIVE TO BE RECOGNIZED AND APPRECIATED FOR THEIR EFFORTS.
❧ *Broken people have a sense of their own unworthiness; they are thrilled that God would use them at all.*

14. PROUD PEOPLE GET WOUNDED WHEN OTHERS ARE PROMOTED AND THEY ARE OVERLOOKED.
❧ *Broken people are eager for others to get the credit, and they rejoice when others are lifted up.*

15. PROUD PEOPLE ARE ELATED BY PRAISE AND DE-FLATED BY CRITICISM.
❧ *Broken people know that any praise of their accomplishments belongs to the Lord and that criticism can help them grow into spiritual maturity.*

ATTITUDES ABOUT THEMSELVES

16. PROUD PEOPLE FEEL CONFIDENT IN HOW MUCH THEY KNOW.
❧ *Broken people are humbled by how very much they have to learn.*

17. PROUD PEOPLE ARE SELF-CONSCIOUS; THEY WORRY ABOUT WHAT OTHERS THINK OF THEM.

☙ *Broken people are not preoccupied with what others think of them.*

18. PROUD PEOPLE ARE CONCERNED ABOUT APPEARING RESPECTABLE; THEY ARE DRIVEN TO PROTECT THEIR IMAGE AND REPUTATION.

☙ *Broken people are concerned with being real; they care less about what others think than about what God knows—they are willing to die to their own reputation.*

19. PROUD PEOPLE CAN'T BEAR TO FAIL OR FOR ANYONE TO THINK THEY ARE LESS THAN PERFECT. THIS CAN DRIVE THEM TO EXTREMES—WORKAHOLIC TENDENCIES, PERFECTIONISM, THE TENDENCY TO DRIVE OTHERS OR TO PLACE UNREALISTIC EXPECTATIONS ON THEMSELVES OR OTHERS.

☙ *Broken people can recognize and live within God-given limitations.*

ATTITUDES ABOUT RELATIONSHIPS

20. PROUD PEOPLE KEEP OTHERS AT ARM'S LENGTH.

☙ *Broken people are willing to take the risks of getting close to others and loving intimately.*

21. PROUD PEOPLE ARE QUICK TO BLAME OTHERS.

☙ *Broken people accept personal responsibility and can acknowledge where they were wrong in a situation.*

22. PROUD PEOPLE WAIT FOR OTHERS TO COME AND ASK FORGIVENESS WHEN THERE IS A MISUNDERSTANDING OR A BREACH IN A RELATIONSHIP.

☙ *Broken people take the initiative to be reconciled, no matter how wrong the other party may have been.*

23. PROUD PEOPLE ARE UNAPPROACHABLE OR DEFEN-
SIVE WHEN CORRECTED.
❧ *Broken people receive correction with a humble, open spirit.*

24. PROUD PEOPLE FIND IT DIFFICULT TO DISCUSS
THEIR SPIRITUAL NEEDS WITH OTHERS.
❧ *Broken people are willing to be open and transparent with others as
God directs.*

25. PROUD PEOPLE TRY TO CONTROL THE PEOPLE AND
THE CIRCUMSTANCES AROUND THEM—THEY ARE
PRONE TO MANIPULATE.
❧ *Broken people trust in God—they rest in Him and are able to wait
for Him to act on their behalf.*

26. PROUD PEOPLE BECOME BITTER AND RESENTFUL
WHEN THEY ARE WRONGED; THEY HAVE EMOTIONAL
TEMPER TANTRUMS; THEY HOLD OTHERS HOSTAGE
AND ARE EASILY OFFENDED; THEY CARRY GRUDGES AND
KEEP A RECORD OF OTHERS' WRONGS.
❧ *Broken people give thanks in all things; they are quick to forgive
those who wrong them.*

ATTITUDES ABOUT SIN

27. PROUD PEOPLE WANT TO BE SURE THAT NO ONE
FINDS OUT WHEN THEY HAVE SINNED; THEIR INSTINCT
IS TO COVER UP.
❧ *Broken people aren't overly concerned with who knows or who finds
out about their sin—they are willing to be exposed because they have
nothing to lose.*

28. PROUD PEOPLE HAVE A HARD TIME SAYING, "I WAS
WRONG; WILL YOU PLEASE FORGIVE ME?"

❦ *Broken people are quick to admit their failure and to seek forgiveness when necessary.*

29. PROUD PEOPLE TEND TO DEAL IN GENERALITIES WHEN CONFESSING THEIR SIN TO GOD ("DEAR LORD, PLEASE FORGIVE ME FOR ALL MY SINS . . .") OR EXPRESSING SPIRITUAL NEED TO OTHERS ("I NEED TO BE A BETTER CHRISTIAN . . .").

❦ *Broken people are able to acknowledge specifics when confessing their sin: "Lord, I agree with You that I love myself more than I love my mate; I confess that I am addicted to television; I'm a glutton; I have a critical spirit; I am an angry mother. . . ."*

30. PROUD PEOPLE ARE CONCERNED ABOUT THE CONSEQUENCES OF THEIR SIN. THEY ARE DISTURBED OVER THE PROBLEMS CAUSED BY THEIR SIN—FOR EXAMPLE, THE FINANCIAL BONDAGE CREATED BY THEIR OVERSPENDING, OR THE PROBLEMS IN THEIR MARRIAGE THAT HAVE RESULTED FROM SELFISHNESS AND IMMORAL CHOICES.

❦ *Broken people are grieved over the cause, the root of their sin. They are more concerned about how their sin has grieved and dishonored God than about the problems it has created in their lives.*

31. PROUD PEOPLE ARE REMORSEFUL OVER THEIR SIN—SORRY THAT THEY GOT CAUGHT OR FOUND OUT.

❦ *Broken people are truly repentant over their sin, and the evidence of their repentance is that they forsake the sin.*

ATTITUDES ABOUT THEIR WALK WITH GOD

32. PROUD PEOPLE ARE BLIND TO THE TRUE CONDITION OF THEIR HEARTS.

🕏 *Broken people walk in the light and acknowledge the truth about their lives.*

33. PROUD PEOPLE COMPARE THEMSELVES WITH OTHERS AND FEEL WORTHY OF RESPECT.

🕏 *Broken people compare themselves with the holiness of God and feel a desperate need for His mercy.*

34. PROUD PEOPLE DON'T THINK THEY NEED TO REPENT OF ANYTHING.

🕏 *Broken people realize that they need to maintain a continual heart attitude of repentance.*

35. PROUD PEOPLE DON'T THINK THEY NEED REVIVAL, BUT THEY ARE SURE EVERYONE ELSE DOES. (IN FACT, RIGHT ABOUT NOW, THEY ARE MAKING A MENTAL LIST OF THE PEOPLE THEY THINK NEED TO READ THIS BOOK!)

🕏 *Broken people continually sense their need for a fresh encounter with God and for a fresh filling of His Holy Spirit.* [2]

Are you a "broken Christian"? Based on these characteristics, how would you answer that question? How would those in your family or your workplace respond if they were asked, "Is he/she a broken Christian?" Most important, what would God say?

If this list has helped you realize that you are a proud, rather than a broken, person, do not despair. God has been merciful to show you your need. The first step to brokenness and humility is to get honest and acknowledge your need. Walk in the light; agree with God about what He has revealed to be the true condition of your heart. Don't try to cover up, justify, rationalize, compare yourself with your mate, or pretend that you are better off than you really are. "Humble [yourself] in the sight of the Lord, and He will lift you up" (James 4:10). The infinite riches and blessings of the kingdom of God belong to those who recognize their spiritual poverty.

Notes

1. Edwin and Lillian Harvey, comps., *Royal Insignia* (Yanceyville, N.C.: Harvey & Tait, 1992), 87.
2. The key points from this list are available on a bookmark (individually or in quantity). Contact Revive Our Hearts, P.O. Box 2000, Niles, MI 49120; (877) 432-7894; e-mail: info@ReviveOur Hearts.com.

The broken person . . . will find that all of the resources of heaven and all of the Spirit's power are now at his disposal and, unless heaven's riches can be exhausted or the Spirit's power can be found wanting, he cannot come up short.

JENNIFER KENNEDY DEAN[1]

The BLESSING
of BROKENNESS

BY MOST STANDARDS, Brian and Melanie Adams had a good marriage. They were both believers, they were committed to each other, and they were trying to lead their eight children to follow Christ. However, over nineteen years of marriage, the intimacy they had once experienced had gradually eroded. Melanie says, "The dinner table had grown larger and larger between us with the addition of each child, and I had almost come to accept that we would never experience the closeness that we both longed for and needed."

When they had an opportunity to attend a retreat called "Renewing Your Heart—Reviving Your Marriage," Melanie hoped this might be just what they needed. In her "humble" opinion, her husband needed to improve in some areas, and what better place to repair your husband than a marriage retreat!

On the second day of the retreat, the speaker gave a message on bitterness and the need for personal brokenness and humility. As Melanie and Brian walked back to their room together following the session, Melanie was mentally preparing a lecture for Brian on the need for brokenness in his life.

What followed can only be described as a supernatural work of the Spirit in Melanie's heart. She writes: "God began to peel back the layers of my heart, and what was revealed was not pretty: bitterness, hardness of heart, hate, rebellion, and most of all a dependence on my own righteousness, and an underlying pride that corrupted all."

What kinds of blessings does brokenness bring?

As God showed Melanie the true condition of her heart, she began to cry, then to weep. Sobs of grief and despair racked her body. Her shocked husband held her close as she poured out her confession. Like an infection being drained from a lanced cyst, the pride and self-righteousness were purged from her spirit.

From that place of humility and brokenness before God and her husband, Melanie cried out to God to take away her heart of stone and give her a heart of flesh. She describes what happened next: "In His mercy, like a refreshing, cleansing wind, the Spirit of God swept through my heart. My tears of anguish were transformed to tears of joy, forgiveness, and freedom. God had chosen to reveal His glory—and I will never be the same. Never."

Why would anyone choose to be broken? Well, why would a man check into a hospital and allow the surgeon to start cutting? Is it because he loves pain? Of course not. It is because he knows that surgery is the only way to experience healing and to be physically restored. What makes a woman willing to endure long hours of intense labor? She knows that beyond the labor there will be the joy of a new life.

So why would anyone choose the pathway of brokenness? Because, as Melanie discovered, *brokenness brings blessedness.* Jesus said, *"Blessed are the poor in spirit"*—contrary to what we would expect, brokenness is the pathway to blessing! There are no alternate routes; there are no shortcuts. The very thing we dread and are tempted to resist is actually the means to God's greatest blessings in our lives. What kinds of blessings does brokenness bring?

God Draws Near to the Broken

Again and again in the Scripture, we learn that God "resists the proud" (see Proverbs 3:34; James 4:6; 1 Peter 5:5). The concept here is that

God sets Himself in "battle array" against those who are proud; He stiff-arms the arrogant; He keeps them at a distance. God repels those who are self-sufficient and who take unholy pride in their accomplishments.

On the other hand, He pours grace on the humble. He comes to the rescue of the humble. Like an ambulance racing to the scene in response to a call for help, so God races to the scene when His children humble themselves and acknowledge their need. As Charles Spurgeon reminds us, "He that humbles himself under the hand of God shall not fail to be enriched, uplifted, sustained, and comforted by the ever-gracious One. It is a habit of Jehovah to cast down the proud, and lift up the lowly."[2]

Over and over again, I have experienced the grace of God poured out in response to my need. I recall one particular day when I found myself physically and emotionally depleted in the midst of an especially grueling season of ministry. I was getting ready to leave on yet another trip when I "hit the wall," feeling that I just could not go on. I collapsed into a chair in my study and began to sob uncontrollably. At that point, I had two options. I could try to pull myself together, put on a strong front, put one foot in front of the other, and somehow muster up the strength to do what I had to do.

However, I knew that acting in self-sufficiency would cause me to forfeit the grace and presence of God in my life. I knew how much I needed His grace, and I could not bear the thought of going on without His presence. So in my weakness and desperation, I chose option two: I made the conscious decision to humble myself, to acknowledge my need, and to cry out to the Lord for grace. After praying and confirming that He indeed wanted me to make the trip, I asked Him for the supernatural enabling to do what He had called me to do.

The next day I stood and addressed an audience of full-time Christian workers. My topic was "The Potential Pitfalls of Ministry." The reality was, at the time, that I had fallen into or was perilously close to several of those pitfalls myself. I was tempted to try to protect my image before those Christian workers—to leave them with the impression that I had somehow avoided all those pitfalls and that *they* were the ones who needed this message.

But I knew that I was the one who really needed that message, and that if I wanted God's grace to meet me at my point of need, I needed to humble myself before Him (roof off) and before those in the audience (walls down) and be honest about the condition of my own life.

This mystery is that death brings life.

Do you wonder why God sometimes seems so far away? Could it be that He has withdrawn His presence and is resisting you because of lingering pride in your heart? "Though the Lord is on high, yet He regards the lowly; but the proud He knows from afar" (Psalm 138:6).

Do you want to be close to God? Even as the father of the Prodigal Son drew his broken, repentant boy to his chest and embraced and restored him, so our heavenly Father draws near to those who come to Him with humble, broken hearts.

New Life Is Released

Recently a friend wrote to tell me how God had brought him to a fresh point of brokenness. In describing the difference brokenness has made in his life, he used a vivid word picture:

> Prior to this time, I struggled with low-grade depression. I had turned so much anger inward that it had become churning hatred, which affected my entire attitude. However, since God brought me to a new point of brokenness, I have described my life as one that has moved from being in a black-and-white movie, to being lived in a *full-color motion picture!*

My friend's experience illustrates another blessing of brokenness. When we are faced with the prospect of being broken with Christ at the cross, we are tempted to believe that will be the end for us. And in a sense, it is the end—the end of our pride, our self-life, and the rule of our flesh. But in reality, it is just the beginning. Through our willingness to be united with Christ in His death, new life is released through our brokenness—the supernatural, resurrection life of Christ.

THE BLESSING OF BROKENNESS

In John 12, immediately following the triumphal entry into Jerusalem, Jesus turned to His disciples and began to speak of His imminent death. He introduced the subject by saying, "The hour has come that the Son of Man should be glorified" (verse 23). Glorified? Why would anyone describe his *death* as the hour in which he would be glorified? Hadn't Jesus just been glorified when He was escorted into Jerusalem by throngs of adoring worshipers?

Jesus understood something that His disciples would not grasp until after His death, resurrection, and ascension back into heaven—something the Bible calls a "mystery." This mystery is that *death brings life*, and that there can be no real life apart from our willingness to die. To help explain this principle, Jesus used an illustration from the world of farming: "Unless a grain of wheat falls into the ground and *dies*, it remains alone; but if it *dies*, it produces much grain" (verse 24, italics added).

I can take a grain of wheat and clean it up, put it on a beautiful piece of china on my dining room table, shine lights on it, play music for it, pray for it, and what will happen to it? Absolutely nothing! It will always just sit there "alone." What has to happen to that grain if it is to bear fruit? It must go down into the ground and *die*. If that grain of wheat had feelings, I can imagine it might say, "Hey, it's dark down here! It's cold down here! It's lonely down here!" But in that dark, cold, lonely place, the grain will shed its hard outer husk so that the life within it may be released. Then—after it has "died"—it will put down roots, and the first shoots of new life will finally spring forth.

By the way, I believe one of the reasons that so many people live with chronic loneliness is that they are unwilling to die. As Jesus pointed out, if a grain of wheat does not fall into the ground and die, it "remains alone." Our natural instinct is to hold on protectively to our own lives. When we refuse to shed that hard, outer shell called "self," no one can get close to us; no one can penetrate or enter into our life. Just as pride repulses God, so pride keeps others from getting close to us.

Years ago, when I was a college student, I heard Pastor Ray Ortlund say, "Most churches are like a bag of marbles—all hard and clanging up against one another. Instead, we ought to be like a bag of grapes— *squished* together so that the juice of His Spirit may flow out through us." True Christian community, as Pastor Ray described it, is something few believers ever experience, because it requires that each individual let go of "self" and pour out his life on behalf of others.

What does this kind of death mean? It means that we must be willing to die to our own interests, die to our own reputation, die to our own rights, die to our own ways of doing things, die to our own comfort, convenience, hopes, dreams, and aspirations. To "die" means to lay it all down. To give it all up. To let it all go. This may seem difficult, perhaps even unthinkable, to our self-protective, individualistic, rights-oriented minds. But, as Jesus went on to tell His disciples, "He who loves his life will lose it, and he who hates his life in this world will keep it for eternal life" (John 12:25).

What was Jesus saying? The only way to gain your life is to give it up. The only way to win it is to lose it. We think we are giving up so much by dying. But in reality, it is those who refuse to die who are giving up everything. When we choose the pathway of brokenness and humility, we are choosing to receive new life—His supernatural, abundant life—flowing in us and through us.

Of course, the ultimate picture of that kind of brokenness is the Lord Jesus Himself. He is the One who said, "This is My body which is *broken* for you" (1 Corinthians 11:24, italics added).

The prophet Isaiah spoke of the Lord Jesus when he said, "He was wounded for our transgressions, He was *bruised* for our iniquities. . . . It pleased the Lord to *bruise* Him" (53:5, 10, italics added).

The cross became the site of Christ's true glorification.

Interestingly, the word translated "bruised" in Isaiah 53 is a variation of the word used in Isaiah 57:15, where God says, "I dwell . . . with him who has a *contrite* and humble spirit, to revive the spirit of the humble, and to revive the heart of the *contrite* ones." As we have seen, that word means to be crushed or broken in pieces. Jesus was willing to be crushed, to die, so that through His death, eternal life could be released for us.

In both the natural and supernatural realms, *death brings life*. The petals of the rose must be crushed for the perfume to be released, and the caterpillar must die to its life as a caterpillar and surrender to the confines of a chrysalis so it can be metamorphosed into a butterfly. The apostle Paul said that if "the rulers of this age" (including Satan and his demons) had known this mystery, they would have never crucified the Lord Jesus (1 Corinthians 2:8). They thought the cross was Jesus' ultimate defeat and their final triumph. In fact, it proved to be just the reverse.

Because Jesus understood the ways of God, He did not resent or resist His death. He reminded His disciples that no man took His life from Him, but that He laid it down willingly (John 10:18). When the time came, in obedience to the will of His Father, He turned His face toward Calvary and went as a lamb to the slaughter. He knew that beyond the cross there was life everlasting. For this reason, the cross became the site of His true glorification—the place where He conquered death and gave birth to eternal life.

So, too, when you and I are willing to be broken in union with Him, His abundant life is released to flow through us to others. Brokenness is the entrance into life. Not until we are broken can we begin to experience the free flow of the power of His Spirit in and through our lives.

Deeper Love, Deeper Worship

When Melanie Adams finally came to the end of herself and was broken before God and her husband, God began to increase her capacity for love and for worship. Several months after that initial point of brokenness, Melanie wrote to tell some of the changes that had taken place in her life as a result:

> I have fallen in love with my husband more deeply than ever. It was quite a rude awakening to realize the chasm in our marriage was my fault, born of an unforgiving heart. My husband has forgiven me and I smile at the future.
>
> I have developed the somewhat frustrating habit of crying all the time—not a normal response for me. In church, a song of worship or a meaningful message finds me borrowing my husband's handkerchief as he gently pats my hand.

God's Word jumps off the page every time I open His Holy Book—it is personal now. I enjoy a sweet communion with the Lord and have heartfelt gratitude for His love and sacrifice that I never knew before. I have peace and joy, and He has given me a new song.

Like Melanie, the "sinner woman" who anointed Jesus' feet was able to love much because she had been forgiven much. We see in this unnamed woman of Luke 7 a freedom and an abandon that many believers never experience. She was oblivious to the rejection or the disapproval of anyone around her. Her expressions of worship and love were extravagant and lavish. All that mattered to her was Jesus.

Have you ever known someone who worshiped the Lord with great abandon, who was unusually free to express her love to God and to others? Perhaps you envied her freedom. Or perhaps you found yourself feeling critical—questioning her motives or the appropriateness of her behavior, even as Simon the Pharisee was critical of the woman who "crashed" his dinner party.

Why is it so hard for us to express our love and worship?

So many of us are bound up in our ability to express love and worship. And it's odd, because many of us have no difficulty cheering till we're hoarse at a ball game. But to *sing* aloud in church? To lift our hands in adoration before the Lord? To pray aloud in front of others? To step out of our comfort zone and engage someone we don't know in a spiritual conversation? To express verbal appreciation for what another believer has meant in our life? That's another matter altogether.

Why is it so hard for us to express our love and worship? Perhaps it is because we still have the roof on and the walls up. Pride causes us to erect barriers between ourselves and God, and walls between ourselves and others. It makes us so concerned about what others think that we are imprisoned to our inhibitions.

"But that's just my personality—I'm naturally shy," someone might counter. Let's get honest. Is it really a matter of personality, or could it be a matter of pride? When our personality is surrendered to the Holy

Spirit, He will express the heart of God in and through us. We will no longer be self-conscious but entirely God-conscious.

There is a lot being said today about freedom, love, and worship, and a fervent attempt is being made in many circles to cultivate love in the body of Christ and create worshipful experiences. However, true freedom, love, and worship cannot be manufactured or engineered. Part of the problem is that we are short-circuiting the process God has established that leads to these things.

True worship begins with *brokenness and humility* over whatever God reveals to us in His Word. Poverty of spirit and mourning over our sin lead to genuine *repentance*, which in turn leads to *forgiveness*. Forgiveness will produce *freedom*—freedom from guilt and bondage. When we have freedom that has been birthed out of brokenness, repentance, and forgiveness, we will have a greater capacity for *love*—supernatural ability to love God and to love those who are unlovable—and for *worship*. And of course, true love and worship will lead us back to a new level of brokenness, which leads to greater and deeper repentance, increased forgiveness, newfound freedom, and an even greater capacity for love and for worship.

Brokenness is the starting place for a lifelong cycle. We cannot experience true freedom, love, and worship if we do not enter by way of humility, repentance, and forgiveness.

One of the most memorable things to me about the Campus Crusade gathering in 1995 is the obvious way that personal and corporate brokenness resulted in a new capacity for love and worship. Initially, as people began to mourn and grieve over their sin, the atmosphere was heavy, as God's hand of conviction settled in on that auditorium. Nobody felt much like singing. But over the next couple of days, people began to sing—not because a worship leader said it was time to sing but simply out of gratitude and devotion to Jesus. Many of the songs focused on the grace of God and the wonder of His love and forgiveness.

Rarely have I heard more beautiful or heartfelt music than that which poured forth from those freshly cleansed hearts and lives. As the week progressed, the spirit of praise and worship began to intensify. On the final evening of the conference, the celebration was unforgettable.

Strains of "Shout to the Lord All the Earth!" nearly lifted the roof off the building.

The night of weeping turned to shouts of joy (Psalm 30:5); the bones that He had broken began to rejoice (Psalm 51:8); hearts that had been delivered from guilt were freed to sing aloud of His righteousness (Psalm 51:14); the spirit of heaviness was replaced with the garment of praise (Isaiah 61:3). So it will be in the lives of all who choose the pathway of brokenness.

Able to Be Used by God

One of the recurring themes of Scripture is that God uses things and people that are broken. That is His way. The turning point of Jacob's life took place in a wrestling match in the middle of the night at the river Jabbok (Genesis 32). Years earlier God had promised to bless Jacob, but he had never been able to enjoy that blessing because he had been trying to control and manage life on his own terms.

Now, at Jabbok, Jacob came to a situation over which he had no control and which he could not manage. The next morning he was to meet his estranged brother who was approaching with an army. Jacob the conniver was cornered, and he was terrified. God had his attention. That night God, in the form of an angel, met Jacob and engaged him in hand-to-hand combat, while Jacob struggled to elicit the blessing that already belonged to him.

In conceding defeat, Jacob won his ultimate victory.

The real victory was won when Jacob was overcome by the angel, and when the angel asked Jacob his name. At that moment, I wonder if Jacob had a flashback to the day years earlier when he had been trying to wrest a blessing from his elderly, blind father. Isaac had asked him, "Who are you, my son?" (Genesis 27:18), and Jacob had deceived his father by claiming to be his brother Esau. The pride of his heart had caused him to pretend to be somebody he wasn't.

This time, Jacob had met his match. No longer controlling, he had come under the control of One infinitely stronger than he, and he finally spoke the truth about who he was:

"What is your name?"

"*Jacob.*"

No pretending, no trying to leave a good impression, no explaining, no justifying. Jacob spoke the bare, naked truth. "Jacob—the schemer, the deceiver, the manipulator, the con artist. That's who I am." And in conceding defeat, Jacob won his ultimate victory. At that point, he was a new man. With Jacob's natural strength broken down, God was able to clothe him with spiritual power. Once he admitted the truth about who he was, God gave him a new name—*Israel,* meaning "prince with God"—representative of a new character. Now he was usable in God's hands.

Like Jacob, Moses also knew the power of brokenness. After forty years in the palace where he was part of the royal court, it took forty more years in the desert to strip him of all his natural assets—giftedness, contacts, position, reputation. Moses lost it all. But he emerged at the burning bush a broken man, usable in the hands of God.

When the children of Israel arrived at Mount Horeb and found no drinking water, Moses got another lesson in brokenness (Exodus 17). "Strike the rock," God said, "and water will come out." Anybody knows you don't get water out of a rock. But obediently, Moses struck the rock—a picture of Christ being smitten, broken for us—and water came gushing out to quench the thirst of two million thirsty Israelites in the desert.

And then there was the unlikely military leader named Gideon. Hopelessly outnumbered by the Midianite army, Gideon's ragtag assortment of soldiers had no chance of survival, much less of victory. But as is so often the case, brokenness was the name of God's battle plan. Break down the army until there are so few that you look ridiculous. Break the pitchers so that the light of the lanterns within can shine forth. Out of brokenness comes light, and in that light the enemy is thrown into disarray, the victory is won. In the end, everyone knows who won the battle.

Our greatest example, of course, is the Lord Jesus. When His body was broken on Calvary, eternal life was released for the salvation of the world. Do you want to live a fruitful life? Do you want the fragrance of the life of Christ to be released through you? Do you want the power of God to flow through you? Do you want to be a usable instrument in His hands? Follow the Savior to the cross. His death and the resurrection that followed bear eternal witness that brokenness brings increased fruitfulness.

Yes, God uses things and people that are broken. In a sense, revival is really nothing more than the release of God's Spirit flowing through broken lives. Historical records of revivals bear this out over and over again, as these few snapshots will reveal.

Rivers of Revival

During the Welsh Revival in 1904–5, a song rang out from the contrite hearts and lips of God's people. "Bend me lower, lower, down at Jesus' feet," they sang. Through that brokenness, God released a great floodtide of His Spirit that encompassed the entire principality and overflowed in untold blessing to the world.

Perhaps you have read or heard about the Shantung Revival in China in the late 1920s and early 1930s.[3] Dr. C. L. Culpepper was the director of a large denominational mission in that province. He was part of a group of Christian leaders and missionaries who had been praying for revival.

One night after the prayer meeting, Dr. Culpepper returned to his home and felt pressed to seek the Lord into the late hours of the night. He sensed spiritual need and dryness in his life, but he couldn't put his finger on what the issue might be. He asked, "Lord, what is it in me?"

He listened to the Lord's counsel, and he was shattered by what he heard.

The next morning, he returned to the prayer meeting and confessed to his fellow missionaries and leaders his sin of spiritual pretense and the spiritual impotence that had resulted. He acknowledged that their praise of him as a "good missionary" had caused him to be proud and to steal glory from God. He later said, "My heart was so broken I didn't believe I could live any longer."

Out of Dr. Culpepper's brokenness, God brought brokenness to that entire group of missionaries and national Christian leaders. That, in turn, resulted in a great outpouring of God's Spirit in conviction, confession, and fullness throughout the province. God revived their hearts and countless hearts among those whose lives they touched.

Twenty years later, in another corner of the world, a small band of church leaders prayed earnestly for revival in their community. They were gathered in a small town on the Isle of Lewis, the largest isle of the Outer Hebrides, just off the coast of Scotland. These believers were particularly burdened for the young people of the island who had no interest in spiritual matters and scorned the things of God.

Your brokenness may be the very thing God uses.

For eighteen months these men met, three nights a week, praying through the night, right on into the early hours of the morning, beseeching God to come and visit in revival. For eighteen months there was no evidence of any change.

Then one night, a young deacon rose to his feet, opened his Bible, and read from Psalm 24: "Who may ascend into the hill of the Lord? Or who may stand in His holy place? He who has clean hands and a pure heart. . . . He shall receive blessing from the Lord" (verses 3–5). Facing the men around him, this young man said, "Brethren, it seems to me to be just so much 'humbug' to be waiting and praying as we are, if we ourselves are not rightly related to God."

There in the straw, the men knelt and humbly confessed their own sins to the Lord. Within a short period of time, God had begun to pour out His Spirit in an extraordinary awakening that shook the entire island.

The most dramatic, widespread revival movements in history have begun with a handful of humble-hearted believers whose revived lives and prayers have become sparks that ignited the lives of those around them.

Interestingly, the "most godly" men and women on the scene have generally been the first to humble themselves and have then been used as instruments of revival. Have you been waiting for your mate or children or church leaders to humble themselves so there can be revival in your home or your church? God may be waiting for you to humble yourself; your brokenness may be the very thing He uses to provoke the brokenness of those around you. The greatest hindrance to revival is not others' unwillingness to humble themselves—it is *our* need to humble ourselves and confess our desperate need for His mercy.

Are you seeking to know God in a more intimate way? Do you want the supernatural life of His Spirit to be released through you? Do you long to be able to worship God and to love Him and others with greater freedom? Do you have a desire to be usable in God's hand? Are you conscious of a need for revival in your family, in your church, and in our world? Revival blessings flow to and through those who are truly broken before God. Andrew Murray said it well: "Just as water ever seeks and fills the lowest place, so the moment God finds you abased and empty, His glory and power flow in."

Notes

1. Jennifer Kennedy Dean, *He Restores My Soul: A Forty-Day Journey Toward Personal Renewal* (Nashville: Broadman & Holman, 1999), 27.
2. Charles H. Spurgeon, *Cheque Book of the Bank of Faith: Daily Readings* (Scotland, Great Britain: Christian Focus Publications, 1996), 210.
3. An account of this revival is recorded in C. L. Culpepper, *Spiritual Awakening: The Shantung Revival* (Atlanta: Home Mission Board, SBC, 1982).

Being broken is both God's work and ours.
He brings His pressure to bear, but we have to
make the choice. . . . All day long the choice
will be before us in a thousand ways.

———————

ROY HESSION[1]

JOURNEY
into BROKENNESS

THROUGHOUT THIS BOOK you have been introduced to believers who came to a place of brokenness before the Lord. What about you? Have you seen glimpses of your own life in these pages? Can you honestly say that you have been truly broken before God?

Perhaps you have experienced genuine brokenness in the past. Are you continuing to walk in a lifestyle of brokenness today?

You may be saying, "I recognize my need for a broken and a contrite heart; I want to choose the pathway of brokenness. Where do I begin?"

Brokenness requires both God's initiative and our response. According to the Scripture, there are three primary instruments God uses to bring us to the point of brokenness.

First, *the Word of God* has the power to soften the hardened soil of our hearts and shatter our stubborn self-life. God says, "Is not my word . . . like a hammer that breaks the rock in pieces?" (Jeremiah 23:29). The psalmist stood in awe of the power of His Word: "The voice of the Lord is powerful . . . the voice of the Lord breaks the cedars" (Psalm 29:4–5). Each time we open God's Word, whether in private or public settings, it should be with the intent of allowing the Word to break us. The same Word that serves as a hammer to break us will then become a balm to heal our hearts and a light to guide our footsteps in the pathway of humility.

Second, God uses *circumstances* to expose our need and bring us to the end of ourselves. The circumstance He uses may be a stressful job, a difficult marriage, a chronic illness, a financial crisis, or some other issue that brings pressure to bear on our lives. In the face of such pressure, we can choose to respond in pride, by resisting and resenting the circumstance, or by giving in to despair. Or we can choose to respond in humility, to submit to the hand of God and allow Him to mold and shape us through the pressure.

> *When we step into the light of God's holiness, our lives are brought into sharp relief.*

Third, God has given us *the body of Christ*. As we walk in the light with our fellow believers, they can help us see areas where we need to be broken. "Faithful are the wounds of a friend" (Proverbs 27:6)—whether that friend is a pastor, a parent, a partner, or another believer—who loves us enough to point out our spiritual blind spots.

The Word, circumstances, and other believers—these can all be tools to show us our need and create opportunities to choose the pathway of brokenness. The Spirit of God is the arm that wields each of these instruments to bring us to a point of brokenness. However, we must respond to His initiative. How can we cultivate a broken, contrite heart? The following four suggestions will help us enter into a deeper level of personal brokenness:

1. Get a Fresh Vision of God

The closer we get to God, the more clearly we will see ourselves as we really are. As long as we compare ourselves to others, we can always find someone who makes us feel good about how well we are doing. But when we step into the light of God's holiness, our lives are brought into sharp relief. What once may have seemed clean and pure suddenly looks soiled and tarnished. The pure light of His holiness exposes the nooks and crannies, the cracks and crevices of our innermost being.

Throughout the Scripture, when even the holiest men and women were confronted with the awesome holiness of God, they were moved to deep contrition and brokenness before Him.

Take Job, for example. Job was a righteous man; he feared God and lived a blameless life. For reasons known only to God, Job became a bit player in a cosmic drama, acted out between heaven and hell. When he could not fathom God's purposes for the excruciating pain he was forced to endure, and when his so-called friends wrongly assumed that he was being punished for some failure on his part, Job began to reveal a self-righteous heart.

In extended dialogue and debate, Job protested his innocence and begged for the opportunity to defend himself in the courtroom of heaven. Finally, God stepped in—as if He had been patiently waiting for someone to give Him a chance to speak. Through a series of questions that neither Job nor his friends could possibly answer, God revealed Himself in a way that Job had never experienced. God unveiled His greatness, His infinite power, His superior wisdom, His mighty acts, and His unfathomable ways.

When God had finished, Job could hardly breathe. He had been stopped dead in his tracks: "Behold, I am vile; what shall I answer You? I lay my hand over my mouth. . . . I have heard of You by the hearing of the ear, but now my eye sees You. Therefore I abhor myself, and repent in dust and ashes" (Job 40:4; 42:5–6). Job was no longer defensive, no longer claiming innocence or seeing himself as a helpless victim. In the brilliant light of God's majesty, Job was exposed; he now saw himself as a perpetrator and a vile sinner, desperately in need of mercy.

Job had been a good man—his lifestyle was above reproach and his suffering was not directly caused by his sin. Suffering did, however, serve to lift the lid off his heart and expose a deeper level of depravity than he might have otherwise seen. As a result of his encounter with God, Job was not only a good man and a religious man; now he was a broken man.

The prophet Isaiah had a similar experience. In the early chapters of Isaiah, we see this great servant of God pronouncing "woes" on the apostate nation of Israel—"woe" to those who are materialistic; "woe" to those who are relativistic; "woe" to those who are hedonistic; "woe" to those who are sensual and immoral. And he was right. These were terrible blots on the nation, even as they are in our world today.

Then we come to the first verse of Isaiah chapter 6, where Isaiah encounters God in a way he has never seen Him before. The prophet is struck with a vision of the holiness of God—holiness so intense that even the pillars in the temple had the good sense to tremble.

Isaiah no longer sees himself in contrast to all the depraved people around him. Now he sees himself in the light of the holy, high, supreme God of the universe. And what are the first words out of his mouth? No longer is it "Woe to *them*." Now it is "Woe is *me!*"

After his experience, Isaiah confessed not the sins of the nation but his own sins—"*I am a man of unclean lips.*" In response to his contrite, broken heart, God sent an angel who took a hot coal from the altar of sacrifice. In one searing, painful moment, the hot coal was applied to Isaiah's lips and he was cleansed. Prior to that point, Isaiah had been a good man; he was gifted and committed to God. But in chapter 6, Isaiah came to true brokenness. From then on, he operated not out of natural strength or superiority but out of an intense sense of his own neediness. Isaiah was a broken man.

To know God, to live in His presence, and to be occupied with a vision of His holiness is to know how foolish and frail we are apart from Him and to be broken from a preoccupation with ourselves.

2. Don't Wait for God to Break You—Choose to Be Broken

Jesus identified Himself as the rejected Stone spoken of in the Old Testament: "The stone which the builders rejected has become the chief cornerstone. This was the Lord's doing; it is marvelous in our eyes" (Psalm 118:22–23). He stressed the importance of how we choose to respond to His lordship: "Whoever falls on that stone will be broken; but on whomever it falls, it will grind him to powder" (Luke 20:18).

Some people who may seem "broken" have not been broken at all. Rather, they have been crushed by their circumstances because of their unwillingness to voluntarily fall on the Rock and be broken. Don't wait for God to break you. "*Humble yourself* under the mighty hand of God" (see

1 Peter 5:6). Fall on the Rock—Christ Jesus, who was broken for you—and cultivate the habit of crying out with the tax collector, "God, be merciful to me a sinner" and with David, "Have mercy on me, O God."

The fact is, we will all be broken—sooner or later. We can choose to be broken or we can wait for God to crush our pride. If we resist the means God provides to lead us to brokenness, we do not avoid brokenness—we simply make it necessary for God to intensify and prolong the process.

We have considered the blessings of brokenness. But we also need to be reminded of the painful price paid by those who refuse to be broken: "He, that being often reproved hardeneth his neck, shall suddenly be destroyed, and that without remedy" (Proverbs 29:1 KJV).

> *We must learn to live with the roof off and the walls down.*

For a time, we may succeed in resisting the will of God; He may allow us to continue walking in the pride of our hearts. But eventually God will bring down everything that exalts itself against Him. There will come a day when every knee will bow and every tongue will confess that Jesus Christ is Lord (see Philippians 2:10–11).

> *The lofty looks of man shall be humbled,*
> *The haughtiness of men shall be bowed down,*
> *And the Lord alone shall be exalted in that day.*
> *For the day of the Lord of hosts*
> *Shall come upon everything proud and lofty,*
> *Upon everything lifted up—*
> *And it shall be brought low.*
> —Isaiah 2:11–12

What is the alternative? Choose the pathway of brokenness. Jennifer Kennedy Dean encourages us to see the difficult circumstances of our lives as "crucifixion moments":

> Every time you are confronted with a crucifixion moment, choose to lay down your self-life. Choose to surrender your pride, your

expectations, your rights, your demands. Choose the way of the cross. Let someone else get the credit you deserve; forego the opportunity to have the last word; die to the demands of your flesh.[2]

3. Acknowledge Spiritual Need—to God and to Others

If we want to live a lifestyle of humility and brokenness, we must learn to live with the roof off and the walls down. One practical way to do that is to make a habit of acknowledging and verbalizing our spiritual need to God and to others.

Living with the "roof off" toward God is having a heart attitude that says, "It's not my father, not my brother, not my mate, not my kids, not my roommate, not my boss, not the youth director or the pastor—it's *me*, oh Lord, standin' in the need of prayer!" To live with the roof off toward God means that I no longer blame others, but I take personal responsibility for my sin. There is no brokenness where the finger of blame is still pointed at another; brokenness means no excuses, no defending, no rationalizing my sin.

When I acknowledge my need to God, I say,

> *Nothing in my hand I bring,*
> *Simply to Thy cross I cling;*
> *Naked, come to Thee for dress,*
> *Helpless, look to Thee for grace.*
> *Foul, I to the fountain fly;*
> *Wash me, Savior, or I die.*[3]

For many of us, it is easier to live with the roof off than it is to let the walls down—to be transparent and honest with others. We work so hard at leaving a good impression; we want others to think well of us. But once we have really been contrite and humble before God, it will not be threatening to be humble and honest with others—we have nothing to lose, no reputation to protect—because we have *died*. The broken person is willing to say, "Will you pray for me? I have a need in my life—God is dealing with me in this specific area." Brokenness toward God produces openness toward others. Living with the walls down toward others can become a wonderful means of God's grace in our lives.

When I was in my midtwenties, God's Spirit began to convict me that I had developed a habit of "exaggerating the truth" in certain situations. ("Exaggeration" is actually a proud, unbroken word for "lying.") Driven to make a good impression on others, I was frequently guilty of "stretching" the truth. Though no one else knew of my deception, and though others might have considered my offenses relatively inconsequential, I experienced an almost suffocating (and blessed!) sense of God's conviction in my heart, and I knew this was something I had to bring into the light.

I agreed with God, confessed my deception, and purposed to begin speaking the truth in every situation. But I soon discovered that lying was a stronghold in my life—it was deeply ingrained. I was hooked and couldn't seem to get set free. Ultimately, the freedom that I needed and longed for began when I was willing to let the walls down. God brought to mind the principle of James 5:16: "Confess your trespasses to one another, and pray for one another, that you may be healed."

I will never forget approaching two godly individuals, acknowledging to them my sin of lying, and asking them to pray for me. It was one of the most difficult things I had ever done, and I would certainly have preferred to work things out alone with the Lord. But the very pride that didn't want to be exposed was the same pride that was causing me to lie. The moment I humbled myself and let down those walls, the pride that had kept me in bondage had its back broken, and I was set free to begin speaking the truth.

Even now, it is not easy for me to put this story in print. But I know that every opportunity to humble myself is an opportunity to get more of His grace, which will enable me to obey God in every area of my life—including being truthful.

4. Do Whatever You Know God Wants You to Do

In most of our lives, there are specific issues about which we know God has revealed something that we have not fully obeyed. Pride causes us to resist or delay our obedience. The humble, broken heart says simply,

"Yes, Lord"; "Have Thine own way, Lord. Thou art the Potter; I am the clay."

A number of years ago, I began to realize that the television had become a barrier in my relationship with the Lord. I live alone and had been using the television as a "companion" when I got home after a long day of work. I knew that I would be better off in my walk with the Lord if I turned the TV off—but, for some reason, I resisted yielding to Him. I'm ashamed to admit that I wrestled with this issue for months before I finally surrendered. My resistance had been based on some twisted sense that I would be giving up something I wanted. But the incredible freedom and increased fruitfulness that flowed out of that point of surrender have far surpassed anything that I may have "lost" by giving up my TV viewing.

Some might think, *What's the big deal? Are you trying to tell me I can't watch TV anymore?* I'm not telling you what you can or can't do. Nor am I suggesting that watching television is inherently sinful. I am saying that if we want the blessings of brokenness, we must obey God whenever He begins to deal with our hearts about an issue, regardless of what the issue may be or how hard it may be for our flesh to say yes to God.

For me, the "big deal" was not so much *what* I was watching on television (though when I finally turned it off, I began to realize how desensitized I had become to things that were displeasing to the Lord). The big deal was that I was resisting the direction of the Holy Spirit. The big deal was that I had not considered His authority to be a big deal in my life.

I had not shaken my fist in God's face. However, over a period of time, by ignoring His conviction, I had stiffened my neck and hardened my will against Him. My heart was no longer soft, pliable, and responsive to His leading. The real issue was not whether or not I would watch television. The issue was whether I was going to walk in pride or in brokenness.

You see, though some of us may never blatantly defy God by committing adultery or embezzling money from the church or committing some other egregious sin, all it takes for me—or for you—to get into a position where God is forced to resist us is to refuse to humble ourselves and be broken before Him in one "little" matter. God always resists the proud—whether that proud person is a blasphemer or an adulterer, or a pastor or a homeschooling mom.

"Carl" is a Texas businessman who found himself under the hand of God's conviction a number of years ago. Years earlier, he had been summoned as a witness in a federal court. Under oath, he had purposely given vague answers to direct questions, out of a desire to protect one of the parties involved. He did not tell "the whole truth," as he had sworn to do.

Now, years later, in the middle of the night, God surfaced in his heart this issue that Carl had thought was a "closed case." He knew that if he came clean, he would risk going to prison for perjury. He tried to reason with God; he tried to negotiate a compromise by confessing other sins and offering to surrender other areas of his life. But God wouldn't let him off the hook. Finally, he said, "Yes, Lord." He called the judge's office and explained the situation to an assistant, acknowledging that he had been dishonest on the witness stand and that God had convicted him of the need to make it right. Carl had to wait twelve months before a decision was made that neither side wished to re-open the case.

During that year that seemed to go on forever, God took Carl through a much-needed process of deepening brokenness in his life. When he was first confronted with this issue, by his own testimony, Carl was a proud man. He was a demanding husband and father who was convinced that he was doing fine spiritually and that his wife and children

Has God's Spirit been tugging at your heart?

were the ones with the real spiritual needs. He admits now that the reason he was concerned about issues in their lives was that he wanted them to make him look good in his community and in his church, where he served as a deacon.

That initial choice to humble himself and call the judge's office proved to be just the first step in an extended process of God stripping away the layers of pride that Carl had been blind to in his life. His obedience in that one difficult issue opened the door for God's grace to be poured into every area of his life. His heart was turned toward his wife and children in a new way and their hearts were turned toward the Lord. He began to experience a deeper level of freedom, compassion, and sensitivity to the Lord and others.

What Is God Saying to You?

As you have been reading, has God's Spirit been tugging at your heart? Is there a step of brokenness He is leading you to take? That step of brokenness may mean:

+ Slipping to your knees and acknowledging to God that you *need* Him—that you have been trying to live the Christian life by your own effort, that you have been self-sufficient and tried to live independently of Him.

+ Discussing a spiritual need in your life with another believer and asking him or her to pray for you and to help hold you accountable.

+ Making a phone call or a visit to humble yourself and seek forgiveness from someone you have sinned against—a parent, a child, a mate, an ex-mate, a friend, a pastor, a neighbor, an employer, or someone else God has laid on your heart. (I had to make one such call today, as I was working on this book.)

+ Going before your family, your church family, your discipleship group, or your fellow employees and admitting that you have been a hypocrite and that you have not been living the kind of life you have professed before others.

+ Clearing your conscience over something in your past that you have never made right.

+ Surrendering your will to God in relation to your future, your career, your marriage, or some other specific issue that He has been speaking to you about.

+ Calling off divorce proceedings.

✦ Selling some possession so you can give more to the Lord's work or help another believer in need.

✦ Sharing the gospel with a neighbor or colleague.

✦ Agreeing to lead a small group or to accept some other responsibility for which you feel inadequate.

✦ Acknowledging that you have never been truly converted and need to be born again.

You may be thinking, *There's no way I can do that!* Or perhaps you find yourself negotiating with God: "I'll go to anyone, but not that person . . . I'll do anything, but not that one thing . . ."

Dear friend, if you want to experience the blessings of brokenness, if you want to have a revived heart, you must choose to run head-on into whatever it is that your pride is telling you not to do.

As I speak on this message on brokenness in women's conferences all across the country, I generally ask at the close, "How many of you know there is some step of brokenness God wants you to take, but there's a battle going on inside, and your pride is keeping you from taking that step?" Invariably, many hands go up all across the room. I tell them the same thing I want to tell you: The battle inside will stop the moment you wave the white flag of surrender and say "Yes, Lord." The longer you delay, the harder you resist, the more difficult it will be to obey God. Don't hesitate a moment longer. You can't begin to imagine the joy that awaits you on the other side of the cross, the power of His resurrection life that will be released through your death to self, and the wholeness that will emerge out of your brokenness.

Oh Father, we confess our great need of Your grace—grace to let You search our hearts; grace to offer to You the sacrifice of a broken, contrite heart; grace to put to death our pride and self-will; grace to walk in the pathway of humility, as our beloved Savior humbled Himself for us; and grace to keep looking to Him as our only hope of eternal salvation.

Through our brokenness, may Christ be seen, magnified, loved, and worshiped by others, till He returns to make all things new. Amen.

Notes

1. Roy Hession, *The Calvary Road* (Fort Washington, Pa.: Christian Literature Crusade, 1990), 23, 25.
2. Jennifer Kennedy Dean, *He Restores My Soul: A Forty-Day Journey Toward Personal Renewal* (Nashville: Broadman & Holman, 1999), 33.
3. "Rock of Ages" by Augustus M. Toplady.

For, as to have a broken heart, is to have an excellent thing, so to keep this broken heart tender, is also very advantageous.

JOHN BUNYAN[1]

Afterword:
A PERSONAL TESTIMONY

IN A SENSE, I wish I had waited another twenty years or so before agreeing to write this book. As I have written, I have been faced with the reality that my life is still wading around in the shallows of a vast, deep subject. It seems that I have only touched the hem of the garment of His ways, when it comes to understanding and experiencing what it means to have a "broken and contrite spirit." But I do know that such a heart is something that God treasures and seeks and empowers. And, in spite of frequent failures, I have embarked on a daily, lifelong pilgrimage to cultivate the kind of heart He revives.

I have described the gathering in July 1995 when God moved in such a gracious way to bring men and women to a point of brokenness before Him. During that week, hundreds of men and women were revived as they offered to God the sacrifice of a broken and contrite heart.

As is generally the case when we minister to others, God's purpose that week was not just to change those who heard me speak. He knew there was a need for a deeper level of humility and brokenness in my own life.

That occasion resulted in some significant changes and challenges in my life and ministry. In the weeks and months that followed, tens of thousands of audio- and videotapes of the message on brokenness were distributed throughout the nation and around the world. As word spread of what had happened, I was presented with many new ministry opportunities, including a dramatic increase in invitations to speak at other gatherings.

Many people who had heard the message, either in Colorado or on tape, wrote to tell their stories. Others stopped me along the way to share how God had used the message in their lives or in their church family. I was truly grateful and deeply awed by what God had done. But all the publicity poured fresh fuel on a fire I had battled most of my life—a craving for human applause and recognition, or what the Bible calls "love of the praise of men."

Long before 1995 I had repented of this sin, and out of that brokenness had experienced a great measure of freedom and victory. But in the months following the Campus Crusade conference, I gradually found myself once again in bondage to this lust for human praise. I would find myself relishing hearing people talking about how God had used me. I was quick to pass along to others complimentary letters, e-mails, and write-ups about my ministry with the motive of having them think highly of me. I loved seeing my name in print, and at times would take steps to ensure that full credit was given. Even as I write this, I am grieved by the tendency of my heart to embezzle the glory that rightly belongs only to Him.

As the scope of my ministry grew exponentially, so did the battle with pride and self-exaltation—even as I was traveling around the country delivering what had become a "signature message" on humility and brokenness. As is always the case with sin and pride, the answer is to get out "into the light"—to let the roof off and the walls down. I had stepped into the light with God, but I realized I needed to humble myself before others in order to put the ax to the root of this poisonous pride in my heart.

One morning I sensed the Lord directing me to write a letter to about a dozen of my "praying friends"—men and women who I knew cared for my soul. I admitted this matter to them and asked them to pray that I would be delivered. The simple act of writing and sending that letter was an important step of brokenness for me and began a process of personal revival and restoration. That initial step of humility became a means by which God brought much-needed grace into my life.

One of those individuals wrote and gave an idea that had come to him as he had prayed for me:

> Perhaps for a season you might collect letters of commendation, praise, and anything that could be the occasion for pride. Do you have a fireplace? If so, once a week, light the fire, and then read through at least a few of them. Then tell the Lord that you know everything will someday be tried by fire and only the gold, silver, and truly precious things will last.

> At that point, toss some or all of the letters into the fireplace as a symbolic gesture. You might pray (in your words): "Lord, I put the fire to all of these words that could be a cause to puff me up or create pride. You alone know what is pure before You and what is truly lasting. I want only that which truly pleases You to flow out of my life!" Somehow I sense that this gesture of denial or submission would deeply impact your heart.

As I read this suggestion, I had an unmistakable sense that God had spoken through His servant. My mind went immediately to a particular bulging file in my study that contained "memorabilia" related to that week in the summer of 1995. In that file, I had placed many flattering letters, published accounts and articles about the event, reprints of my message in other publications, requests for permission to reproduce, and other complimentary responses.

God showed me that the contents of that file had served to fuel my pride and had been a means of the Enemy gaining a foothold in my life. I don't think I had opened that file in the two years that had passed, except to add items to it. But its very existence had been meaningful to me. It was symbolic of the enhanced reputation I had experienced and relished in the wake of that divine visitation. I had always known I could go back at some low point and be affirmed by the praise contained within that manila folder.

As the Lord would have it, a couple of weeks after receiving his letter I was scheduled to be in the city where this man and his wife live (never having been there before). I contacted them, explained how the Lord had spoken to me, and asked if they would be willing to meet with me when I was in town to witness the burning of this material. They graciously agreed.

A journal entry I made at that time gives a personal glimpse into what was going on in my heart:

> There is a dying involved in walking through this process—dying to being able to ever go back and reread the words of praise, dying to anyone else ever reading and being impressed by what's in there, dying to ever being able to draw affirmation or a sense of personal worth from those flattering words.
>
> This exercise gets to the heart of some of the deepest needs in my life. Flesh dies hard—but I know that beyond the brokenness, there will be wholeness; beyond the death, there will be a new experience of His abundant life.
>
> Grant, oh God, I pray, a deeper level of brokenness, repentance, and humility than I have previously known. Put the ax to the root of the pride in my life. I do repent of that hideous, self-congratulating, self-exalting, self-seeking pride that has so deeply tainted my motives, my thoughts, and my service for You. Please break the bondage of pride in my life. Set me free to love, exalt, and worship You, and You alone. More than anything, I want You to be glorified in my life.

A couple of weeks later, that couple and I met together in their living room, seated in front of the fireplace. Following a time of Scripture reading and prayer, I placed all the contents of that file—one handful at a time—into the fire, having already offered it all up to the Lord in my heart.

In the days that followed, God began to grant an unusually sweet sense of His presence, I found my heart growing in tenderness for Him, and His Word was quickened to my heart in richer and more personal ways than had been true in a long time. Shortly after that particular breaking process, God began to provide fresh insight and direction in relation to future ministry.

You may or may not particularly relate to my battle with craving recognition and praise. The pride in your heart may manifest itself in ways that are quite different. Regardless of the specific nature of the battleground, the point is that pride and self must die. Then, through our brokenness, we will experience the release of the resurrection life and the sweet fragrance of the Lord Jesus and the free-flowing power of His Holy Spirit.

Note

1.John Bunyan, *Acceptable Sacrifice; or the Excellency of a Broken Heart,* vol. 1 (Edinburgh: Banner of Truth Trust, 1999), 712.

BROKENNESS
DISCUSSION GUIDE

As You Begin

The whole concept of brokenness can be intimidating and threatening, especially once you start to discuss it with others! We all face the common temptations to be more concerned about what others think than about what God thinks, to fear our needs or failures being exposed, and to sinfully compare ourselves to each other.

Be aware of these temptations, and ask God for grace to cultivate an atmosphere of humility and transparency in your group. Respect God's work in one another's lives, by not discussing each others' struggles or sins with those who are not a part of the process.

As you open your heart to the Lord and to those in your group, remember that brokenness and humility are the keys that will unlock some of God's richest blessings in your life and relationships.

Goals for Your Group

This guide provides suggestions for discussing *Brokenness* with others. But hopefully, your time together will not just be for the purpose of discussion, but for the purpose of spiritual growth! Ask the Lord to do a deep, penetrating work in the heart of each group member, and to show you how to apply these truths to your life.

The objective is not to master the message of this book, but to let this message master you and to be transformed into the image of Christ. Keep your focus on Christ and the life-transforming power of the gospel, for apart from this glorious hope, your efforts to change will produce mere self-righteousness or even greater failure and frustration.

Tips for Group Leaders

Open and close each meeting by praying together. Ask the Holy Spirit to guide you through the Word, to help you be real with one another, and to bring about any needed change in each heart.

Seek to lead by example. You can serve your group best by modeling personal humility—being the first to confess your own sin and the first to encourage others in God's grace at work in them.

Some of the questions in this discussion guide call for a level of transparency and openness that many people are not accustomed to. Encourage the members of your group to respect each other's privacy by not discussing others' contributions outside of this group. Remind them that God is patient and gracious with us as He conforms us to the image of His Son, and that we need to extend the same patience and grace toward each other.

This discussion guide is designed to be used in a variety of contexts—from small groups to Sunday school classes. Feel free to direct the discussion based on the size of your group and the allotted time. Avoid rabbit trails into secondary or unrelated issues. However, don't feel pressured to get through all the questions each time you meet. Depending on your available time and the size and openness of your group, you may end up only discussing two or three questions.

The goal is to grow together in your understanding of God and His ways and to experience individually and as a group the reality of the message of this book.

Keep your group centered on the truth of the gospel: We are *all* sinners in need of a Savior. Help your members steer clear of self-righteous responses to the confessions of others in the group and from condemnation about their own performance by pointing them to the One who is both the author and perfecter of their faith (Hebrews 12:2).

INTRODUCTION

Getting Started

What motivated you to read *Brokenness* or to be a part of this group? What, if any, fears or reservations have you had about doing so?

Opening Prayer

Read aloud the prayer found in the front of the book from *The Valley of Vision*—either as a group in unison, or have one or more individuals read while others listen.

How does this prayer illustrate that God's thoughts and His ways are different than our thoughts and our ways?

Going Deeper

1. Have you ever been in a setting that you would describe as true revival among a group of God's people? Describe briefly what it was like.

2. What things stood out to you in the account of what took place at the Campus Crusade gathering in July of 1995? What were the marks or characteristics of that gracious visitation of God's Spirit?

3. Have you ever experienced the kind of intense conviction over sin that took place in many who participated in the Campus Crusade gathering? What was He illuminating in your life and what was the fruit of it?

4. What was your response to the description of the public confessions that took place? In a similar setting, do you think you would have participated or hung back? Why?

5. *"[Humility] is God's prescription for nearly every condition that ails human hearts and relationships"* (p. 26). What Scriptures come to mind that support this point? Why do you think this is the case?

6. *"Throughout that vast auditorium, hundreds of men and women*

humbled themselves before God and before one another. Husbands and wives, parents and young people, colleagues, supervisors and subordinates—people got serious about being honest with God and with each other. Over the next few days, long-standing grievances were confessed and breaches were reconciled—some of them going back for decades. . . . Pretense and masks were stripped off in His presence" (p. 24).

Try to imagine what it would be like if millions of God's people throughout this country and around the world were to humble themselves in this way. How would our churches be different? How would our homes be different? How would your life be different? What would be the impact in the lost world?

For Next Time

Page 26 lists a number of problems/issues that have their root in pride—but which can crumble through genuine brokenness and humility. Identify any of those issues you see in your own life. In the coming days, note any passages you encounter in the Word where the Lord either addresses that matter directly or promises to help you change by His grace. Be ready to share those items with the group next time.

Grace Note

The introduction closes with a reference to the perspective in the prayer from *The Valley of Vision*—that the way up is down, that death brings life, and the broken heart is the healed heart. This might be an uncomfortable concept for you, but God promises to pour His grace on *the humble*. The very thing we naturally resist—being humbled—is precisely what will produce the blessings we long to experience and that He longs to give us.

Chapter One:
THE HEART
OF THE MATTER

Getting Started

On page 31, Wayne Stanford reports his response to the biblical account of Naaman, saying Naaman did what he would typically do in a bind—try to buy his way out of a problem. Can you recall a time when you responded that way yourself or saw someone else do so? What did that look like? (If you're describing someone other than yourself, be sure to speak generically and avoid confessing someone else's sin!)

Since Last Time

Your assignment last time was to identify specific issues in your life or relationships that could be rooted in pride, and to be alert to biblical passages that address those areas. Spend a few minutes sharing what God may have shown you since your last meeting.

Going Deeper

1. By all *appearances*, Wayne and Gwyn Stanford were "good Christians" before the experience they described in 1982. Based on their subsequent testimony, what was wrong? How would you describe their *true* condition at that time?

2. Either now or in the past, can you relate to anything about Wayne's or Gwyn's spiritual condition prior to their encounter with God in 1982?

3. Can you recall a time when your relationship with someone was hindered by your pride or anger? How was it resolved?

4. In order to appreciate the gospel and the One who is our Savior, we must come to see ourselves as "sinful and desperately needy of [God's] grace" (p. 31), as Gwyn did. Describe one such moment in your life, either at the point of conversion or subsequently.

5. What was the fruit of that moment? How has the grace of repentance affected your relationship with God?

6. In Gwyn's case, she realized that "in spite of her religious appearance and activity, she had never been truly born again" (p. 31). Do you think this is a rare or a common condition in the church today? Why might it be more common than it should be?

7. Why does the Scripture put such an emphasis on the *heart*, rather than mere external appearances?

8. What were some of the changes that took place in Wayne's and Gwyn's lives after God transformed their hearts (pp. 34–35)?

9. *"What about you? What is the condition of your heart?"* (p. 35). If you feel the freedom, share an area of your life where the outward appearance is satisfactory, but God knows—and you know—that your *heart* is not what it should be. Then take time to pray for a fresh work of humility, grace, and revival in each others' lives.

For Next Time

At the close of the chapter, you were encouraged to make an appointment with the Great Physician to ask Him to examine your heart, according to Psalm 139:23—"Search me, O God, and know my heart." Before the next meeting, set aside some time to do this; wait quietly on the Lord and let Him show you what He sees. Then read Psalm 32:1–5 to be reminded of how God responds to those who humble themselves and confess their sin.

Grace Note

As you do this assignment, and throughout this study, you may be surprised to find the Holy Spirit showing you areas of your life or certain motivations or heart attitudes that you had not considered before. Remember that the Great Physician does not uncover or expose us without intending to heal and restore us. It is a Father's loving correction that is at the heart of any "diagnosis" you may receive in this homework assignment.

Chapter Two:
WHAT IS BROKENNESS?

Getting Started

Chapter 2 uses the analogy of a horse being broken. Has anyone in your group actually ever broken a horse or seen it being done? What was it like?

Since Last Time

Did you set aside time to hear from the Great Physician? What did He reveal to you? How have you responded to that "diagnosis"?

Going Deeper

1. What was your idea of brokenness before you started reading this book? Did you have any misconceptions? How did this chapter help you gain a better understanding of true brokenness?

2. Why do you think we have a natural aversion to the concept of brokenness? Why might some people be afraid of brokenness?

3. What do you know about God and His ways that could help alleviate those fears and should motivate believers to choose the pathway of brokenness?

4. Read James 4:6–10 together. Discuss the contrast between this passage and the prevailing way of thinking in our culture. What evidences and results of pride do you see in this passage? What evidences and results of humility?

5. What is meant by "roof off, walls down"? Which do you think is more difficult? Why? Why are both important?

6. What insights about the process and fruit of brokenness can be gleaned from the account of Jordan in this chapter?

7. Are there areas in your life that are still dominated by self-will? Do you see that affecting your relationships with others?

8. How has this chapter affected your view of God and His work in your life?

For Next Time

Before the next meeting, practice letting the "walls down:"

Go to a close friend or family member that you trust—a spouse, child, accountability partner, roommate, etc.—and do one (or both!) of the following:

• Share a specific area of spiritual need, sin, or area of recurring defeat in your life, and ask that person to pray for you.

• Ask your friend to share any specific area(s) of concern that she has about your life—perhaps a "blind spot" she may have observed.

If you've not done this before, you may want to do two things: (a) Ask God for the grace to receive the person's input with humility; (b) Assure the person you ask that you really desire to know the truth and will not become offended at her remarks.

Grace Note

Generally, it's a lot easier to see areas of weakness or pride in others than to see them in ourselves! If you've never asked anyone close to you for observations about your character or areas that need change, you may be reluctant to do so. But remember that spiritual blindness is usually unilateral. Others can see clearly those things we may not recognize about ourselves or may be unwilling to address.

Asking for honest input into our lives is a way to demonstrate the horizontal dimension of brokenness and usually strengthens our relationships with others.

Hard as it may be to open our hearts to others or receive candid feedback, it provides an opportunity to humble ourselves. Remember . . . you can never go wrong on the pathway of humility, because God promises to pour out His grace on the humble!

Chapter Three:
BIBLICAL PORTRAITS: BROKEN AND UNBROKEN

Getting Started

Think about the way we tend to measure or categorize sins. What are some sins we usually think of as "big" sins? What are some sins that are generally considered relatively insignificant? How is God's perspective on sin different than ours?

Since Last Time

How did God meet you as you asked someone close to you for observations about any blind spots in your life or you shared a spiritual need and asked someone to pray for you? Did this step of humility strengthen your relationship with that person? How did this step affect your relationship with God?

Going Deeper

1. In this chapter, we "unpacked" some well-known biblical accounts and parables and examined them through the lens of pride and humility. Did you gain fresh insights into any of these stories?

2. This chapter draws attention to several biblical illustrations that contrast broken people with proud people. In each of those "pairs," the difference was not so much in the magnitude of their sin, but in their response when confronted with their sin.

Can you think of a time when you responded in pride when confronted by God or another person over your sin? What did that look like? What would a humble response to reproof look like?

3. In some of the biblical characters we considered in this chapter, we saw the effects of a proud, unbroken heart: blindness toward their own sin and their need for a Savior, criticism of the message and the messenger, an inability to rejoice when others repented, and a lack of joyful worship. Did any of these points

"hit home" with you? If so, in what way?

4. *"Jesus was always drawn to those whose sin seemed to be more egregious (from a human point of view), but who were repentant over their sin. On the other hand, He was repulsed by those who looked like perfect saints but whose hearts were proud and unbroken"* (p. 61). Why do you think this is so? How is this different from the way we often view people?

5. By its very nature, pride tends to make us blind to the fact that we are proud. What are some ways we can be helped to identify more clearly the pride in our lives?

6. *"For most of us, the subtle encroachment of pride is more dangerous, and more likely to render us useless to God and others, than any other kind of failure"* (p. 60). In what areas of your life can you see this subtle encroachment of pride? (Hint: It's probably what you'd be most defensive about if criticized.)

For Next Time

In this chapter we examined three accounts in the Gospel of Luke. Before the next meeting, skim through Luke's gospel and look for the other encounters Jesus had with the Pharisees. (You'll find them in almost every chapter, beginning with chapter 5.) Make a list of the evidences and effects of pride you discover in those accounts.

Grace Note

It's easy to become discouraged when God reveals pride (or other sins) in our lives. (In fact, even that discouragement may be an evidence of self-absorption or pride—we expected better of ourselves, we despair of our ability to change, etc.)

Our failure and need should always cause us to turn to Christ, who is God's only and all-sufficient provision for our sin, through His death on the cross! Remember, too, that God doesn't reveal anything to us that He does not intend to change by His grace. In those moments, we need to remember that through these revelations our Father is lovingly conforming us to the image of His Son.

Chapter Four:
AM I A PROUD OR
A BROKEN PERSON?

Getting Started

This chapter opened with a story about how the national believers in one region of Africa would inquire when hearing of another believer, "Is he a broken Christian?" That question would probably seem strange to most Christians in our culture! What kinds of questions are we more likely to ask?

Since Last Time

What evidences or characteristics of pride did you discover in your study of Jesus' encounters with the Pharisees in the Gospel of Luke? How does that help us understand why Jesus and the Pharisees were always at odds with each other? Did God point out any of those same evidences in your own life?

Going Deeper

1. What qualities would cause you to say of another person, "He/she is a 'broken' Christian"?

2. Walk together through each of the eight categories in the list of characteristics of proud and broken people (starting on p. 64). In each category, share any particular expressions of pride that you found especially convicting, or any specific characteristics of humility that you see a need to cultivate in your life. (If you find it difficult to be honest and "real" about these issues with the others in your group, remember that this is an opportunity to humble yourself—to live with the "walls down"—and to receive more of God's grace in your life!)

    a. Attitudes toward others

    b. Attitudes about rights

    c. Attitudes about service and ministry

    d. Attitudes about recognition

    e. Attitudes about themselves

    f. Attitudes about relationships

    g. Attitudes about sin

    h. Attitudes about their walk with God

3. If someone who did not know you were to ask your friends, family members, or coworkers, "Is [your name] a 'broken' Christian?" how do you think they would respond?

4. Close your time in prayer. Confess any pride you are recognizing or struggling with in your own heart; pray for a broken and contrite heart; pray for God's grace to be poured into the lives of others in your group as they humble themselves before Him.

For Next Time

Take time to pray over this list (even if you've done so before!) and ask God where He wants you to start receiving His grace to change and applying His Word to at least one specific area of your life. Share what God shows you with someone in your group or another accountability partner and ask for prayer in that area.

Grace Note

"If this list has helped you realize that you are a proud, rather than a broken, person, do not despair. God has been merciful to show you your need" (p. 70). Thank God for loving you enough not to let you stay the way you are! And thank Him that He not only exposes our need, but that He also supplies us all the grace we need—both the desire and His supernatural power—to transform us and to enable us to live a humble, Christlike life. Therefore, "humble [yourself] in the sight of the Lord, and He will lift you up" (James 4:10)!

Chapter Five:
THE BLESSING
OF BROKENNESS

Getting Started

Has anyone in your group ever had to let a doctor break a bone in order for it to be reset properly, or watched someone else go through that experience? What was it like? Was it worth the pain?

Since Last Time

With regard to one area where you are seeking to change with God's help, how have you experienced His grace since your last meeting?

Going Deeper

1. The concept that "brokenness brings blessedness" runs counter to our natural thinking. What does the Enemy want us to believe will happen if we humble ourselves?

2. Review the five blessings of brokenness highlighted in this chapter and comment on any that you particularly desire or need in your life.

3. How does each of the following illustrate the principle, the process, or the blessings of brokenness?

    a. A grain of wheat being put into the ground
    b. The metamorphosis of a caterpillar
    c. Fruit being turned into juice
    d. The death of the Lord Jesus on the cross

4. How does Melanie Adams's testimony illustrate the following "cycle" (described on pp. 79–80)?

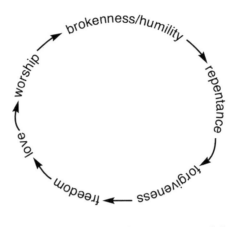

Describe how you have experienced some aspect of this cycle in your life.

5. Who do you know (or know of) who has become a more effective, fruitful servant of the Lord as a result of being broken?

6. What is the connection between brokenness and personal or corporate revival? How is pride a barrier or hindrance to true revival?

7. "*The greatest hindrance to revival is not others' unwillingness to humble themselves—it is our need to humble ourselves and confess our desperate need for His mercy*" (pp. 85–86). Can you identify any way(s) that your pride may have been a hindrance to revival? As God prompts, share with the group any specific ways that you know you need to humble yourself before Him or others.

For Next Time
"*Have you been waiting for your mate or children or church leaders to humble themselves so there can be revival in your home or your church? God may be waiting for you to humble yourself . . .*" (p. 85).

Is there any situation or relationship where you need to take the initiative to humble yourself, rather than waiting for the other person to change or move? If so, would you be willing to follow the example of Melanie Adams and take that first step?

Grace Note

It's worth stating again: *Brokenness brings blessedness* (Matthew 5:3)! Sometimes what it takes to humble ourselves may seem awkward, difficult, or embarrassing. However, it is always more than worth it to obey God and choose the pathway of brokenness.

Chapter Six:
JOURNEY INTO BROKENNESS
Afterword: A Personal Testimony

Getting Started
How has this study been helpful to you? In what ways have you found it difficult or challenging?

Since Last Time
What is one "blessing of brokenness" you have experienced since you started this study?

Going Deeper
1. Proverbs 29:1 warns that those who resist God's reproof and harden, or stiffen, their necks will be destroyed suddenly and without warning. Can you think of an individual who might be an illustration of this verse? (Do not identify the person by name or share unnecessary details.)

2. How has God used His Word, circumstances, or His people as an instrument to help bring about greater brokenness in your life?

3. Seeing God as He is helps us see ourselves as we really are and results in deeper contrition and humility. What are some ways we can get a fresh vision of God's awesome holiness, power, majesty, and love?

4. As is illustrated in the afterword, sometimes our greatest defeats and failures can come on the heels of our greatest victories. Why might that be the case? Can you think of a time when that was true in your own experience?

5. We have seen that brokenness is not a onetime, crisis experience, but a way of life. What might a "lifestyle of brokenness" look like in

practical terms? What are the greatest obstacles or hindrances to that kind of lifestyle?

6. Numerous examples have been given in this book of individuals choosing to "walk in the light" with God and others about specific sins or issues in their lives.

Is there any area of darkness in your life that needs to be brought into the light? Anything you know God wants you to do that you have been resisting? Any specific step of brokenness that the Lord put on your heart as you read this chapter?

It will never be easier to take a step of brokenness than with a group of friends who love you and are aware of their own need for humility. As God prompts, take time to share those areas openly and honestly within your group and to have the group pray specifically for each one who shares.

Grace Note

Though this concludes your study of *Brokenness: The Heart God Revives,* it may be just the beginning of a new walk of humility. In the days ahead, you will face many opportunities to choose the pathway of brokenness, each created by our Sovereign Lord who also promises that His grace is sufficient for anything and everything He requires of us. Never forget that whatever God commands you to do, He will also enable you to do.

As you "walk in the light" with Him and other believers, remember that His light not only exposes our ugly sin and pride, but it also shines on the person and the cross of Christ. As His cross is brought to bear in our lives, we will experience the joyful fruit of brokenness and experience true revival.

Closing Prayer

Close your time by reading aloud again the prayer from *The Valley of Vision* found at the beginning of *Brokenness*.

SURRENDER
The Heart God Controls

All Scripture quotations, unless otherwise indicated, are taken from the *New King
James Version.* Copyright © 1982, 1992 by Thomas Nelson, Inc. Used by permission.
All rights reserved.

Scripture quotations marked NIV are taken from the *Holy Bible, New International Version*®. NIV®. Copyright © 1973, 1978, 1984 by International Bible Society. Used by permission of Zondervan Publishing House. All rights reserved.

Scripture quotations marked NASB are taken from the *New American Standard
Bible*®, © Copyright The Lockman Foundation 1960, 1962, 1963, 1968, 1971,
1972, 1973, 1975, 1977, 1995. Used by permission.

Scripture quotations marked ESV are taken from *The Holy Bible, English Standard Version.* Copyright © 2000, 2001 by Crossway Bibles, a division of Good News
Publishers. Used by permission. All rights reserved.

Scripture quotations marked TLB are taken from *The Living Bible* copyright ©
1971. Used by permission of Tyndale House Publishers, Inc., Wheaton, Illinois
60189. All rights reserved.

Editor: Cheryl Dunlop
Interior Design: BlueFrog Design
Cover Design: Smartt Guys
Cover Photo: Douglas Walker/Masterfile

Library of Congress Cataloging-in-Publication Data

DeMoss, Nancy Leigh.
    Surrender : the heart God controls / Nancy Leigh DeMoss.
      p. cm.
    Includes bibliographical references.
    ISBN-10: 0-8024-1280-7
    ISBN 13: 978-0-8024-1280-5
    1. Christian life. 2. Spiritual warfare. I. Title.
  BV4501.3.D45 2003
  248.4—dc21
                                                    2003007130

O God whose will conquers all,
There is no comfort in anything
    apart from enjoying thee
    and being engaged in thy service;
Thou art All in all, and all enjoyments are what to me
    thou makest them, and no more.
I am well pleased with thy will, whatever it is,
    or should be in all respects,
And if thou bidst me decide for myself in any affair
    I would choose to refer all to thee,
    for thou art infinitely wise and cannot do amiss,
    as I am in danger of doing.
I rejoice to think that all things are at thy disposal,
    and it delights me to leave them there. . . .
I can of myself do nothing to glorify thy blessed name,
    but I can through grace cheerfully surrender soul
    and body to thee.

—From *The Valley of Vision: A Collection of Puritan
Prayers and Devotion*

CONTENTS

FOREWORD

I WILL NEVER FORGET that special visit to Lima, Peru. I was on my way to preach in Argentina but stopped for a few days to attend the annual conference of a national movement of churches dedicated to spreading the gospel of Christ throughout all of Peru.

The service that evening was a blessing, even though I had to depend greatly on an interpreter sitting next to me. In the middle of the meeting, the leadership called to the platform a young couple who seemed to be in their late twenties. As the leaders introduced them to the audience and prepared to pray for them, the congregation began singing a beautiful Spanish chorus of worship to the Lord.

Suddenly, the presence of the Lord descended on that service in a palpable and fresh way. I turned to my friend and asked what exactly was going on. It turned out the young couple had been trained to minister God's Word and were leaving after much prayer to pioneer a church in a remote jungle area in Peru. I learned later that they had no church building or congregation waiting for them, nor a home prepared to live in.

With only the few dollars the conference gave them, this man and his wife were stepping out in faith and total surrender to God's purpose for their lives. A hundred and one things we might worry about were as nothing to them. I still remember their shining faces and the tears of joy in their eyes. I also can never forget how God melted and ministered to my own heart through their surrender to Jesus.

The highest possible worship and service to God is when we obey the apostle Paul's plea in Romans 12:1 (NIV, italics added): "Therefore, I urge you, brothers, in view of God's mercy, to *offer your bodies as living sacrifices*, holy and pleasing to God—*this* is your spiritual act of worship."

Christianity without this principle of heart surrender to our living Lord is a contradiction of the very essence of following Jesus. It produces spiritually bankrupt lives and churches that are listless and impotent. It does require grace to sing "Hallelujah" to God, but far more grace is needed to sincerely sing "I Surrender All."

Many years ago, a young Methodist minister was struggling with his calling and a severe attack of discouragement. He was hoping his assignment from God might change, but his superiors reappointed him to the same difficult place of ministry. As the spiritual crisis deepened within him, he came to the breaking point of *surrender to God's will* no matter what that might mean. That day, he also wrote a hymn that is one of the first I remember hearing in church as a child:

> *Would you have Him make you free,*
> *And follow at His call?*
> *Would you know the peace*
> *That comes by giving all?*
> *Would you have Him save you*
> *So that you can never fall?*
> *Let Him have His way with thee.*
>
> *His power can make you what you ought to be,*
> *His blood can cleanse your heart*
> *And make you free,*

His love can fill your soul,
And you will see
'Twas best for Him to have His way with thee.
—"His Way With Thee," C. S. Nusbaum

I am so happy that Nancy Leigh DeMoss has written this powerful book on surrender to God and its implications for each of us and the kingdom of God. May the Lord use it around the world for His glory!

—Jim Cymbala, Senior Pastor
The Brooklyn Tabernacle

ACKNOWLEDGMENTS

LIKE ALL NEW BIRTHS, every book has its own gestation, labor, and delivery process, with a variety of professionals and friends supporting and assisting along the way. This book is no exception. I owe special thanks to . . .

+ *My friends at Moody Publishers*—you are kindred spirits and true partners in ministry.

+ *Lela Gilbert* for your input during the developmental stage and for your contribution to parts of chapter 5, in particular.

+ *Carolyn McCulley* for your valuable help with the initial shaping of the discussion guide.

+ *Holly Elliff, Andrea Griffith, Tim Grissom, and Dr. Bill Thrasher* for reading various drafts and offering helpful suggestions.

+ The wonderful men and women who serve on the staff of *Revive Our Hearts*. I am especially grateful to *Dawn Wilson* for your research assistance and to *Mike Neises* for your godly, wise management of our publishing efforts.

✦ *Dr. Bruce Ware* for the safeguard of your careful theological review.

✦ *Bob Lepine* for your help in developing, shaping, and refining this message. Your contribution has been substantial and invaluable.

✦ *My "praying friends"*—you'll never know this side of eternity how much I need and count on your prayers and encouragement. You have helped me stay the course and have made me a far more fruitful servant than I ever could have been without you.

*There will likely be a time in our Christian
journeys when, like Jacob, we will wrestle with
God all night long. . . . But there must eventually
come a dawn when we say, "OK, God,
You win. . . . Not my will but Thine be done."*

INTRODUCTION

ON MARCH 10, 1974, almost thirty years after the end of World War II, Lt. Hiroo Onoda finally handed over his rusty sword and became the last Japanese soldier to surrender.

Onoda had been sent to the tropical island of Lubang in the Philippines in 1944, with orders to conduct guerrilla warfare and prevent enemy attack on the island. When the war ended, Onoda refused to believe the messages announcing Japan's surrender.

For twenty-nine years, long after all his fellow soldiers had either surrendered or been killed off, Onoda continued defending the island territory for the defeated Japanese army. He hid in the jungle, living off the land, stealing food and supplies from local citizens, evading one search party after another, and killing at least thirty nationals in the process. Hundreds of thousands of dollars were spent trying to locate the lone holdout and convince him that the war was over.

Leaflets, newspapers, photographs, and letters from friends were dropped in the jungle; announcements were made over loudspeakers, begging Onoda to surrender. Still he refused to give up his fight. Some thirteen thousand men had been deployed in the effort before Onoda finally received a personal command from his former commander and was persuaded to give up the futile, solitary war he had waged for so many years.[2]

In his autobiography entitled, *No Surrender: My Thirty-Year War*, Onoda describes the moment that the reality of what had transpired began to sink in:

> I felt like a fool. . . . What had I been doing for all these years? . . . For the first time I really understood. . . . This was the end. I pulled back the bolt on my rifle and unloaded the bullets. . . . I eased off the pack that I always carried with me and laid the gun on top of it.[3]

The war was finally over.

Our Personal War

From our vantage point today, Hiroo Onoda seems to have been sadly mistaken at best, absurdly foolish at worst. The best years of his life—thrown away, fighting a war whose outcome had already been determined.

Every human being has an inborn determination to run his own life.

Yet, in a sense, Onoda's story isn't unique to him. It's our story as well. We all begin life as members of a rebellious race, fighting our own personal war against the Sovereign King of the universe. For most, that resistance unfolds into a lifelong story that could be titled *No Surrender*.

Some express their resistance overtly, perhaps through a lifestyle of unbridled lust and perversion. Others are more subtle—they are upstanding citizens and community leaders; they may even be active in church work. But beneath the surface, every human being has an inborn determination to run his own life and an unwillingness to be mastered by Christ, the King of Kings.

The decision to give up the fight is no small matter, especially after years of resistance. In Onoda's case, he had become accustomed to living as a lone guerilla soldier, moving from one jungle hideout to another, dodging all attempts to subdue him. By the time he was fifty-two years old, he scarcely knew any other way to live. Resisting, running, and hiding had become the *norm*—the way of life with which he was most familiar and comfortable. For Onoda, surrender meant nothing less than a radically altered lifestyle.

It's time to hand over your sword.

Surrender to Christ as Savior and Lord is no less life-changing. Whether we first wave the white flag at the age of eight or eighty-eight, that surrender involves a transfer of allegiance and a transformation of perspective that ought to affect every aspect of our lives.

I assume that most who are reading this book have come to that initial point of surrender that the Bible identifies as being born again: You have placed your faith in Christ's sacrifice for your sin, relinquished control of your life to Him, and been converted into the kingdom (the control) of God. My hope is that you will grow in your understanding of what it means to live out the implications of that surrender on a daily basis.

I have no doubt, however, that some who are reading these words have never come to that point: You may have made a profession of faith; you may have long considered yourself a Christian, and others may assume that you are a Christian, but you have never truly been born into the family of God—you have never waved the white flag of surrender to Christ; you have never relinquished the right to run your own life.

My appeal to you is to recognize the foolishness and futility of further resistance and to believe and obey the gospel that *Jesus is Lord. The war is over* . . . it's time to hand over your sword to the King of Kings!

A Lifetime of Surrender

You may be thinking, *I gave my life to Christ years ago; tell me something new.*

Here's what's new for many. That initial surrender to Christ (which we often refer to as the point of salvation) was not the end of the story. In fact, it was really the starting place.

That point of surrender simply set the stage for a lifetime of surrender. Having surrendered our lives to Christ as Savior and Lord, we must now learn what it means to live out a surrendered life—to continually say *no* to self and *yes* to God.

Many Christians live perpetually discouraged, defeated lives because they have never realized (and therefore are not living out) the implications of their initial surrender to Christ. Having once surrendered control of their lives to Christ, they have reverted to trying to manage their own lives. As a result, they are living out of alignment with the Lord who created, redeemed, and owns them.

It may be that even at this moment you are living in a chapter called "Unsurrendered." Oh, that may not describe your whole way of life—you can probably point to specific areas where you are obeying God. But could it be that there are some issues on which you are reserving the right to control your own life?

Reasons for Lack of Surrender

At certain points in their journey, those who have professed faith in Christ may find themselves "unsurrendered" to God's control in particular areas of their lives. The reasons for this may vary.

For example, though they may have truly surrendered their lives to God, they may have never realized some of the specific implications of that surrender—*You mean, my money belongs to God? My kids? My body? My time? I'd never thought about that!* As you read the pages that follow, I pray God will open your eyes to see the practical outworking of a surrendered life in ways you may never have considered.

In some cases, believers know what it means to live under God's control, but they are afraid of what might happen if they surrender some particular area—*If I surrender my family to the Lord, what will happen to them? If I surrender my finances, will my needs be met?* If you are wrestling with fears about the will of God, I want to encourage you with the promises of God and to help you understand that He is worthy of all your trust.

In a third scenario, some people claim to be surrendered to God, and may even believe that they are, but (perhaps subconsciously) they are justifying and rationalizing certain habits, values, attitudes, or behaviors that are contrary to the Word of God. *What about the stuff I watch on movies and TV? I don't think it's really that bad. OK, I admit I have a chronic struggle with overeating and with controlling my temper. But I'm just human. None of us is going to be perfect until we get to heaven.*

To some extent, we all find ourselves in this "deceived" condition at times. We so easily become desensitized to God's standards or feel that compared to the world's standards we are doing fine.

In fact, writing this book has forced me to face a number of matters in my own life that I had been overlooking, tolerating, or excusing that are really "surrender issues" at heart.

If you claim to be a follower of Christ while living in denial about certain areas of your life that are not pleasing to Him, my desire is to help you see the truth—that you are not living a fully surrendered life, no matter how many people may think of you as a "good Christian." (A word of caution here: If, over a period of time, you continue to be deceived and are unwilling or unable to acknowledge the truth, it may well be that your *profession* of faith falls short of *true* belief.)

Finally, some professing believers are living in willful rebellion against God's control in specific areas of their lives—*I know what God wants me to do, but I'm just not going to obey.* If that is true of your life, you are in one of two dangerous conditions:

(1) You are not really a Christian—you are deceiving yourself and others about the true state of your soul, and you are living under the wrath of God and facing eternal judgment, despite any profession of faith you may have made (Matthew 7:21–23); or

(2) You are a rebellious child of God, and you can expect to experience the loving correction and discipline of God until you repent or until God ends your life (1 Corinthians 11:27–32; Hebrews 12:6).

Either way, the consequences of persisting in willful rebellion are severe. To live in conscious resistance against God is no trivial matter. In fact, if that characterizes your lifestyle, it is likely you have never truly been born again. At best, you have no basis for claiming to be a child of God or for having assurance of salvation.

Genuine saving faith is always accompanied by repentance and must be followed by ongoing growth in obeying God (2 Peter 1:4–8); that does not mean perfect obedience, to be sure, but a desire to move from rebellion toward greater surrender to and satisfaction in God.

Whatever the reason for your lack of surrender (whether in isolated issues or as a way of life), you may have settled into that lifestyle for so long that you don't know any other way to live. Maybe you even think this is *normal*—after all, your life may not be so different from lots of other people you know. In fact, compared to many other professing Christians, you may seem like a spiritual giant.

However, regardless of what seems to be typical, *the fully surrendered life is intended to be—and can be—the norm for every one of God's children.*

The High Price of Holding Out
Do you fear what a lifestyle of full surrender might cost you? Then consider the cost of holding out on God. I think of professing believers I know who have tragically wasted what could have been the most productive, fruitful years of their lives, much as Hiroo Onoda did. They have been satisfied to fend for themselves and forage off the land when they could have been feasting at His banquet table. They have settled for wartime conditions when they could have been enjoying the blessings of peace.

As was true in Onoda's case, others' lives are invariably affected by our resistance. I have watched men and women whose refusal to surrender has left a trail of broken relationships—with parents, mate, children, friends, fellow church members, and others.

Onoda might understandably have feared the consequences he would face if he were to surrender. Would he be tried as a war criminal? Might he be sentenced to death? Imagine Onoda's relief when he finally turned over his sword and surrendered to President Marcos of the Philippines, and the president immediately issued him a full and complete pardon.

The truth is that resistance is far more costly than surrender. To reject God's gracious provision of salvation and to refuse His command to repent means eternal punishment for sin. For those of us who are followers of Christ, any resistance to the will of God will keep us from enjoying an abundant life and will create barriers in our fellowship with God.

But our God abounds in mercy and grace; He is willing to offer a full and complete pardon to those who lay down their weapons.

In eternity, knowing what we cannot see now or what we have refused to believe, any holding out on our part will appear no less misguided and foolish than a Japanese officer spending three decades of his adult life holed up in a tropical jungle, living like an animal, fighting a war that had long since ended.

As we consider the meaning of Christian surrender, I pray that your heart will be captured with a compelling vision of the One who claims the right to run the universe. May you experience an irresistible sense of the joys and blessings that can be yours through relinquishing control to this God who loves you and who holds your very life in His hand.

Notes

1. Gary Thomas, *Seeking the Face of God* (Eugene, Oreg.: Harvest House, 1999), 84.
2. "Old Soldiers Never Die," *Newsweek*, March 25, 1974, 49, 52.
3. Hiroo Onoda, *No Surrender: My Thirty-Year War* (New York: Kodansha International Ltd., 1974), 14–15.

Surrender is not the surrender of the external life,
but of the will; when that is done, all is done.
There are very few crises in life;
the great crisis is the surrender of the will.

———————

OSWALD CHAMBERS[1]

THE BATTLE
for CONTROL:
KINGDOMS AT WAR

+ **MINDY, A CHRISTIAN** college senior, can't believe she ended up in bed with her fiancé last night—again—after promising herself she wouldn't give in and praying about the matter with her accountability partner just last week. Mindy and Jeff are planning to get married after graduation and had hoped to serve as short-term missionaries before having children. But now . . . the whole idea seems hypocritical.

+ Angie steps on the scales, sighs, and heads for the kitchen, where she opens the refrigerator. She starts to pick up a bag of carrots, then reaches instead for a piece of carrot cake that seems to be calling her name. Just then, the phone rings; her sister is calling to offer a ride to their weekly Bible class tomorrow morning.

+ Something inside Dan knows he really shouldn't be going out for "business lunches" with his attractive young assistant—especially since their recent conversations have been less about business and more about the problems in her marriage. Dan is nervous about being seen with Stacie by someone from the church where he is a respected elder. But some unseen force is drawing him to spend more time with her.

✦ Both Tamara and Rod would like for her to be able to quit her job so she can stay at home when their first child is born next month, but they just don't see how they can swing it financially. Their pastor recently preached a message from Matthew 6 about trusting God to provide for basic needs. But they are afraid to step out—and his parents have said she'd be crazy to quit her job.

✦ Reggie is still fuming as he flies down the freeway at eighty miles per hour. He knows he shouldn't have lost his temper with Carla—especially with their three-year-old son standing there watching the whole scene. But he can't believe she has overdrawn their checking account again. Why can't she exercise some self-control when it comes to spending? Reggie gets scared when he thinks about what he might do someday when he is in one of his fits of rage. Recently his anger has started coming out with the students at the Christian school where he coaches football.

✦ Corrie is troubled by the attitudes and language her children are picking up from other children in preschool and second grade. She wants her children to have a heart for God and really feels she should consider home-schooling them, but she can't handle the thought of being tied down with kids all day every day.

The Real War

These men and women are not alone in their struggles. Every day, in big or little ways, even as believers, you and I find ourselves engaged in a battle (Galatians 5:17).

The battle is real and dangerous. We are like a soldier in a foxhole, with bullets whizzing past his head, but our battle is actually part of a larger war that has been going on since the creation of the world.

In fact, one of the megathemes that emerges repeatedly in Scripture is that our battles here on earth are merely a reflection of a cosmic war between the kingdom of God and all other kingdoms. That is true whether we are talking about kids squabbling on a playground, embattled parents and teens, estranged mates in a divorce court, warring desires within our own hearts, power struggles in the church, or nations at war.

This bigger war—the "real war"—begins in the opening pages of the Word of God and continues unabated, gaining in intensity, almost to the final page. It is, in essence, a battle for control.

In the first recorded act in time and space, God *exercised control.* He spoke with authority and power . . . bringing light, life, and order to the darkness and chaos of the universe. When He said, "Let there be light," there was light. When He said, "Let the trees bring forth fruit," the trees brought forth fruit. All creation, including—initially—the first man and woman, lived in glad, wholehearted surrender to the sovereign control and will of the Creator.

This surrender did not strip the creation of dignity or freedom; to the contrary, surrender was—and still is—the source and means of true freedom and fullness. The sovereign Creator God ruled over His creation with tender love, inviting His creatures to engage with Him in a divine dance-of-sorts, in which He led and they followed. They responded to His initiative with trust, love, and surrender. In turn, their needs were abundantly met, they fulfilled their created purpose, and they existed in harmony with God and with each other.

Psalm 104 describes this original, ideal state. In that passage, we see a definite, unquestioned hierarchy in which God—the gracious Sovereign—acts, initiates, directs, sets boundaries, supervises, and lovingly rules over His creation. The creation looks to Him, waits for Him, bows before Him, surrenders to His control, and simply does as He directs.

The oceans stay within the boundaries He has established for them. The grass and the trees grow according to God's direction and provide nourishment for man and animals, also in surrender to God's will. The sun and moon keep their appointed seasons; the animals get up when God tells them to get up and they lie down when God directs them to do so.

What is the result? "The earth is satisfied" (verse 13); "they are filled with good" (verse 28). Did you catch that? To surrender to the Creator's control is not onerous or burdensome; it is, in fact, the place of blessing, fullness, and peace. There is no evidence in this passage of any stress, struggle, or strain. Why? Because the creation is not vying with the Creator for control.

Don't miss this picture. It is what the old gospel song describes as "perfect submission, perfect delight!"[2]

The Battle Begins

Let's go back to the Genesis account. The first blip on this perfect screen came when one of God's created beings—already a rebel himself—approached the happy couple and challenged God's created order. Until that point, there had never been any question about who was in charge and who was taking direction. Now the suggestion was made that the man and woman could be in charge of their own lives, that they didn't have to take direction from anyone else. *You don't have to live a surrendered life; you can be in control,* the tempter implied.

So the man and the woman—created beings—tried to wrest control from the hands of their sovereign Creator. Control that didn't belong to them. They resisted the will of God and insisted on sharing His throne. The battle had begun.

From that point to this, man has been engaged with his Creator in a battle for control—dueling wills, we might call it.

God has opted first to woo and win the hearts of His creatures.

Mercifully, we are dealing with a Creator who is not only sovereign, but also compassionate. God knew that if we tried to run our own lives, we would reap misery and conflict, and that our drive to be in control would render us hopelessly enslaved and would ultimately destroy us. He knew that the only hope for man was through surrender.

From that very first skirmish, God set into motion a plan devised in eternity past to restore man back to a place of surrender to His control. Possessing absolute power, He could have chosen to bludgeon His rebellious creatures into submission. However, because He desires a loving, personal relationship with men and women, created in His likeness, He has opted first to woo and win the hearts of His creatures. He wants their willing, volitional surrender.

We know that one day "every knee [will] bow" and "every tongue . . . confess that Jesus Christ is Lord" (Philippians 2:10–11). Those who refuse His overtures of love and grace will do so under coercion. But those who love and trust Him will find ultimate, eternal joy in that glad-hearted surrender.

The King and His Kingdom

The very thought of God being bent on exercising control over His creation raises an obvious question. If you or I were to attempt to bring the whole planet under our control, we would rightly be labeled "control freaks." So why is it acceptable for God to insist on "world domination"? Why is it considered selfish and rebellious for us to want control, but absolutely appropriate for God to assert control? The answer is simple:

He's God—
and we're not.

In that profound, unalterable, eternal reality lies the key to understanding and dealing with this cosmic war, as well as handling our personal, daily struggles for control.

No one would consider it unreasonable for a mother to insist on being in control of her mini-van while her four children are seat-belted in place. That's because she knows what she's doing. She knows how to drive and her children don't. She is the only one in the vehicle capable of keeping everyone safe. The fact that she doesn't share the driving with her preschoolers doesn't make her a control freak!

> *He is the only One capable of running the universe.*

In the same way, God exercises His sovereign control over the universe because He is the only One capable of running the universe.

Inherent in His being is absolute sovereignty—the right to rule. He is the Creator—we are His creatures. He is eternal—we are finite. He is all-powerful—we have no power of our own. He is autonomous, independent, and self-existent, needing no one and nothing—we are dependent on Him for our next breath (Acts 17:24–25).

The God revealed in the Scripture is King—not a king on a level with other kings, each with their own sphere of control—but *the* King over all kings. This King has a kingdom. That kingdom—the realm over which He has lawful jurisdiction—includes every molecule of the planet on which we live; it includes the farthest-flung reaches of our galaxy and of every galaxy; it includes those regions that are inhabited by the angelic hosts (both fallen and holy).

In his commentary on the Gospel of Luke, twentieth-century Bible expositor G. Campbell Morgan suggests that the kingdom of God really means the *kingship of God*.

> It means that God is King now, and always. The Kingdom of God is in existence. God has never been dethroned; and this is what Jesus preached. . . . He was proclaiming the Kingship of God, the rule of God, the fact that the Lord reigneth. . . .
>
> What this age needs is the proclamation of the sovereignty of God, the Kingship of God, the Kingdom of God. . . . When a man yields himself up to that sovereignty, nobody can tyrannize over him.[3]

The concept of a Sovereign King who exercises absolute control over His subjects is one that our egalitarian, Western minds find difficult to embrace. We want to have a say in the matter—to vote for the leader of our choice. We don't want to bow before an all-powerful monarch. To the contrary, what we really want is to *be* the king—or at least to have a representative form of government.

But whether we buy into it or not, the sovereign rule of God and the lordship of Jesus Christ is a nonnegotiable reality that is as determinative and binding as the law of gravity—and more so. It is an irrefutable truth with which every human being must come to terms, sooner or later. And, as Morgan suggests, those who resist His sovereign Lordship set themselves up to be tyrannized by other lords.

One Woman's Control Crisis

"Lynda," a forty-something mother of four, learned the hard way that to resist surrender to the perfect will of God is to become controlled by tyrants. I received a letter from Lynda in which she told her story. She has been married for twenty-five years to a man she calls "saintly." However, she grew up in a home with an alcoholic father who was extremely controlling of her and her passive mother.

As she became an adult, she resolved that she would never submit to another human. She recalls, "I had a huge problem when it came time to say our wedding vows—'to love and obey.' Love? Yes, absolutely! *Obey?* I don't think so!"

In retrospect, Lynda can see how her drive to be in control created numerous problems from the outset of her marriage and led to choices that ultimately caused her life to career out of control. She admits that she began to turn to other men

> to make me feel in control again, and to show my husband that I—and no one else—was in charge of my life. Little did I realize that I was "out of control" in many ways—including sexually and with alcohol abuse. And I was not ever in charge of my life or body.
>
> You see, while I refused to submit to my husband, I *was* submitting to other men—but not in loving relationships. I was not in control of my body or my life—other men were. "Meet me here, Lynda." "OK." "You drive today, Lynda." "OK." "You check us in at the motel." "OK." "Wear this, do that, call me. . . ." "OK, OK, OK."

Lynda's experience poignantly illustrates that as long as we refuse to surrender our will to the will of God, we are never truly free. Rather, we find ourselves dominated by ungodly appetites and forces. When we throw off the restraints of our wise, loving God, we become slaves to terrible taskmasters that are intent on our destruction. That is exactly what happened to the Old Testament Israelites:

*Because you did not serve the Lord your God joyfully and gladly in
the time of prosperity, therefore in hunger and thirst, in nakedness
and dire poverty, you will serve the enemies the Lord sends against
you. He will put an iron yoke on your neck until he has destroyed
you.*

—Deuteronomy 28:47–48 NIV

You don't want to surrender to God's control? You won't bow to His
will in relation to your marriage, your morals, your attitudes, your
tongue, your eating habits, your spending habits, or the way you spend
your time? Then count on it—the very points on which you refuse to
surrender will become "enemies" that rule over you—lust, greed, possessions, food, sloth, immorality, anger, etc.

After more than twenty years of turmoil in every area of Lynda's life,
the Lord brought matters to a head by causing her husband to discover
her unfaithfulness. In an incredible display of the
heart and ways of God, her husband not only extended mercy, but he tenderly and firmly exerted
the wise, loving leadership that Lynda needed to
get her life back in order.

*What is the
turf in which
you are in a battle
for control?*

Lynda hardly knew how to respond to such
grace. But in that crisis of surrender, she says, "I
repented. I knew I had to submit completely to
God and to my husband—in that order!"

Though she had always feared what would happen if she were to relinquish control of her life, Lynda began to experience blessings she had
never known in all the years she was trying to hold on to the reins.

A *huge* weight was lifted off my shoulders. I didn't want to be in
control any more. My journey has not always been easy, but it
has been wonderful and life-changing. I had to "let go" of a lot of
people in my life—but I have God and my family. I have a beautiful peace of mind and serenity. And I hold my head high every
day, because I know I have been forgiven. I will *never* be the same
person again—ever.

156

Lynda's whole perspective on this matter of control has changed. Today she tells others, "Even if you are stubborn and think you will not submit to anyone, you will always be submitting to someone or something—and that can be extremely dangerous. Even life-threatening."

Surrendering her will to Christ's control in relation to her marriage brought about a dramatic change in Lynda's life. "Your kingdom come; Your will be done" replaced her former motto of "I am in charge of my own life."

What is the turf in which you are in a battle for control? Perhaps it is in relation to your marriage—you may be bent on changing your mate, refusing to accept him/her as God's choice for your life, or resisting your God-given responsibilities in that relationship.

Your battle for control may be in another relationship—perhaps with a parent, a child, an employer, a pastor, or a friend.

Or you may be resisting God's right to control your body—your eating, sleeping, exercise, or moral habits—or your tongue, your time, your future plans, or your finances.

Whether in our relationships, personal disciplines, daily decisions, or recurring habit patterns, our choice to resist or to voluntarily surrender to the control of the King has far-reaching implications.

When we play "king"—when we insist on establishing our own kingdom and asserting our right to rule—we set ourselves unavoidably at war with the Sovereign God of the universe—a battle, I might add, that we cannot possibly win. Invariably, we will end up being ruled by tyrants.

However, when we bow to His kingship—when we recognize His kingdom as being supreme, when we surrender to His wise and loving control—then we can live at peace with the King. And only then will we be free from all other tyrannies.

MAKING IT PERSONAL . . .

✦ What is one example of a battle for control in your life?

✦ What is one area of your life that has ended up ruling you as a "tyrant" because of your lack of surrender?

Notes
1. Oswald Chambers, *My Utmost for His Highest,* September 13.
2. Fanny J. Crosby, "Blessed Assurance."
3. G. Campbell Morgan, *The God Who Cares* (Old Tappan, N.J.: Revell, 1987), 153, 172.

I have been before God, and have given myself, all that I am and have, to God; so that I am not, in any respect, my own. . . . I have given myself clear away, and have not retained any thing as my own.

———————

JONATHAN EDWARDS[1]

The TERMS
of CHRISTIAN
SURRENDER:
UNCONDITIONAL AND LIFETIME

THE HOME OF WILMER and Virginia McLean in the village of Appomattox Court House, Virginia, was the scene of a historic meeting that resulted in bringing to an end the bloodiest conflict in this nation's history. On April 9, 1865, after four years of hostilities that had claimed some 630,000 lives and inflicted more than one million casualties, General Robert E. Lee signed an agreement surrendering the Confederate Army of Northern Virginia to General Ulysses S. Grant.

That defining moment in the Civil War was the culmination of an intense series of exchanges between the two commanders. Six days earlier, Richmond had fallen to Union troops. The battle continued as Lee led his army in retreat, pursued by Grant and his men. On April 7, Grant sent a message to Lee suggesting that further resistance by the Confederate Army was hopeless and requesting that Lee surrender his portion of the army, to avoid further bloodshed.

Although Lee would not concede that his situation was hopeless, he responded the same day by asking Grant to spell out the conditions of any possible surrender.

In his reply early the following morning, Grant clearly stated the terms for surrender:

> Peace being my great desire, there is but one condition I would insist upon—namely, that the men and officers surrendered shall be disqualified for taking up arms against the Government of the United States.

Grant offered to meet Lee at any place he wished, for the purpose of working out the details of the surrender.

Lee responded later that day by saying that he wished to meet Grant at ten o'clock the following morning to discuss how to bring about the "restoration of peace," but that he did not intend to surrender.

Grant's response early the next morning, April 9, made it clear that there was no point in meeting if Lee was not willing to surrender. Grant appealed to the Southern commander to accept his conditions:

> The terms upon which peace can be had are well understood. By the South laying down their arms, they would hasten that most desirable event, save thousands of human lives, and hundreds of millions of property not yet destroyed.

Within hours, a messenger overtook Grant on the road to Appomattox Court House with Lee's reply. The inescapable reality was that Lee's army was surrounded and his men were weak and exhausted. His army was badly in need of food and basic provisions for both men and animals. Lee was left with little choice but to agree to meet for the purpose of surrendering.

We . . . were estranged from the Sovereign God of the universe.

Lee's decision to accept Grant's terms of surrender that afternoon resulted in the conclusion of the Civil War, as Lee's Army of Northern Virginia laid down their arms, followed over the next few months by the surrender of the remaining Confederate armies.

Of course, an arduous, lengthy process of rebuilding the divided

Union lay ahead. Nonetheless, at that decisive moment, once the terms of surrender were accepted, the course of the war and of the Union was changed and the ultimate outcome was assured.

Peace Through Surrender

Lee's surrender paved the way for peace to be restored to a war-torn nation. In the spiritual realm, there can be no peace with God, nor can there be peace in our hearts, apart from unconditional surrender. Refusing to surrender merely compounds our losses; delayed surrender only prolongs the conflict.

According to the Scripture, from the moment we were conceived, we were at war with God (Psalm 51:5). We had conflicting goals, desires, philosophies, strategies, and loyalties. Our will was opposed to His will. We were intent on going our own independent way, and as a result, were estranged from the Sovereign God of the universe.

Even when the Spirit opened our eyes to recognize our rebellious condition, we may have sought a way to bring about peace apart from surrender. We did not want to continue suffering the unpleasant consequences of our resistance, but neither did we want to lay down our arms.

Then the message was sent to our hearts: *There can be no peace until you are willing to accept My terms—unconditional surrender.*

Christian surrender means that we come to Him on His terms.

Realizing that surrender was our best—and ultimately our only—option, we finally agreed to accept His terms. We waved the white flag; we owned Christ as Lord; we gave our lives to the One who gave His life for us on the cross—the One who demands and deserves our wholehearted allegiance.

The handover of power was not merely an external act, as was the case at Appomattox. Through an internal work of the Spirit and the grace of God, our willful, rebellious hearts were conquered and we were each given a new heart—a heart to love God and to obey and follow Christ as our Captain and sovereign Lord.

This is what the Bible calls being *born again—regenerated*. It is what theologians refer to as *conversion*, or what many people call the *point of salvation*. At that decisive moment, though he may not fully comprehend all that is taking place, the rebel repents of his anarchy against the King; the sinner surrenders to the loving lordship of his sovereign Creator and Savior.

In no way does that act of surrender save us. It is Christ's work on the cross, His sacrifice for sin, that is our only means of forgiveness and salvation. But His death is the provision that frees us from sin and enables us—yes, compels us—to surrender ourselves wholly to God.

The person who has never acknowledged Christ's right to rule over his life has no basis for assurance of salvation. He may claim to be a Christian; he may have walked an aisle or prayed the sinner's prayer; he may know how to speak "Christianese"; he may be heavily involved in Christian activities; but if he thinks he can have a relationship with God by retaining control over his life and somehow trying to fit Jesus in with everything else, he is deceived and is still at war with God.

Sadly, for the past 150 years or more, evangelicalism has developed a theology that offers assurance of salvation to almost anyone who prays a prayer or "makes a decision for Christ," even though he may still be clinging to his rights, holding on to his sin, and bent on running his own life. The Scripture does not recognize such a profession as genuine.

Jesus warned, "Not everyone who says to me, 'Lord, Lord,' will enter the kingdom of heaven, but only he who *does the will of my Father* who is in heaven" (Matthew 7:21 NIV, italics added). Surrender to the will of God is a mark of the truly converted.

The terms of our surrender to the Lord Jesus are nonnegotiable and unconditional. What does He ask us to surrender? In a word, *everything*. Christian surrender means that we come to Him on His terms, as the conquering general of our soul, and say simply, "I surrender all." We lay down our arms; we hand over everything we have, everything we are, everything we hope to be.

And, unlike Lee's surrender at Appomattox, our surrender to Christ does not involve a sense of genuine loss. To the contrary, Christian surrender brings us what we now see is beauty, life, joy, and true good. We are given eyes to see the glory of Christ we previously despised (2 Corinthians 4:4–6), and in surrendering to Him, we finally see the "surpassing value" of Christ over all that the world ever could have given us (Philippians 3:8 NASB).

Foundation for a Lifetime of Surrender

As every believer soon discovers, that initial point of surrender to the Lord Jesus is not the final chapter—any more than Robert E. Lee's signature on a piece of paper on April 9, 1865, immediately resolved all the deep issues between the Union and the Confederacy.

As we have indicated, that crucial point must be followed by an ongoing process of working out the reality of our surrender in practical, day-to-day ways. However, that daily lifestyle of surrender is birthed out of a foundational, unconditional, lifetime surrender to Jesus as Lord.

I have seen this to be true in my own life.

My first conscious memory is kneeling by my bed on May 14, 1963, as a four-year-old child, and trusting Christ as my Savior. I don't recall the words I prayed that day—I'm sure they didn't reflect any deep theological understanding. But I had been nurtured in an environment of the Word of God, which the Spirit of God had used to show me my sinful condition and to draw my heart to Christ, who was my only hope.

Throughout those early years following my conversion, I had a growing, inescapable awareness that my life belonged to God, and by the age of seven or eight, I was conscious of having made a volitional, lifetime, unconditional surrender to Jesus as Lord of my life. That surrender was the fruit of the seeds of repentance and faith that God had planted in my heart when I was born again.

At that young age, I had little comprehension of the implications of full surrender. I had no idea what God would ask of me down the road. What I did know was that Jesus is Lord, that my life belonged to Him, and that to surrender myself completely to One who possessed infinite wisdom, love, and power was the only course that made any sense. With all my heart, I knew that I wanted to follow Christ—*whatever that might mean, whatever it might require, and wherever it might lead me.*

As my faith has matured, I have faced many situations that have required a fresh affirmation and expression of that initial surrender to the will of God. Most of those instances have been simply the daily choices to obey the Word of God and the promptings of His Spirit. . . .

+ Hold your tongue—don't try to prove your point.

+ You've had enough to eat—stop!

+ Assume the best of that person—don't give a negative report.

+ Open your home to that couple who need a place to stay.

+ Spend time in the Word and prayer before starting the business of your day.

+ Seek forgiveness from that person you treated roughly.

+ Make a financial contribution to that young person going on a mission trip.

On occasion, the pathway of obedience has required a more costly surrender.

+ Forgive that person who defamed your reputation.

+ Go to that person who has a grievance against you and seek to be reconciled.

+ Give a large portion of your personal library to a Third World pastor who has few books.

+ Sacrifice the security and blessings of a home to travel in full-time itinerant ministry.

+ Yield the right to be married and to have children of your own.

Whether large or small, those points of surrender over some forty years have been greatly simplified because of that initial surrender to the lordship of Christ when I was a little girl.

In the natural realm, the dieter who has made a firm commitment not to eat desserts has an easier time saying, "No, thank you!" when the tantalizing dessert tray is passed than the person who is frustrated with being overweight but has not determined his course of action.

In much the same way, once that lifetime surrender has been made, many of our battles will be much less difficult to fight, because the outcome—*Jesus is Lord*—has already been established. That fundamental acknowledgment of His sovereign right to reign and rule over us will serve us well as our allegiance to the King is tested on a daily basis.

Signing Our Surrender

One of the challenges of complete surrender to Christ is that we don't know what lies ahead. Doubtless, some of us might be more inclined to surrender if God would hand us a contract with all the details filled in. We'd like to know what to expect: "What will this cost me? Where will God expect me to go? What will He ask me to do?" We want to see all the fine print so we can read it over, think about it, and then decide whether to sign our name on the dotted line.

We have nothing to lose by signing the blank contract.

But that's not God's way. God says instead, "Here's a blank piece of paper. I want you to sign your name on the bottom line, hand it back to Me, and let Me fill in the details. Why? Because I am God; because I have bought you; because I am trustworthy; because you know how much I love you; because you live for My glory and not your own independent, self-promoting pleasure."

Signing that blank paper is risky . . . *if* God dies or *if* He ever falls off His throne or *if* He is not, in fact, trustworthy. But the reality is that we have nothing to lose by signing the blank contract. Oh, we may lose some things that the world considers valuable or essential. But in the eternal scheme of things, we cannot lose, because He is a God who can be completely trusted. If we will let Him, God will fill in the details of our lives with His incomparable wisdom and sovereign plan, written in the indelible ink of His covenant faithfulness and love.

Those Who Signed the Contract

Some of the most stirring language in the pages of church history has come from the pens and hearts of men and women expressing their desire to be unreservedly surrendered to God.

For example, in 1753, John Wesley, greatly used of God in the first Great Awakening, published a "Covenant Prayer," based on a Puritan text written almost one hundred years earlier:

I am no longer my own, but thine.
Put me to what thou wilt, rank me with whom thou wilt.
Put me to doing, put me to suffering.
Let me be employed by thee or laid aside for thee,
Exalted for thee or brought low by thee.
Let me be full, let me be empty.
Let me have all things, let me have nothing.
I freely and heartily yield all things to thy pleasure and disposal.
And now, O glorious and blessed God,
Father, Son, and Holy Spirit,
Thou art mine, and I am thine. So be it.
And the covenant which I have made on earth,
Let it be ratified in heaven. Amen.[2]

French missionary Charles de Foucauld (1858–1916) expressed his heart this way:

Father, I abandon myself into Your hands; do with me what You will. Whatever You may do, I thank You: I am ready for all, I accept all. Only let Your will be done in me, and in all Your creatures—I wish no more than this, O Lord.

Betty Scott grew up in China, where her parents were missionaries. She returned to the United States at the age of seventeen for her last year of high school, followed by college and Bible institute. During those years, Betty penned a prayer that has become the petition of many other believers who long to live a life of unconditional surrender to Jesus as Lord:

Lord, I give up my own plans and purposes, all my own desires, hopes and ambitions, and I accept Thy will for my life. I give up myself, my life, my all, utterly to Thee, to be Thine forever. I hand over to Thy keeping all of my friendships; all the people whom I love are to take second place in my heart. Fill me now and seal me with Thy Spirit. Work out Thy whole will in my life at any cost, for to me to live is Christ. Amen.

After completing her schooling, Betty returned to China to serve with the China Inland Mission. Two years later, in October of 1933, she married John Stam, also a CIM worker. In December of 1934, just weeks after the birth of their baby girl, John and Betty were taken hostage by hostile Communist soldiers, and within a few days were beheaded. Betty was twenty-eight years old.

When she wrote, "Work out Thy whole will in my life *at any cost*," she had no way of knowing what full surrender would cost her. Although some might consider the cost exorbitant, I am confident that Betty, having laid down her life for Christ, would not think the price too high.

His Forever

Fourteen years after the death of John and Betty Stam, another young couple exchanged wedding vows in a small town in Oklahoma. Although they were deeply in love, at that point their focus was different from the Stams'. By his own admission, as a young adult, Bill was motivated by selfish goals and materialistic pursuits. When they got engaged, this enterprising young man had promised his wife-to-be that she would have everything her heart could desire—they would travel the world and own a home in upscale Bel Air, California.

However, during the first two years of their marriage, their desires and interests slowly began to change. Looking back nearly fifty years later, Bill explained what brought about the change: "We had both fallen in love with Jesus."[3]

At the time, Bill was pursuing a graduate degree at a nearby theological seminary, while also running a successful business he had started. Both he and his wife found themselves deeply stirred and motivated by the challenge of the Lord Jesus, recorded in the Gospel of Mark:

> *"If any of you wants to be my follower,"* he told them, *"you must put aside your own pleasures and shoulder your cross, and follow me closely. If you insist on saving your life, you will lose it. Only those who throw away their lives for my sake and for the sake of the Good News will ever know what it means to really live."*

Mark 8:34–35 TLB

One Sunday afternoon in the spring of 1951, as the young couple talked, they were gripped by the realization that knowing and serving the Lord Jesus was more important than any other pursuit in life. There in the living room of their home, they knelt together and prayed a simple, but heartfelt prayer:

> Lord, we surrender our lives irrevocably to You and to do Your will.
> We want to love and serve You with all of our hearts for the rest of our lives.[4]

At that moment, the kneeling pair could not have imagined the extent to which that prayer and the surrender it represented would change the whole course of their lives.

Bill describes one further step they took that day as an expression of their hearts' intent:

> We actually wrote and signed a contract committing our whole lives to Him, relinquishing all of our rights, all of our possessions, everything we would ever own, giving to Him, our dear Lord and Master, everything. In the words of the Apostle Paul, [my wife] and I became that Sunday afternoon voluntary slaves of Jesus.[5]

Once that contract was signed, the die was cast. There was to be no turning back. Decades later, Bill and Vonette Bright had become household names in the Christian world; they had founded and led one of the largest Christian organizations in history, with seventy different ministries, 26,000 full-time staff, and 226,000 trained volunteers serving in 190 countries of the world. Yet, in spite of his many achievements, when Dr. Bright was diagnosed with a terminal lung disease, he made it known that the only epitaph he and his wife wanted on their tombstone was "Slaves of Jesus Christ."

Bill and Vonette Bright have never served Christ out of a sense of drudgery or mere duty. Passionate love for Christ has been the spring of their desire to be His devoted slaves. In our day of Christian celebrities, public relations campaigns, and nationally telecast awards ceremonies, few professing believers are enthralled with the idea of being simply a slave of Jesus Christ. However, as we will see, if we overlook or reject that calling, we forfeit one of life's greatest privileges and our only means to true freedom.

MAKING IT PERSONAL...

✦ In your own words, write out a prayer expressing your heart's intent to be wholly surrendered to Christ. Then date and sign your "contract" with the Lord.

Notes

1. *The Works of Jonathan Edwards, Volume 1,* "Memoirs of Jonathan Edwards: Chapter IV: His Diary" (Carlisle, Pa.: Banner of Truth Trust, 1976), xxv.
2. *The United Methodist Hymnal,* #607, taken from the Wesleyan Covenant Renewal Service; published in 1753 by John Wesley.
3. From an acceptance speech by Dr. William R. Bright, receiving the 1996 Templeton Prize for Progress in Religion. Delivered in Rome, Italy, at The Church of St. Maria in Trastevere, 9 May 1996.
4. Ibid.
5. Ibid.

Lord, send me anywhere, only go with me;

lay any burden on me, only sustain me;

and sever every tie, but the tie that

binds me to Thy service and Thy heart.

DAVID LIVINGSTONE

A HOLE *in the* EAR:
BONDSLAVES FOREVER

ROMANIAN PASTOR and Christian leader Josef Tson was exiled from his native country in 1981, after experiencing prolonged persecution at the hands of one of the most repressive Communist regimes in history. He immigrated to the United States, where he ministered for nearly a decade, until he was able to return to his homeland, where he continues serving today.

I first met Josef and his wife, Elizabeth, in the early 1980s when he was speaking to a gathering of Christian workers. I have never forgotten his response when he was asked how he wished to be introduced. Though his academic and professional credentials are impressive, Josef did not offer a printed bio sketch. Rather, this articulate, Oxford-educated theologian, who had suffered so greatly for his faith, said simply, "I wish to be introduced as 'a slave of Jesus Christ.'"

During his years in exile, Josef was taken aback by some of the traits of evangelical Christianity in the United States that were foreign to what he had experienced in Eastern Europe. As he studied the historical development of American evangelicalism, he discovered that those contemporary characteristics were the fruit of a series of spiritual paradigm shifts.

> The emphasis on pursuing holiness shifted to a desire for upliting, ecstatic experiences.

The first of those changes took place at the beginning of the twentieth century, when the nineteenth-century emphasis on pursuing holiness shifted to a desire for uplifting, ecstatic experiences.

A second change took place in the 1950s and 1960s, which Josef identifies as a "shift from the call to *full surrender*, to the call to *commitment*." He explains the difference this way:

> Christian *surrender* means that a person lifts his or her hands and says to God, "Here I am; I surrender; You take over; I belong to You; You dispose of me!"
>
> But this is America, the country of the independent people! This is the place of "Nobody should command me! . . . I belong only to myself!"
>
> A call to surrender, and even more, to full surrender, simply doesn't go well with such people. Therefore, the preachers, who wanted "results," and wanted them in big numbers, felt (and gave in to) the temptation to soften the demand, to reduce the cost, to make the message more "palatable." And they hit the word "commitment."
>
> You see, *commitment* means "I engage myself to do something for you," or, even lighter, "I promise to do something for you," but I remain myself and I may keep my promise or not. We can speak of weaker or stronger commitment, but be it as strong as possible, it is still my independent self that engages itself in a tentative promise.[1]

This subtle change paved the way for other shifts in the Christian culture. Josef Tson goes on to say:

> One of them came quietly, almost unobserved, through the new versions of the Bible. Translators did not like the term "bondslave" to be applied to people. Who wants to be somebody else's slave? Therefore, they replaced it with "servant."

Again, a reflection and demand of the independent spirit!

In the Greek, "slave" is *doulos*; "servant" is *diakonos*. In the Greek Bible one never, never *diakoneo* to God—one never *serves* God; one only *douleo* to God—that is, one *slaves* to God.

Jesus makes it clear in Luke 17 that however much you do for God, at the end of the day you say: "I am an unworthy slave; I only did what is the duty of the slave to do!" But all that is gone now, by the replacement of the word "slave" with the word "servant."

Webster's dictionary bears out the difference in meaning between these two words. A *servant* is defined as "a person employed to perform services . . . for another." A *slave*, on the other hand, is a "human being who is owned as property by and is absolutely subject to the will of another."

As Josef Tson points out, slavery is a concept we resist in the West. We can barely swallow the idea of a servant, but the word *slave* sticks in our throat—as it should, if we were speaking of coerced or involuntary slavery of a person who is owned against his will by another. That is an abhorrent relationship between two individuals, both of whom are created in the image of God. But it is absolutely appropriate that human beings should choose to be the slaves of the Lord Jesus, whom they love and long to serve for all their lives.

Pierced Ears

The twenty-first chapter of Exodus includes a lengthy list of regulations regarding Hebrew servants. Among them is a dramatic scenario that vividly illustrates what it means to be a bondslave in the spiritual sense:

> *Now these are the rules that you shall set before them. When you buy a Hebrew slave, he shall serve six years, and in the seventh he shall go out free, for nothing. . . . But if the slave plainly says, "I love my master, my wife, and my children; I will not go out free," then his master shall bring him to God, and he shall bring him to the door or the doorpost. And his master shall bore his ear through with an awl, and he shall be his slave forever.*
>
> —Exodus 21:1–2, 5–6 ESV

On occasion, poverty-stricken Jews were forced to sell themselves into service to their fellow Jews. The law of God required that all servants be treated with justice and kindness, and that they be freed at the end of six years. In this passage, we have a description of an unusual option provided for a servant who had fulfilled his obligation to his master and was due to be released from servitude.

The servant was free to leave. In this case, however, he had developed a strong, loving relationship with his master and with the wife and children he had acquired during his years of service, and he did not wish to be released from his master's service. Presumably, he admired his master and was grateful for the way he had been treated and provided for—so much so, that he wanted to continue serving in his master's household.

Knowing his master as he did, the bondslave trusted that all he needed would be provided, that he would never want for food, shelter, clothing, or any other basic needs.

He was under no obligation to stay, but he *wanted* to stay—he *loved* his master and made a voluntary choice to become his master's *bondslave*. In doing so, he was not just signing up for another six-year stint—he was making a lifetime commitment. He was surrendering himself and giving up all his rights—permanently—to his master.

> *Christ humbled Himself and offered Himself to be a bondslave.*

This was not merely a contractual agreement. This was not about being hired help. This was the act of a man who voluntarily said to someone he had come to know and love and trust, "I am yours—I belong to you, and I want to spend the rest of my life fulfilling your wishes."

There could be no secret about the nature of the servant's new relationship to his master. The transaction was made in a public ceremony where the surrender was recognized in a visible—and painful—way. A sharp instrument was used to pierce a hole in the servant's ear, signifying obedience to the voice of his master. The decision was irreversible. From that point on, he would always be branded as a bondslave.

If the bondservant ever had second thoughts—if a week or a month, or a year, or ten years later he decided, "I think I want out of this deal"— he would always have a hole in his ear to remind him that he was not his own and never would be again. To acquire this mark of ownership involved a degree of suffering, but the servant was willing to endure the physical pain, in order to formally establish and demonstrate his relationship with his master. The hole spoke of lifetime ownership.

The Picture Fulfilled

Nowhere in the Scripture or in ancient historical records do we find a single instance in which a servant made this choice referred to in Exodus 21. So why did God even suggest such a scenario? Like so many other Old Testament pictures, I believe it was intended to point us to Christ and to depict our relationship with Him.

The New Testament tells us that when the Lord Jesus came to this earth, He took "the form of a servant [*doulos*—the lowest form of slave]" (Philippians 2:7). In obedience to His Father's will and out of love for His Father—and for the bride and family His Father had given Him— He humbled Himself and offered Himself to be a bondslave, so He could deliver those who were in bondage to sin (Hebrews 2:10–18).

Speaking prophetically of the atoning death of Christ, the psalmist wrote, "Sacrifice and offering you did not desire, but *my ears you have pierced.* . . . I desire to do your will, O my God" (Psalm 40:6, 8 NIV, italics added). As far as we know, no one had ever opted to have his ear pierced in the ceremony described in Exodus 21—until *Christ* came to earth! In His desire to do the will of God and His willingness to suffer and bear the marks of that submission, He became the bondslave who symbolically fulfilled the literal exchange described in the Old Testament law.

In the New Testament, the apostles Peter and Paul, along with James and Jude (both half brothers of the Lord Jesus) all followed in the steps of that Great Bondslave when each identified himself as a *doulos*—a bondservant, a slave of Jesus Christ. Paul said, "I bear in my body the marks of the Lord Jesus" (Galatians 6:17). What was he saying? "I'm a man with a hole in my ear. I am the bondslave of Jesus Christ."

Certainly these men understood that they were also sons of God and coheirs with Jesus Christ—but, like Josef Tson, they wanted to be known first and foremost as the slaves of the Lord Jesus Christ.

No Higher Calling

I have come to believe that there is no greater calling than to be marked as His slave—to choose to give my life in the service of the Master I have grown to know and love and trust. For many years, my prayer has been, "Oh, God, make me a woman with a hole in my ear; I want to be identified as a slave of Jesus Christ."

That is not to say that living as a bondslave of Jesus Christ has always been easy. Among other things, for me, that choice has meant:

+ Spending the majority of my adult life on the road, living out of suitcases in temporary accommodations

+ Seldom being able to put down roots; difficulty maintaining deep, long-term relationships

+ Relinquishing any "right" to a private life; virtually always being on display and "on call" to minister to the needs of others

+ Living with relentless deadlines; little "free time" for entertainment, recreation, or personal pleasures; working when others are relaxing or socializing; few days or nights "off"

+ Forgoing the privilege of marriage and childbearing

+ Carrying an ever-pressing burden for the condition of the church and the spiritual needs of others

Do I sound as if I am complaining? I'll confess that I've done more than my share of whining about the "pressures and demands" of serving Christ, but the foundational reality that both motivates and drives my choices is the same perspective that motivated that bondservant in Exodus 21: *I love my Master!* I truly cannot imagine a more wonderful, gracious, kind, giving, loving Lord than He.

Are His requirements sometimes hard? Absolutely. Are they sometimes different from what I would have chosen for myself? No question. Do I sometimes wish to be free from the constraints placed upon me in His service? Definitely. Yet, in the deepest part of my heart, I truly want nothing more than to be His lifelong, loyal bondslave.

Now don't think that makes me some kind of supersaint. Nothing He has ever required of me could begin to repay the debt I owe Him. Besides, the heart He has given me ought to be—and can be—the heart of every child of God.

And, by all means, don't feel sorry for me! I can hardly begin to calculate the incredible gifts and joys He has lavished upon me since I first became His willing slave as a young girl. What a privilege it is:

- ✦ To know and love Him, and to be known and loved by Him
- ✦ To have His companionship at all hours of the day and night
- ✦ To live under His watchful, protective care
- ✦ To bring Him pleasure
- ✦ To be entrusted with the infinite riches of His glorious gospel and to be called to make it known to others
- ✦ To have an eternal home awaiting me in heaven
- ✦ To serve alongside so many precious fellow servants
- ✦ To have assisted in the birth and nurture of countless spiritual children

These are just a handful of the treasures I have received from His hand. Would I not be a fool to leave His service and choose to serve anything or anyone else in this world? As C. S. Lewis reminds us,

Those Divine demands which sound to our natural ears most like those of a despot and least like those of a lover, in fact marshall us where we should want to go if we knew what we wanted.[2]

For you to be the slave of Jesus Christ will likely mean a different set of assignments than those He has given me or someone else. We must resist the temptation to compare what He asks of us with what He may require of others. He may ask you, as His bondservant, to:

✦ Forgo a fulfilling career or to make a name for yourself, in order to devote the prime years of your life to serving your husband and children

✦ Be "on call" 24/7 to meet the needs of your children or an elderly parent, having "no life of your own"

✦ Get out of your comfort zone and teach a Sunday school class or lead a small-group Bible study or develop an outreach to inner-city "at risk" youth

✦ Serve Him in a secular work environment that is antagonistic to Christian beliefs and values, or to be a faithful witness as the only believer in your extended family

✦ Serve faithfully for years in a needed but thankless and obscure position in your local church

✦ Reduce your living expenses so you can give more generously to the Lord's work

Regardless of whether He calls you to serve Him in ways that seem menial or significant, hidden or visible, beneath your skills or light-years beyond your abilities, routine or exciting, common or unimaginable . . . whatever He asks, wherever He sends . . . the surrendered heart will say with Mary of Nazareth,

> *"I am the bondservant* [marginal note] *of the Lord;*
> *Let it be to me according to your word."*
> —Luke 1:38 ESV

Leonard Ravenhill was a faithful servant of the Lord whose books and sermons on revival have inflamed the hearts of millions. At four o'clock one morning, just days before he went to meet the Master at the age of eighty-nine, he penned these words that I have displayed in my study as a reminder of what it means to be a bondservant of the Lord:

> Lord, engage my heart today
> with a passion that will not pass away.
> Now torch it with Thy holy fire
> that nevermore shall earth's desire
> invade or quench the heaven born power.
> I would be trapped within Thy holy will,
> Thine every holy purpose to fulfill,
> that every effort of my life
> shall bring rapturous praise to my eternal King.
> I pledge from this day to the grave
> to be Thine own, unquestioning slave.

Lord, grant that this prayer shall be our own. Amen.

MAKING IT PERSONAL . . .

✦ Are you a man/woman with a "hole in your ear"?

✦ Would your relationship with Christ be better characterized by the word *commitment* or *surrender*?

Notes

1. E-mail from Josef Tson, 30 July 2001. In his book *The Closing of the American Mind,* university professor Allan Bloom makes a similar point from a secular perspective: "Commitment is a word invented in our abstract modernity to signify the absence of any real motives in the soul for moral dedication. Commitment is gratuitous, motiveless, because the real passions are all low and selfish" (New York: Simon & Schuster, 1987), 122.
2. C. S. Lewis, *The Problem of Pain* (London & Glasgow: Collins Clear-Type Press, 1940), 41.

We must train men and women who will devote to the revolution, not merely their spare evenings, but the whole of their lives.

———————

LENIN[1]

The WHOLE of OUR LIVES:
A LIVING SACRIFICE

IN 1917, A SMALL HANDFUL of men set out to bring about a world-wide revolution. Within just a few decades, they had succeeded in building an empire that held more than one-third of the world's population in its grip. How did it happen?

At least in part, the answer lies in their devotion to a cause and their willingness to sacrifice their lives for that cause. Their mission and the outcome of their efforts were undeniably evil. Yet the rise of the Communist Party is one of the most striking examples in human history of the meaning of total surrender.

Douglas Hyde was a onetime Communist Party leader in England. In 1947, he defected from the party and spent the rest of his life endeavoring to expose the movement. In his thought-provoking book, *Dedication and Leadership,* Hyde highlighted some of the principles practiced by the Communist Party that he felt Christians would do well to embrace.

The theme of wholehearted dedication and sacrifice is a recurring one in Hyde's book. He pointed out, for example, that "practically every

PART

BROKENNESS SURRENDER HOLINESS

party member is a dedicated man in whose life, from the time he rises in the morning until the time he goes to bed at night, for 365 days a year, Communism is the dominant force."[2] Hyde described Communists as "100 percenters in a world of 50 percenters."[3]

Is our relationship with Jesus Christ the center of our existence?

Years ago, I came across a letter written by a young Communist Party member to his fiancée, explaining why he felt compelled to break off their engagement. His letter illustrates the type of sacrificial mind-set that was characteristic of many who devoted themselves to the Communist revolution:

> There is one thing about which I am in dead earnest and that is the Socialist cause. It is my life, my business, my religion, my hobby, my sweetheart, my wife, my mistress, my bread and my meat. I work at it in the daytime, I dream of it at night. Its hold on me grows, not lessens as time goes on. I shall be in it the rest of my life.
>
> When you think of me, it is necessary to think of Socialism as well because I am inseparably bound to it. Therefore, I can't carry on a friendship, a love affair, or even a conversation without relating it to this force which both drives and guides my life. I evaluate people, books, ideas and notions according to how they affect the Socialist cause and by their attitude toward it.
>
> I've already been in jail because of my ideas, and if necessary, I'm willing to go before a firing squad. A certain percentage of us get killed or imprisoned; even for those who escape these harsher ends, life is no bed of roses. A genuine radical lives in virtual poverty. He turns back to the party every penny he makes above what is absolutely necessary to keep him alive. Radicals don't have the time or money for many movies or concerts or t-bone steaks or decent homes or new cars.
>
> We've been described as fanatics. We are. Our lives are dominated by one great over-shadowing factor—the struggle for Socialism.

184

The meteoric rise of Communism in our world cannot be explained, in my opinion, apart from a willingness to make what most would consider extreme sacrifices for a cause.

The example of those devoted to the cause of Communism prompts those of us who claim to believe the truth to examine our own level of sacrifice and surrender: Is our relationship with Jesus Christ the center of our existence? Like the young Communist, does our every act revolve around "the cause"—in our case, the cause of Christ?

Sacrifices and Offerings

The Scriptures provide a number of word pictures that help us understand what it means to be a true follower of Jesus Christ. One of the most compelling images is that of a *burnt offering.*

Old Testament Jews knew all about sacrifices and offerings. Virtually every aspect of life—"secular" or "spiritual"—was tied in to a system of worship that revolved around sacrifices and offerings, words that appear in their various forms more than sixteen hundred times in the Old Testament alone.

Volumes have been written on the significance of the different offerings prescribed by God for His people. Ultimately, all those offerings were pictures intended to point people to their need for a Savior—an innocent One who would sacrifice His life as a substitute for sinners, making it possible for them to have fellowship with a holy God.

The most frequent form of sacrifice offered in the Old Testament was the burnt offering (Leviticus 1), so-called because the sacrificial animal was placed on the altar and totally consumed by the fire.

Often offered in conjunction with sin or guilt offerings, burnt offerings were intended to express the worshiper's total dedication and consecration to the Lord. They pictured complete surrender to the will of God.

Sacrifices Pleasing to God

Though the New Testament does not speak explicitly of burnt offerings, it does reveal the fulfillment of that Old Testament picture in two senses. First, Christ, the Lamb of God, offered His body as a burnt offering, in complete consecration and surrender to the will of God (see Hebrews 9:14; 10:5–7). Second, in light of Christ's sacrifice for us, New Testament believers are exhorted to make an offering of their own:

> *Therefore, I urge you, brothers, in view of God's mercy, to offer your bodies as living sacrifices, holy and pleasing to God—this is your spiritual [reasonable] act of worship.*
>
> —Romans 12:1 NIV

This is the manifesto for the Christian's surrender to God. Our "bodies" represent the sum total of all that we are, all that we have, and all that we do. As those Old Testament believers signified their consecration by offering up sacrifices to be utterly consumed on the altar, so we are to offer ourselves in totality to be consumed by God.

Unlike the Old Testament sacrifices, however, we are to offer ourselves as *living sacrifices*—that is, we are to go on living in these bodies, recognizing that they are not our own, that they belong to God, whose temple we are.

This passage suggests both an initial and an ongoing aspect of consecration—a surrender that is made once and for all, as well as a daily, recurring sacrifice of our lives to God.

Offering our bodies speaks of a complete presentation of ourselves to God. It means devoting to the Lord Jesus, not just our "spare evenings," but "the whole of [our] lives."

Being a *living sacrifice* pictures living out that devotion, one day at a time, as God actually asks us for more than our "spare evenings," and we respond to Him on the basis of that initial consecration.

"I Do"—A Moment and a Lifetime

This twofold aspect of surrender—an initial point, followed by an ongoing, lifetime process—can be seen in marriage. When a man and woman stand before a minister to join their lives together, they affirm a series of vows, usually by saying "I do." At that moment, they make a full surrender of their lives to each other. They pledge to love each other, to be faithful to each other, and to serve each other.

The exchange of vows at the altar is just the starting place. But it *is* the starting place. Until a man and woman say "I do," they have no legal or spiritual basis for an ongoing, intimate, fruitful relationship.

However, once a couple says "I do"—once they come to that point of initial surrender—they begin a lifetime process of keeping those vows, every day, for the rest of their lives. After the candles are blown out, the rice is thrown, and the rented tuxes are returned, they must begin to live out the implications of those vows in the nitty-gritty context of real life—for better *and* for worse.

> *We are new people, under new ownership, bound to Christ eternally.*

Over time, they will grow in their understanding of what those vows really meant. Undoubtedly there will be moments when both partners will think back to the moment they stood at the altar and exchanged their vows, and will say to themselves, *I had no idea it would mean this! It never occurred to me that he would want me to do that! I never dreamed loving her would involve this!*

Likewise, in our relationship with the Lord, there is a starting place, a point at which we say to Him, "I do"; a point at which we enter into an eternal, covenantal relationship with Him. From that moment on, we are new people, under new ownership, bound to Christ eternally. Our lives are no longer our own; we belong to the One who created us and redeemed us by the blood of His Son.

Yet, at the point of conversion, no one can possibly be aware of all the implications of that transaction, any more than a couple standing at the altar is fully aware of all that their vows will mean down the road.

Our initial surrender to Christ was the launching pad for a lifetime of continual surrender and sacrifice. Now, on a daily, perpetual basis, we are called to live out that consecration, by responding to the various circumstances and choices of life in obedience and surrender to His will.

Sacrifice—Different Sizes and Shapes

One preacher illustrated the ongoing, daily dimension of sacrifice and surrender this way:

We think giving our all to the Lord is like taking a $1,000 bill and laying it on the table—"Here's my life, Lord. I'm giving it all."

But the reality for most of us is that he sends us to the bank and has us cash in the $1,000 for quarters. We go through life putting out 25 cents here and 50 cents there. Listen to the neighbor kid's troubles instead of saying, "Get lost." Go to a committee meeting. Give up a cup of water to a shaky old man in a nursing home.

Usually giving our life to Christ isn't glorious. It's done in all those little acts of love, 25 cents at a time.[4]

God may be asking you simply to sacrifice the next thirty minutes to call your widowed mother-in-law who can be so negative . . . or your afternoon to help a family who is packing for a move . . . or your evening to help your child with a science project . . . or your normal night's sleep to care for a sick child . . . or your weekend to watch your neighbor's kids. . . . Twenty-five cents here. Fifty cents there.

At times, the Lord will ask you to lay down several quarters or even several dollars at once: Instead of taking that expensive vacation or buying that car or that new piece of furniture, give the money to a mission project or to a family in need . . . instead of settling into that comfortable retirement life, volunteer your services to a ministry in your local church or community . . . embrace God's gift of yet one more child . . . adapt your standard of living to make it possible for Mom to be at home with the children.

Periodically, the Lord may ask for a sacrifice that makes all the previous sacrifices seem insignificant: Quit your secure job and move your family to some place you never dreamed of living to serve the Lord in a mission organization . . . release your son or daughter to serve the Lord in a country where Christian witness is restricted . . . faithfully love your unbelieving mate who perpetually ridicules you and your faith . . . accept with gratitude the gift of a physically disabled child who will require constant, lifelong care . . . relinquish your dream of ever being able to conceive and bear children. . . .

Whether they fall in the category of twenty-five-cent pieces or hundred-dollar bills, the sacrifices God asks of us are never pointless. We can be assured that each one serves God's higher, eternal purposes for our lives and for the furthering of His kingdom. Realizing that every act of obedience is significant in God's economy and that it is all for *Him* will add a sense of purpose and joy as we bring our sacrifices and offerings.

A Complete Sacrifice

God's call to lay down our lives on the altar of sacrifice means that we give Him all that we are—our rights, our reputation, our desires, our future plans; everything that concerns us—first, for a lifetime, and then, day by day, moment by moment, decision by decision.

Dr. Helen Roseveare is one of my spiritual heroines. During the 1950s and 1960s, she served as a missionary doctor in Belgian Congo (now Democratic Republic of the Congo), where she suffered great atrocities during the Simba Rebellion. When I need to be reminded what it means to live a surrendered life, I go back and reread her compelling story, Living Sacrifice. Dr. Roseveare's practical description of what it means to be a living sacrifice applies to every believer—whether a missionary, a homemaker, a student, a business owner, or an office worker:

> To be a living sacrifice will involve all my time. God wants me to live every minute for Him in accordance with His will and purpose. . . . No time can be considered as my own, or as "off-duty" or "free." . . .
>
> To be a living sacrifice will involve all my possessions. . . . All should be available to God for the furtherance of His Kingdom. My money is His . . . He has the right to direct the spending of each penny. . . . I must consider that I own nothing. All is God's, and what I have, I have on trust from Him, to be used as He wishes.
>
> To be a living sacrifice will involve all of myself. My will and my emotions, my health and vitality, my thinking and activities all are to be available to God, to be employed as He chooses, to reveal Himself to others. Should He see that someone would be

helped to know Him through my being ill, I accept ill health and weakness. I have no right to demand what we call good health. . . . All rights are His—to direct my living so that He can most clearly reveal Himself through me. God has the right, then, to choose my job, and where I work, to choose my companions and my friends. . . .

> *Shall we devote to such a Savior only our spare evenings?*

To be a living sacrifice will involve all my love. . . . I relinquish the right to choose whom I will love and how, giving the Lord the right to choose for me. . . . Whether I have a life partner or not is wholly His to decide, and I accept gladly His best will for my life. I must bring all the areas of my affections to the Lord for His control, for here, above all else, I need to sacrifice my right to choose for myself. . . .

I need to be so utterly God's that He can use me or hide me, as He chooses, as an arrow in His hand or in His quiver. I will ask no questions: I relinquish all rights to Him who desires my supreme good. He knows best.[5]

A Reasonable Response

Does that seem too much to ask? Truthfully, there are moments when I feel something God is asking of me is unreasonable. It may be to provide a listening ear and a caring heart for one more woman who wants to talk, when I am emotionally and physically spent at the end of a long day of ministry; it may be to provide substantial financial support to help a couple in Christian work provide a Christian education for their children; it may be to stay engaged in a relationship with a difficult, demanding person.

In those moments, my emotions sometimes cry out, "I've already given so much! I just can't give more." That's when I need to take a trip to Calvary and look into the eyes of a bleeding God who gave everything to reconcile me to Himself. That is why the apostle Paul says,

I urge you . . . in view of God's mercy, to offer your bodies as living sacrifices . . . this is your reasonable [marginal rendering] *act of worship.*

—Romans 12:1 NIV

The Greek word translated "reasonable" is the word *logikos.* In light of the incredible mercy of God poured out on us (past, present, and future mercies), a full and complete sacrifice of our lives is the only *logical* response we can make.

Willis Hotchkiss was a pioneer missionary in East Africa in the late 1800s who made what we would consider extraordinary sacrifices for the sake of Christ. On one occasion, he described some of the conditions he and others had faced in the early days of their work: living for more than two months on beans and sour milk, enduring without basic necessities for extended periods of time, fearing attacks from man-eating lions, watching many colleagues lose their lives. Then he concluded,

But *don't talk to me about sacrifice.* It is no sacrifice. In the face of the superlative joy of that one overwhelming experience, the joy of flashing that miracle word, Saviour, for the first time to a great tribe that had never heard it before, I can never think of these forty years in terms of sacrifice. I saw Christ and His cross and I did this because I loved Him.[6]

God may never call you to a foreign mission field; He may never ask you to endure the conditions that Willis Hotchkiss faced in Africa. Nonetheless, He does ask that you offer up your life and your daily circumstances as a living sacrifice—a burnt offering—signifying your wholehearted consecration and surrender to the Savior who gave His life for you.

Shall we devote to such a Savior only our spare evenings? Is He not worthy of the whole of our lives? In the words of Isaac Watts's immortal hymn,

Were the whole realm of nature mine,
that were a present far too small.

Love so amazing, so divine,
demands my life, my soul, my all![7]

MAKING IT PERSONAL . . .

✦ Have you devoted to Christ "the whole of your life," or are you merely giving Him your "spare evenings"?

✦ What might it mean for you today to offer yourself as a "living sacrifice" to God?

Notes

1. Cited in *The Whole of Their Lives*, epigraph. From *Lenin on Organization* (Daily Worker Publishing Co., 1926), 44. Lenin first wrote these words in the Social Democratic newspaper *Iskra*, No. 1, in 1900.
2. Douglas Hyde, *Dedication and Leadership* (Notre Dame, Ind.: Univ. of Notre Dame, 1966), 25.
3. Ibid., 40.
4. From a message at a Pastoral Leadership conference, given by Dr. Fred Craddock.
5. Helen Roseveare, *Living Sacrifice* (Minneapolis: Bethany, 1979), 116–18.
6. Cited in T. A. Hegre, *The Cross and Sanctification* (Minneapolis: Bethany, 1960), 179–80.
7. Isaac Watts, "When I Survey the Wondrous Cross."

If there is anything holding you back,
or any sacrifice you are afraid of making,
come to God and prove how gracious your God is.
Never be afraid that He will command from you
what He will not bestow! God comes and
offers to work this absolute surrender in you.

———————

ANDREW MURRAY[1]

FACING OUR FEARS:
FINDING HIM FAITHFUL

AS I WRITE THIS CHAPTER, some of our Christian brothers and sisters in Indonesia are paying an enormous price to follow Christ. In certain villages that have been taken over by militant Muslims, Christians who refuse to convert to Islam are being "allowed" to leave their villages. The cost of that freedom is that they must forsake their homes and everything they own, and they may never again return to their villages. The only way they can stay is if they agree to become Muslims.

Such a price is unfathomable to most of us. We cannot conceive of being required to literally forsake everything for the sake of Christ. Nonetheless, when we consider Christ's call to full surrender, we may wrestle with real fears of what that might mean for us.

"I surrender all . . ."; "Christ is all I need. . . ." The words roll off our lips as we sing them in church. But it's not so easy to choose to place ourselves in a position where we have to find out if He really is all we need. Although we are not likely to find ourselves in the same situation as those Indonesian believers, full surrender to Christ forces us to face the possibility—or the reality—of giving up some of the things we consider most important in life.

Our natural tendency is to hold on tightly, to try to protect and preserve whatever we think we can't live without. We are afraid that if we surrender *everything* to God—our health, our material possessions, our family, our reputation, our career plans, all our rights, our future—He might take us up on it! We have visions of God stripping us of the things we most need or enjoy, or perhaps sending us out to serve Him in the most inhospitable place on the planet.

Many of our fears about relinquishing total control of our lives to God fall into four categories. If I surrender everything to Him, what about . . .

Provision—Will I have what I need? What if I lose my job? What if my husband loses his job? Can we afford to have more children? How will we pay for their education? What if God asks us to give our savings to the church or to a needy family? What if God calls us into vocational ministry—how will we be supported? What if the economy goes under—what will happen to our investments? What if my husband dies—will I have enough to live on?

Pleasure—Will I be happy? If I fully surrender to God, will I be miserable? Will I be able to do the things I enjoy? What if He wants me to give up my career . . . or sports . . . or my favorite hobby . . . or my best friend . . . or the foods I really like? Might God make me stay in this unhappy marriage? Will I be fulfilled if I obey Him?

Protection—Will I (and those I love) be safe? What if my child is born with a mental or physical disability? What if someone abuses my children? What if I have an accident and am maimed for life? What if I get cancer? What if someone breaks into our house? Might God choose to take my mate or my children? If my child goes to the mission field, will he be safe?

Personal relationships—Will my relational needs be met? What if the Lord wants me to be single all my life? How can I live without sex or romance? What if my mate never loves me? What if God doesn't give us children? What if I lose my mate? How can I handle the rejection of my parents? What if my best friend moves away? What if people reject our family because of our commitment to biblical standards?

Overcoming Fear with Faith

The pages of Scripture are salted with the stories of men and women who risked everything to follow Christ. Sometimes we think of these people as if they were merely lifeless figures in a wax museum; we forget that they were real people who had to deal with real-life issues.

Take Abraham, for example. We think of Abraham as a superhero—a man of towering faith. And he was. Yet he had to face many of the same issues and fears that we struggle with. Over and over again, in order to move forward in his relationship with God, Abraham was called to make a fresh surrender to God. To do so required that he let go, relinquish control, step out on a limb, and trust a God he could not see.

Abraham grew up in a pagan, idolatrous environment where there was absolutely nothing to inspire or nurture faith—no study Bibles, no praise and worship CDs, no churches, no Christian fellowship. When an unseen, unknown God spoke and told Abram (as he was known at the time) to venture out and leave behind everything that was familiar and comfortable, he was faced with a choice: to stay or to go.

In making that choice, Abram had to consider the cost of surrender:

+ How will my family's needs be met? (*provision*)

+ Will we be happy? (*pleasure*)

+ Will we be safe? (*protection*)

+ You want my wife and me to leave all our friends and relatives? (*personal relationships*)

The biblical record does not tell us to what extent, if any, Abram wrestled with his decision. All we know is that he went. Genesis 12:1 records God's call to Abram: "Leave your country, your people and your father's household" (NIV). Three verses later we read, "So Abram left, as the Lord had told him" (12:4 NIV).

Without further explanation, with no idea where he was going, how he would get there, or what he would do once he got there, Abram risked everything, cast himself into the arms of Providence . . . and went. He chose friendship with God over all human relationships, earthly attachments, and visible security.

"But," you say, "Abraham had a lot to gain—after all, God had promised to give him a fruitful land and more offspring than he could count." Yes, Abraham was the recipient of grand promises. But keep in mind

> **The promises of God provide a powerful antidote to all our fears.**

that for more than twenty-five years, he didn't have a shred of visible evidence that God's promises would be fulfilled. Acts 7:5 reminds us of the reality that could easily have shaken Abraham's faith: He had "no inheritance" and "no child." But he went anyway. And, in spite of occasional lapses in his faith, he kept going.

Abraham surrendered himself to the purposes and plans of God, with no tangible guarantee that his obedience would ever "pay off." Even when he could not see the outcome of his faith, he *believed God.* He staked his life, his security, his future—everything— on the fact that God was real and that He would keep His promises (Hebrews 11:6). That was the foundation on which his faith rested. That was what motivated his repeated acts of surrender.

It was faith in the character and the promises of God that enabled Abraham and his wife, Sarah, to embrace an itinerant lifestyle—living in tents—for more than twenty-five years.

It was faith in the promises of God that sustained the couple through decades of infertility and unfulfilled longings.

It was faith in the promises of God that motivated Abram to surrender the best land option to his nephew Lot and to trust that God would provide a suitable inheritance for him (Genesis 13:1–11).

It was the character and the promises of God that gave Abram courage (at the age of seventy-five!) to take on the massive military machine of the allied kings of the East, in order to rescue his errant nephew (Genesis 14).

When Abram was tempted to fear reprisals from the defeated kings, God bolstered his faith with a rehearsal of His promises: "Do not be afraid, Abram. I am your shield, your exceedingly great reward" (Genesis 15:1). What was God saying? *I am your protection and your provi-*

sion; if you have Me, you have all you need. So . . . trust Me!

At times, the call of God in our lives may require us to relinquish things or people we can't imagine living without—material possessions, a job or a promotion, good health, a mate or a child, or the respect and understanding of our closest friends. The promises of God provide a powerful antidote to all our fears and free us to step out in faith and surrender.

Stranger on Earth, Friend of God

Abram came to be known by his contemporaries as "Abram the Hebrew" (Genesis 14:13). The word *Hebrew* means "stranger" or "alien." From earth's perspective, he was always something of a "misfit"; he didn't really belong. But that was OK. He understood that everything this world offers is temporary at best. His ultimate citizenship wasn't on this earth. He was living for an eternal home (Hebrews 11:16). He was willing to venture everything this world considers vital— homeland, reputation, position, possessions, family, prestige—in order to be eternally secure and to gain the blessing of God. And that is exactly what happened.

Each "small" step of surrender confirms that God is worthy of our trust.

Though he was an alien on earth, from heaven's perspective Abraham was called the "friend of God" (James 2:23). The development of this man's extraordinary relationship with God can be defined in terms of a series of surrenders made over a lifetime. Each of those surrenders was based on a revelation of the promise-making, promise-keeping God.

Altars of Surrender

Perhaps the most appropriate symbol of Abraham's life is an altar. On four distinct occasions, at different stages in his pilgrimage, we are told that Abraham responded to God by building an altar. First at Shechem (Genesis 12:7), then between Bethel and Ai (12:8), then at Hebron (13:18), Abraham erected altars—silent symbols of surrender and faith.

Then, on a mountain named Moriah, the man who was called the "friend of God" built yet another altar (22:9). On that altar, at God's unmistakable, but incomprehensible direction, Abraham placed his own son. It was the ultimate act of surrender—a relinquishing of all he held dear.

In an act not unlike a resurrection, God spared Abraham's son. The test had been passed. God knew that when Abraham laid his precious, long-promised son on the altar and prepared to plunge the knife into his heart, Abraham himself was on the altar—all that he was and all that he had were God's.

All those earlier altars had been preparing Abraham for the moment when he would be called upon to make a supreme sacrifice. With each act of surrender, the trustworthiness of God and His promises had been established in Abraham's heart. Likewise, each "small" step of surrender that we take confirms that God is worthy of our trust and prepares us to trust Him with bigger surrenders that may be required down the road.

Altars speak of sacrifice and devotion—of being consumed. They speak of a life that is wholly given up to the one for whom the altar is built. Many churches identify a location or an object at the front of the sanctuary as an "altar." Though we don't light fires and offer literal sacrifices on those sites, they are intended to serve as visible reminders of what ought to be a spiritual reality for every child of God—as the hymn writer put it, "My heart an altar, and Thy love the flame."[2]

Promises That Counter Our Fears

The surrender points Abraham faced over the course of his life may be similar to some you have faced: leaving family and friends behind and moving to a new city where you didn't know a soul . . . making choices to sacrifice your own interests for the sake of others . . . staying engaged with and pursuing the heart of a rebellious relative . . . living with infertility . . . turning down a lucrative offer that you know is not pleasing to God . . . giving up the life of a child.

When it comes to the uncertainties that keep us from sacrifice, surrender, and slavery to God, we, like Abraham, have "exceedingly great and precious promises" (2 Peter 1:4) from God's Word—promises that powerfully counteract our deepest fears. If we trust those promises and the God who has made them, we will be given courage to make each sacrifice He asks of us.

If we do not trust God's promises and, therefore, do not step out in faith and surrender, we will ultimately find ourselves in bondage to the very things we refuse to surrender. We will end up being controlled by that which we are seeking to keep within our own control.

Trust or tyranny. That is the option. *Trust* the promises of God—which will free you to live joyfully under His loving lordship—or live under the *tyranny* of that which you will not surrender.

God wants us to experience provision, pleasure, protection, and personal relationships. But He wants us to seek them in the only place they can be found—in Him. And He doesn't want us to settle for substitutes for the real thing.

Provision. Scripture exhorts us to be content with what we have (Hebrews 13:5) and not to worry about how our future needs will be met (Matthew 6:25–34). The basis for contentment and freedom from anxiety is that God has promised to provide all that we need (though not necessarily all that we *want*) (Philippians 4:19). Based on His promise, when we have a need, rather than fretting, striving, or manipulating, we ought to simply and confidently ask Him to provide (Matthew 7:7; Philippians 4:6).

If we are unwilling to trust God in the matter of provision, we may be tyrannized by greed, stealing, cheating, lack of generosity, lying, worrying, coveting, or centering our lives around money.

Pleasure. We cannot escape the fact that pain is unavoidable in this fallen world and that suffering is an instrument that God uses to mold and sanctify those He loves. But God also created us to experience intense pleasure and joy. The problem is that we are prone to seek plea-

> *Those who take refuge in Him are placed under His protection.*

sure in things and people that cannot ultimately satisfy the deep longing in our hearts. For our hearts can never be truly satisfied with less than Him. The unsurrendered heart pursues after what are paltry pleasures, compared with the pure, infinite pleasures God wants to give us:

You will show me the path of life;
In Your presence is fullness of joy;
At Your right hand are pleasures forevermore.

How precious is Your lovingkindness, O God!
Therefore the children of men
  put their trust under the shadow of Your wings.
They are abundantly satisfied with the fullness of Your house,
And You give them drink from the river of Your pleasures.
                                    —Psalms 16:11; 36:7–8

Even fully surrendered saints sometimes experience sorrow, suffering, and struggles. But in the midst of our earthly journey, the joy Christ offers lifts us beyond our circumstances and provides us with a breathtaking foretaste of heaven's eternal pleasures.

However, if we are unwilling to trust God with our happiness and well-being, and we insist on the pursuit of temporal pleasures, we may become dominated by overeating, getting drunk or using drugs, sexual promiscuity, adultery, pornography, obsession with television or films or novels, being irresponsible, or living beyond our means.

Protection. Our God is a refuge, a fortress, a shelter, and a strong deliverer to His children. Psalm 91 speaks of God's amazing protection:

I will say of the Lord, "He is my refuge and my fortress, my God, in whom I trust." . . . He will cover you with his feathers, and under his wings you will find refuge; his faithfulness will be your shield and rampart. You will not fear the terror of night, nor the arrow that flies by day, nor the pestilence that stalks in the darkness, nor the plague that destroys at midday.
                                    —Psalm 91:2, 4–6 NIV

God doesn't promise that we will never face danger, but those who take refuge in Him are placed under His protection. He assures us that He will defend us and keep us free from fear, no matter what comes our way.

However, if we do not entrust our safety to God, but demand human assurance of protection and security, we may be overwhelmed by fearfulness, worry, mistrust of people, obsession with weapons, unwillingness to be vulnerable, fear of intimacy, tendencies toward violence, hatred, prejudice, conspiracy theories, or paranoid-type thoughts.

Personal relationships. It is true that God may lead us into solitude for a season. But His Word makes it clear that an intimate relationship with Him is the basis for the richest of human relationships (1 John 1:3, 7). God Himself has promised to remain with us, to be our constant companion, wherever we go, whatever we do. "I will never leave you nor forsake you," He has vowed (Hebrews 13:5).

Throughout the Scripture, whenever one of His children was fearful to step out alone, without human support, God's simple response was, *I will be with you.* The implication was—*I am enough. If you have Me, you have everything you need.*

The man or woman who trusts His promises can say with the psalmist,

> *Whom have I in heaven but You?*
> *And there is none upon earth that I desire besides You.*
> —Psalm 73:25

If we do not value *Him* as our primary relationship, we will live in fear of losing human relationships and will set ourselves up to be tyrannized by such things as possessiveness, giving or taking abuse, adultery, promiscuity, gossip, obsessive or controlling relationships, lust, dissatisfaction, unforgiveness, bitterness, manipulation, dishonesty, or jealousy.

Things We Can Count On

Ann Blocher was first diagnosed with breast cancer in 1977, when her five children were young adults. After going through chemotherapy, she went into apparent remission. Several years later, the cancer reappeared. After battling to control the cancer with chemo and diet, she finally went home to be with the Lord in 1986.

As she walked through those tempestuous and uncertain years, Ann had to face numerous fears about her future and her family. One of the things she struggled with was her desire to be a part of her children's lives. As she dealt with each issue, Ann discovered that the surrender God was asking of her really came down to a matter of trust. She expressed that perspective in a poem written less than three years before her homegoing:

Yes, Lord! Yes and Amen!

Can you trust Me, child?
Not only for ultimate eternity,
of which you know next to nothing,
and so are not tempted to meddle—
But for the little span of your life between
the Now and Then, where you envision
decline and separations and failures,
impairments, pain, bereavements, disappointments—
Do you find Me qualified to be Lord of your last days?
Oh—yes, Lord! YES, Lord! Yes and amen!

Can you trust Me, child?
Not only to synchronize the unthinkable
intricacies of creation—
But to work together for good the gravities
and tugs within your little orbit,
where your heart is pulled by needs
and lacks you wish, but are destitute, to fill—
Do you find My resources adequate
to feed both the sparrows and you?
Oh—yes, Lord! YES, Lord! Yes and amen!

Can you trust Me, child?
Not only for the oversight of nations
and creations not of this world—

But for those beloved ones I committed
to you and you committed to Me—
Do you believe Me trustworthy to perform
the good work begun in them
until the Day of Jesus Christ?
Oh—yes, Lord! YES, Lord! Yes and amen![3]

As Ann Blocher cast herself upon the character, the heart, and the promises of God, she was enabled to respond to the will of God in whole-hearted surrender—whether that meant being sick or well, living or dying.

Isn't that the heart of the matter for every child of God? *Can you trust Me?*

Whatever your fears, whatever the unknowns or the challenges in your life, God has promised to provide for you, to share His pleasure with you, to protect you, and to give you His enduring presence.

The fact remains that when we sign the blank contract of surrender, there are no guarantees about where God will lead us or how difficult our journey will be. Yet we know the character of the One in whom we've placed our trust. And we know that God's promises more than offset any risks or dangers or challenges that He may allow into our lives.

MAKING IT PERSONAL . . .

✦ Which of the four fears identified in this chapter do you most relate to?

✦ How has that fear caused you to hold back from surrendering some part of your life to God?

✦ What is one promise in God's Word that addresses your fear?

Notes
1. Andrew Murray, *The Believer's Absolute Surrender* (Minneapolis: Bethany, 1985), 78.
2. George Croly, "Spirit of God, Descend upon My Heart."
3. Permission for use granted by Betty and Clarence Blocher.

Full consecration may be in one sense the act of a moment and in another the work of a lifetime. It must be complete to be real, and yet—if real— it is always incomplete. Consecration is a point of rest and yet a perpetual progression.

FRANCES R. HAVERGAL[1]

LIVING *the* SURRENDERED LIFE:
Making It Practical

ONE OF THE CLEAREST statements of the practical terms of surrender for every follower of Christ is found in Luke 14. In verse 25, we find Jesus surrounded by a large crowd. Unlike what we might have been tempted to do, Jesus never played to the audience. He wasn't concerned about His ratings; He wasn't running for office or trying to attract the biggest crowd in town. He knew full well that when some heard His message, they would lose interest in His movement. But that didn't keep Him from being straightforward.

Jesus looked at the crowd of would-be disciples and said, in effect, "If you want to follow Me, you need to understand what's involved": "If anyone comes to me and does not hate his father and mother, his wife and children, his brothers and sisters"—and here's the heart of the matter—"yes, even his own life—he cannot be my disciple. And anyone who does not carry his cross and follow me cannot be my disciple" (verses 26–27 NIV).

There could be no mistaking Jesus' point. He was not offering His listeners some sort of weekend Christian experience, an escape from their problems, an anesthetic for their pain, or fire insurance from hell.

Everyone listening to Jesus knew that a cross meant only one thing—death. He was calling them to come and die to everything that competed with His reign and rule in their lives.

In verse 33 (NIV), He reiterated His call to total surrender: "Any of you who does not give up everything he has cannot be my disciple."

Jesus' words in Luke 14 are penetrating because they are so intensely personal and practical. He did not speak in sweeping generalities; rather, He identified specific issues that must be surrendered by those who call themselves His followers—things like our *relationships*, our *affections*, our *physical bodies*, our *rights*, and our *possessions*.

It is in the laboratory of life that our initial consecration to Christ is tested.

It's one thing to have an emotional experience at a Christian gathering where you are inspired and challenged to surrender control of everything to God. It's another matter to live out that surrender once the emotion of the moment has passed—when the bus gets home from the conference . . . when you lose your job and the bills keep coming . . . when you find out you're expecting your fifth child in seven years . . . when your mate is diagnosed with a terminal illness.

It is in the laboratory of life that our initial consecration to Christ is tested, proven, and demonstrated in daily, moment-by-moment choices and responses, as we surrender to the sovereignty and will of God.

In 1874, when she was just thirty-eight years old, Frances Ridley Havergal penned a hymn that has become a beloved treasure of the church. Written as a prayer, each line focuses on one dimension of what it means to be fully surrendered to Christ. Like Jesus' words in Luke 14, Frances Havergal's words answer the question: *What does a surrendered life look like?*

The following questions are intended to help personalize and apply this wonderful text. I would encourage you not to skim through these questions, but to set aside some time for thoughtful, prayerful reflection and response.

MY LIFE

Take my life, and let it be
consecrated, Lord, to Thee.

✦ Have I ever consciously acknowledged Christ's ownership of my life?

✦ Have I made a volitional, unconditional, lifetime surrender of my life to Christ?

✦ Am I seeking to live out that surrender on a daily basis?

✦ Are there any "compartments" of my life over which I am reserving the right to exercise control?

MY TIME

Take my moments and my days;
let them flow in ceaseless praise.

✦ Do I live with the conscious realization that all my time belongs to God, or have I merely reserved a portion of my time for the "spiritual" category of my life?

✦ Am I living each day in the light of eternity?

✦ Am I purposeful and intentional in my use of time, seeking to invest the moments of my days in ways that will bring glory to God?

✦ Do I seek His direction as to how I should use my "free time"?

✦ Am I squandering time with meaningless, useless conversation or entertainment?

✦ Do I set apart time each day for worship, prayer, and personal devotion?

✦ Do I readily respond to opportunities to serve others, even if it requires sacrificing "my" time?

✦ Do I become resentful or impatient when others interrupt my schedule or when I am faced with unplanned demands on my time?

✦ Do I view my job as an opportunity to serve Christ and bring glory to God?

✦ Have I considered any possible vocational change the Lord may want me to make to devote more time to the advancement of His kingdom?

MY BODY

Take my hands, and let them move
at the impulse of Thy love.
Take my feet, and let them be
swift and beautiful for Thee.

✦ Am I yielding the members (parts) of my body to God as instruments of righteousness (Romans 6:13)?

✦ Do I use the members of my body to express the kindness and love of Christ to others (e.g., using my hands for serving, for gentle touch)?

✦ Are any of the members of my body—eyes, ears, hands, feet, mouth, etc.—being used to sin against God (e.g., stealing, lying, listening to or repeating gossip, inflicting physical harm on mate or children, listening to profanity, viewing pornography, sexual sin)?

✦ Do I treat my body as if it is the temple of the Holy Spirit (1 Corinthians 6:19)?

✦ Am I abusing my body in any way (e.g., with food, alcohol, illegal or prescription drugs)?

✦ Am I willing to be physically spent in serving God and others?

✦ Have I relinquished the right to have a healthy body? Would I accept and embrace physical illness if that would bring glory to God?

✦ Am I submissive to God in relation to what (and how much) I eat and drink, and how much and when I sleep?

✦ Am I morally pure—what I see, what I think, what I do, where I go, what I listen to, what I say?

MY TONGUE

Take my lips, and let them be
filled with messages from Thee.

✦ Do the words that come out of my mouth reveal that my lips and tongue are fully surrendered to God?

✦ Do I habitually verbalize the goodness and greatness of God?

✦ Do I regularly ask the Lord to guard my tongue?

✦ Before I speak, do I ask the Lord what He wants me to say?

✦ Am I filling my mind and heart with the Word of God, so that what comes out of my mouth will be "messages from Him"?

✦ Do I speak words that are critical, unkind, untrue, self-centered, rude, profane, or unnecessary?

✦ Do I look for and take advantage of opportunities to give a verbal witness for Christ?

✦ Do I intentionally use my tongue to edify and encourage others in their walk with God?

MY POSSESSIONS

Take my silver and my gold;
not a mite would I withhold.

✦ Do I treat any of my possessions as if they were mine rather than God's?

✦ Do I give generously, sacrificially, and gladly to the Lord's work and to others in need?

✦ Do I own anything that I would not be willing to part with if God were to take it from me or ask me to give it to another?

✦ Am I a wise steward of the material resources God has entrusted to me?

✦ Do I view God as my provider and the source of all my material possessions?

✦ Am I content with the material resources God has given me? If God should choose not to give me one thing more than what I already have, would I be satisfied with His provision?

✦ Do I give my tithes and offerings to the Lord before I pay my bills or spend my income?

✦ Do I become angry or upset if others are careless with "my" possessions?

MY MIND

Take my intellect, and use
every power as Thou shalt choose.

✦ Am I "bringing every thought into captivity to the obedience of Christ" (2 Corinthians 10:5)?

✦ Am I disciplining my mind to get to know God and His Word better?

✦ Am I wasting my mind on worldly knowledge or pursuits that do not have eternal, spiritual value?

✦ Do I habitually think about things that are just, pure, lovely, of good report, virtuous, and praiseworthy (Philippians 4:8), rather than things that are unwholesome, negative, impure, or vain?

✦ Am I guarding the entrance of my mind from impure influences (e.g., books, magazines, movies, music, conversations)?

✦ Am I devoting my mental capacity to serving Christ and furthering His kingdom?

MY WILL

Take my will and make it Thine;
it shall be no longer mine.

✦ Do I consistently seek to know and to do the will of God in the practical, daily matters of life?

✦ When I read the Word of God (or hear it proclaimed), am I quick to say, "Yes, Lord" and to do what it says?

✦ Is there anything God has shown me to be His will that I have been neglecting or refusing to obey?

✦ Is there anything I know God wants me to do that I have not done/am not doing?

✦ Do I become resentful when things don't go my way? Do I have to have the last word in disagreements?

✦ Am I stubborn? Demanding? Controlling?

✦ Am I quick to respond in confession and repentance when the Holy Spirit convicts me of sin?

✦ Am I submissive to the human authorities God has placed over me (e.g., civil, church, home, work)?

MY AFFECTIONS

Take my heart; it is Thine own;
it shall be Thy royal throne.

✦ Am I moody? Temperamental? Hard to please?

✦ Do I love Christ and His kingdom more than this earth and its pleasures? Is there anything or anyone that I am more devoted to than Christ?

✦ Am I allowing Christ to reign and rule over my affections, my emotions, and my responses?

✦ Am I easily angered or provoked?

✦ Am I allowing anyone or anything other than Christ to control my emotions and responses?

✦ Are my desires, appetites, and longings under Christ's control?

✦ Am I in bondage to any earthly, fleshly, or sinful desires or appetites? Am I indulging or making provision for my fleshly desires (Romans 13:14)?

✦ Do I trust God's right to rule over the circumstances of my life?

MY RELATIONSHIPS

Take my love; my Lord,
I pour at Thy feet its treasure store.

✦ Is it my desire and intent to love God with all my heart, above all earthly relationships? Do I enjoy and seek out the friendship of God as much as I do human friendships?

✦ Do I love God more than I love myself? Do I seek His interests, His reputation, and His pleasure above my own?

✦ Have I surrendered to God all my desires, rights, and expectations regarding my family?

✦ Am I willing to let God decide whether I am to be married and to whom?

✦ Have I surrendered the right to have a loving, godly mate?

✦ Am I willing to love my mate in a Christlike way, regardless of whether or not that love is reciprocated?

✦ Have I accepted God's decision to grant or withhold the blessing of children?

✦ Have I released my children to the Lord? Am I trying to control their lives? Am I willing for Him to call them and use them in His service—anywhere, in any way, regardless of the cost?

✦ Is there anyone that I "love" in a way that is not pure? Am I holding on to any friendships or relationships that God wants me to relinquish?

✦ Am I willing to sacrifice friendships, if necessary, in order to obey God and His call in my life?

✦ Am I willing to speak the truth in love to others about their spiritual condition, even if it means risking the loss of the relationship or my reputation?

MYSELF

*Take myself, and I will be
ever, only, all for Thee.*

✦ Have I surrendered all that I am and all that I have to God?

✦ Is there any part of myself—my plans, relationships, possessions, emotions, career, future—that I am knowingly holding back from God?

✦ Have I settled the issue that the ultimate purpose of my life is to please God and bring Him glory?

✦ Is it the intent of my heart, by His grace, to live the rest of my life wholly for Him and for His pleasure, rather than for myself and my pleasure?

MAKING IT EVEN MORE PERSONAL . . .

You may have expressed your desire to be fully surrendered to God many times before. Or you may just now be recognizing what it means to be totally surrendered to Him. Regardless, would you stop—right now, if possible—and slip to your knees before the Lord and pray, *O Lord, afresh this moment, I surrender every part of my being—all I am and all I have—to You.*

As you pray these next words, visualize the place where you are kneeling as an altar of sacrifice, and picture each part of yourself being offered up to God as a living sacrifice: *I consecrate to You my life . . . my time . . . my body . . . my tongue . . . my possessions . . . my mind . . . my will . . . my affections . . . my relationships . . . myself. Take me, have me, do with me as You please. I am Yours for this moment and forever. Please work out that surrender in my life—every day, in every matter, until I bow before You in eternity. Amen.*

Note
1. Frances Ridley Havergal, *Kept for the Master's Use* (Chicago: Moody, 1999 [reprt.]), 23.

*Dear Lord, You be the needle and
I be the thread. You go first, and
I will follow wherever You may lead.*

_____

CONGOLESE BELIEVER

The PATTERN:
THE SURRENDERED SAVIOR

FROM THE TIME I WAS a little girl and was first introduced to *The Shoemaker Who Gave India the Bible* (the story of missionary William Carey), I have had a voracious appetite for biographies of "Christian heroes." My heart has been deeply stirred by the stories of Hudson Taylor, George Mueller, Gladys Aylward, and others whose lives are portraits of complete consecration to Christ as Lord.

However, the pages of history do not contain any more moving and powerful picture of what it means to be surrendered to the will of God than that of the Lord Jesus Himself. From eternity past, through all of time, and through all of eternity future, Jesus' life was, is, and always will be, one of absolute surrender.

Before there was time, the Lord Jesus, though co-equal with the Father, willingly placed Himself under the authority of the Father. At the creation and throughout the unfolding of the Old Testament era, He was by His Father's side, delighting to join the Father in His work. He existed in perfect oneness with His Father, never willing anything contrary to the Father's will.

"I Have Come to Do Your Will"

When Jesus left heaven to come to earth, He had one purpose in mind:

> *"I have come down from heaven not to do my will but to do the will of him who sent me."*
>
> —John 6:38 NIV

> *Then I said, "Here I am . . . I have come to do your will, O God."*
>
> —Hebrews 10:7 NIV

We consider it remarkable when a human being fully surrenders his or her agenda and will to the will of God—probably because such an individual is so rare. But as we have seen, in light of who God is and who we are, such surrender is completely reasonable. What makes the attitude of the Lord Jesus so astounding is that He is God. For Him to surrender His will to that of the Father can only be explained in terms of utter selflessness, trust, humility, and deep devotion to His Father.

Satan attempted to get Jesus to surrender to his control.

Throughout His years here on earth, Jesus maintained this posture of surrender to God. Virtually the only insight we are given into Jesus' life from age twelve till He reached manhood is that He was obedient to His parents (Luke 2:51). That obedience to human authorities was an expression of His surrender to the will of God.

Before He began His earthly ministry, Jesus endured a period of intense temptation in the desert. What was the underlying issue that Satan used to tempt Jesus? It was this matter of control.

As he had done with the man and the woman in the garden of Eden four thousand years earlier, Satan attempted to get Jesus to surrender to his control. And as with the first couple, he started by appealing to Jesus' physical appetites—*you decide what to eat and when.* Though Jesus had not eaten in forty days, He refused to operate apart from the direction of His Father, even in a seemingly insignificant matter.

In his final volley, Satan offered to give Jesus "all the kingdoms of the world and their splendor" (something that was not his to give, for that all belongs to God!), if only "you will bow down and worship me" (Matthew 4:8–9 NIV).

Adam and Eve had failed essentially that same test. Offered an opportunity to control their own lives, they had bowed down and worshiped the one whose sole intent is to usurp the throne of God.

Jesus knew that if He conceded even an iota of control to Satan, He would be rejecting the kingdom and control of God. He understood that that is the essence of sin; it is what separates God from man, and it is what accounts for all the misery in the history of the world.

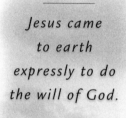

Jesus came to earth expressly to do the will of God.

Jesus acknowledged only one King and was fully surrendered to the will of His heavenly Father; therefore, He would not for a moment concede control to the Father's archenemy. He would not bow before any other so-called king; He would not worship anyone other than God. He would not indulge His human desires for food or comfort or gain, if to do so required Him to operate outside His Father's will.

Jesus came to earth expressly to do the will of God, which required that He offer up His body as a sacrifice. Never for a single moment did He ever resist the will of His Father. Never was there a hint of a power struggle between Father and Son—never a battle for control—just complete, glad surrender. To demonstrate that surrender, the Lord Jesus took upon Himself "the form of a bond-servant." Then, in the ultimate display of relinquishing control, "He humbled Himself by becoming obedient to the point of death" (Philippians 2:7–8 NASB).

The Supreme Surrender

"But what about Gethsemane?" you say. "Didn't Jesus struggle against the will of God as He faced the cross?" To the contrary, next to the cross itself, Gethsemane is the supreme illustration of Jesus' surrender while here on this earth.

Shortly before going to Gethsemane to pray, Jesus predicted His imminent death. Then He said, "Now my heart is troubled, and what shall

I say? 'Father, save me from this hour'? *No, it was for this very reason I came to this hour. Father, glorify your name!"* (John 12:27–28 NIV, italics added).

Before He ever set foot in the garden of Gethsemane, Jesus had settled the issue; indeed, the issue had been settled before He ever set foot on this planet. In eternity past, He had surrendered Himself to the will of God—to become the Sin-Bearer for all mankind. When Jesus knelt in the garden and "offered up prayers and petitions with loud cries and tears to the one who could save him from death" (Hebrews 5:7 NIV), He was not expressing resistance to the will of God; rather, He was expressing *full surrender* to the will of God.

The anguish the Lord Jesus experienced as He sweated drops of blood was that He who had never once disobeyed His Father, He who loved His Father and had been by His Father's side for all of eternity (Proverbs 8:30), He who delighted to do the will of His Father (Psalm 40:8), He who "loved righteousness and hated lawlessness" (Hebrews 1:9)—was about to *become sin*—the very thing He knew His Father hated! The surrendered Son of God was about to take on Himself all the cumulative, compounded resistance and rebellion of all humans who had ever lived or ever would live on this planet.

So He cried out, in effect, "O Father, my Holy Father, I've lived to please You. And because I love You, if it's possible, let this cup pass from Me so that I will not have to be sin, so that I will not have to be separated from You."

The writer of Hebrews tells us that when Jesus cried out, "he was heard *because of his reverent submission*" (5:7 NIV, italics added). That submission was seen as He prayed in the garden: "Not My will, but Yours be done." What was He saying? *I delight to do Your will. That's all that matters. Father, I surrender to Your control.*

Bow the Head

Jesus left the garden under arrest. Not many hours later, He laid down His life on the cross. The Scripture is clear that no man took His life from Him. John's account of the crucifixion gives us a significant detail that is not included in the other Gospels. We are told that after Jesus drank the vinegar, He said, "'It is finished.' With that, *he bowed his head and gave up his spirit*" (19:30 NIV, italics added).

Can you see it? *He bowed His head.* He didn't just slump over. He bowed His head. In that final moment of His life, He performed one last, powerful, volitional act— He bowed His head. He chose the pathway of surrender. "He was heard because of His reverent submission." He surrendered—willingly, freely gave up His life—so you and I could inherit eternal life.

Our Savior will forever be a surrendered servant.

What a God! What a Savior!

And what a calling! As Christ's surrender took Him to the cross, so our surrender will always take us to the cross. Every time your flesh or mine crosses the will of God and we choose to *bow the head* in surrender to the Spirit of God, our will is crucified and Christ is exalted as Lord. So . . .

✦ When your flesh wants to watch that raunchy TV program, and the Spirit says, "Cast off the works of darkness" (Romans 13:12), see it as an opportunity to consciously, volitionally *bow your head* and surrender to God.

✦ When your flesh wants to lash out in anger, and the Spirit says, "Clothe [yourself] with compassion, kindness, humility, gentleness and patience. Bear with each other . . ." (Colossians 3:12–13 NIV), *bow your head* and surrender to God.

✦ When your flesh wants to pass along a critical report about another believer, and the Spirit says, "Speak evil of no one" (Titus 3:2), *bow your head* and surrender to God.

✦ When your flesh is tempted to complain about your circumstances, and the Spirit says, "In everything give thanks" (1 Thessalonians 5:18), *bow your head* and surrender to God.

✦ When your flesh rises up against an authority you think is being unreasonable, and the Spirit says, "Submit [yourself] for the

Lord's sake to every authority" (1 Peter 2:13 NIV), *bow your head* and surrender to God.

✦ When your flesh wants to wound that mate or child or friend who has wounded you, and the Spirit says, "Repay no one evil for evil" (Romans 12:17), *bow your head* and surrender to God.

✦ When your flesh wants to say something that makes you look good, and the Spirit says, "Let another man praise you, and not your own mouth" (Proverbs 27:2), *bow your head* and surrender to God.

✦ When your flesh wants to indulge in sexual fantasies, and the Spirit says, "Blessed are the pure in heart" (Matthew 5:8) and "Take captive every thought to make it obedient to Christ" (2 Corinthians 10:5 NIV), *bow your head* and surrender to God.

✦ When your flesh wants to hoard your financial resources out of fear of the future, and the Spirit says, "He who gives to the poor will not lack" (Proverbs 28:27), *bow your head* and surrender to God.

✦ When your flesh wants to shade the truth to protect your reputation, and the Spirit says, "Each one speak truth with his neighbor" (Ephesians 4:25), *bow your head* and surrender to God.

✦ When your flesh wants to eat in excess, and the Spirit says, "Whether you eat or drink . . . do all to the glory of God" (1 Corinthians 10:31), *bow your head* and surrender to God.

Every time you and I bow our heads in acceptance of and surrender to the will of God, we embrace the cross and we manifest to the world the heart of Christ who bowed His head to the will of His Father.

Eternally Surrendered

We have seen that from eternity past, through His incarnation, in His earthly life and ministry, and in His death on the cross, the Lord Jesus was a surrendered servant. Yet our portrait is not quite finished. Did you realize that for all of eternity, our Savior will forever be a surrendered servant?

Luke's gospel paints a picture that never fails to move me; it describes what will happen when Jesus, our Master, returns for His faithful servants: "I tell you the truth, he will dress himself to serve, will have them recline at the table *and will come and wait on them*" (12:37 NIV, italics added). Can you fathom that? *The King and Lord of the universe* will put on a servant's uniform and will come and wait on *us*? It takes my breath away.

Now let's stand back and watch as the Master Artist adds the final strokes to this exquisite picture of surrender. We see the consummation of that cosmic battle for control that has been intensifying since Lucifer first asserted his will against the will of God:

> *And there were loud voices in heaven, saying, "The kingdoms of this world have become the kingdoms of our Lord and of His Christ, and He shall reign forever and ever!"*
>
> —Revelation 11:15b

And so, the surrendered servant takes His place with His Father on the highest throne in heaven and earth, to rule forever as the Sovereign Lord.

But wait! (As I read these passages, I'm reminded of the final movement of a symphony that progresses from one triumphant, climactic finale to another.)

One more scene completes this portrait. In keeping with the character and heart of our Savior-King, His very last action is not best described with loud, crashing cymbals of majestic conquest, but with the rich, lush, sweeping sounds of . . . *surrender:*

> *Then the end will come, when [Christ] hands over the kingdom to God the Father after he has destroyed all dominion, authority and power. For he must reign until he has put all his enemies under his feet. . . . When he has done this, then the Son himself will be*

made subject to him who put everything under him, so that God
may be all in all.

—1 Corinthians 15:24–25, 28 NIV
(emphasis added)

When all is said and done, the conquering King will turn over to His
Father all the kingdoms He has overcome—all the spoils of war. And
then, once again, as time gives way to eternity, the Son of God, the
Almighty, sovereign Creator and Redeemer, the Lord of heaven and
earth, will bow His head in a final, magnificent act of surrender.

MAKING IT PERSONAL . . .

✦ "Your attitude should be the same as that of Christ Jesus" (Philippians 2:5 NIV). How does your attitude reflect the heart of the
Lord Jesus? How is it different than His?

✦ What is an issue you are currently facing in which you need to
bow your head?

Say "No" to self;
"Yes" to Jesus every time.

WILLIAM BORDEN[1]

YES, LORD!
BOWING THE KNEE

A NUMBER OF YEARS AGO, I was asked to speak to several hundred college students at a conference held between Christmas and New Year's Day. Ordinarily, I do not take speaking engagements over the Christmas holidays; it's the one time of year I don't have to travel, and I look forward to being at home. Although I did not want to make this trip, I felt the Lord wanted me to surrender my desires, so I bowed my will (somewhat reluctantly, I'll admit) and agreed to go.

As I spoke to those students about total surrender, I confessed the emotions I had struggled with in coming to the conference. I shared that, in my humanness, I would have preferred to stay in my house, relax, and look at the river outside my home, rather than having to travel and speak during the holidays, but that it had come down to an issue of surrender.

As I had been preparing to speak, I had a sense that God wanted many of those students to surrender their lives to vocational Christian service. At the close of the message, I told the students what was on my heart and asked them to consider what God might be saying to them and then simply to bow the knee and say, *Yes, Lord.*

Two years later, I received a letter from a young woman who had attended that conference. She was writing to express what God had done in her heart that weekend. At the time she had been a junior in college, preparing for a career in advertising.

> *Am I seeking to know and follow the will of God in every area of my life?*

She recalled, "When you said you believed God was calling many of us to devote our lives to Christian service, I looked around wondering who you could be talking about—knowing it certainly couldn't be me!" But that day God planted a seed in her heart; she began to sense God's call to surrender her career plans and devote her life to the kingdom of Christ. She wanted me to know that she was in the process of raising her financial support to join the full-time staff of a student ministry (where she is still serving today).

I was particularly moved by her closing words: "I'm so glad you didn't choose to sit in your house and look at your river that New Year's holiday, but that you surrendered to God's call in your life."

In retrospect, I'm glad too. But I can't help thinking of other times when I have been slow to surrender to the will of God, and wondering how many more lives He might have touched in significant ways if I had been quicker to bow the knee and say, *Yes, Lord.*

Calling Him "Lord"

What would surrender to God's control look like for you? I asked a number of friends to share a significant point of surrender they had faced in their walk with God. They identified a variety of issues, including the surrender of:

✦ Personal possessions

✦ Spending habits

✦ Personal opinions (e.g., about how my church should be run)

✦ Children leaving home

✦ Schedule and time (e.g., to be a stay-at-home mom or to home-school children)

✦ Health and physical concerns

✦ Addictive habits

✦ The right to control or change a mate

✦ Loss of parents through death

✦ Home and comfort (e.g., to move and serve in a ministry)

The specific issues that God identifies in your life may be similar or different. The question you must answer is, *Am I seeking to know and follow the will of God in* every *area of my life?* The fact is, many professing Christians go through life making decisions and responding to circumstances while rarely considering, "What does *God* want me to do? What does the Scripture say about this?"

Jesus put it this way: "Why do you call me 'Lord, Lord,' and do not do what I say?" (Luke 6:46 NIV). In other words, "Why do you claim that I am in charge of your life, but you run your life as if you were in charge? You don't ask Me what I want you to do, and even when you know what I want you to do, you still insist on doing it your way!"

> *We cannot call Him* Lord *and then proceed to run our own lives.*

To call Him *Lord* means to say *Yes*—to His will, His Word, and His ways. We cannot call Him *Lord* and then proceed to run our own lives.

You say, "If I live a surrendered life, does that mean I'll end up on the mission field . . . or have to quit my job . . . or bring my parents to live in our home . . . or live alone all my life?" Maybe. Maybe not. In a sense, it doesn't really matter. What does matter is saying *Yes, Lord.* Then you will have grace to do the will of God—whatever it is—and joy as you do it!

Surrendering to God may mean being happily married for half a century. Or being faithful in a difficult marriage to an unbeliever. Or being widowed and left to raise young children. Or never marrying. What matters is saying *Yes, Lord.*

It may mean parenting many children. Or few children. Or no children. What matters is, *How many children does God want you to have?*

It may mean you make lots of money and use it for the glory of God. Or that only your essential needs are met and you choose to be content with little.

It may mean you own a lovely, large home and use it to bless and serve others. Or it may mean you live in a two-room efficiency in a Third World country where you spend years translating the Scripture for those who have never heard the Word of God. Regardless, what matters is saying *Yes, Lord.*

Total surrender to Christ as Lord simply means submitting every detail and dimension of our lives to His sovereign, loving rule.

Bowing the Knee

For years, I have made it a practice to kneel before the Lord at least once a day, as a physical expression of my desire to surrender my will to His will.

To be totally surrendered to God means to bow the knee before a Sovereign Lord. It means to say *Yes* to God . . .

- ✦ *Yes* to His choices for your life—even when they don't seem comfortable or convenient

- ✦ *Yes* to difficult or painful circumstances that you cannot understand or change

- ✦ *Yes* to everything that is revealed in His Word

- ✦ *Yes* to His plans, His purposes, and His priorities

- ✦ *Yes* to the human authorities He has placed in your life

- ✦ *Yes* to His disciplines

- ✦ *Yes* to His control over your appetites, your body, your time, your relationships, your future—everything

To some, that type of surrender might seem to be bondage; but those who have bowed the knee—those who have laid down their arms and waved the white flag of surrender—know that it is the only pathway to true freedom. And with that surrender comes a host of blessings that cannot be experienced any other way: the grace to obey God, release from having to run our own world, the peace of God, unexplainable fullness of joy, and greater fruitfulness than we ever dreamed possible.

I have seen this so many times in my own life that I often look back and wonder, *Why did I ever resist the will of God?!*

"Please, Not Me, Lord!"

Someone has said that the will of God is exactly what we would choose if we knew what God knows. The problem is, we don't know what God knows—which is why we so often find it difficult to embrace His will and why we must learn to "trust and obey."

As I look back over my life thus far, I am in awe at the beauty and magnificence of His sovereign plan, and the intricate, loving way that He orchestrates the details of our lives—if we will let Him. Every time we step out in faith to surrender to His will—each time we say *Yes* to God—we move into a realm of greater blessing and fruitfulness.

I'll never forget the time I was first challenged to consider starting a daily radio program for women. From the outset, I had multiple objections to the idea, and was quick to list them to the Lord and others. Some of those reservations were practical—I knew virtually nothing about broadcasting and felt utterly inadequate and incapable of taking on such a responsibility.

Other hurdles were more personal—I was in my early forties and was wishing for a more settled life than I had experienced over more than twenty years of itinerant ministry. In my mind, accepting this responsibility would mean working harder and having less "free time" than ever; it would mean relinquishing any thought of anonymity, of privacy, or of a "normal" life—things I longed to enjoy. I remember thinking, *This would mean having no life of my own!*

Then my heart was pierced. From the time I was a little girl, I had recognized God's ownership of my life and had acknowledged that my life was not my own. Yet here I was trying to protect and preserve part of it for myself.

Years earlier, I had signed that blank contract, giving my life wholly to God to be used for His purposes; now that God was filling in the details, I knew that I could not take it back. Once again, I had to come to a fresh point of surrender to the will of God, regardless of what that might mean or what the cost might be. Finally, I said, "*Yes, Lord.* I am Your servant. You know my weaknesses, my fears, and my personal desires. But I will embrace whatever You reveal to be Your will in this matter."

> My friend,
> *it's all about*
> *complete*
> *surrender.*

Once I came to that point of surrender, God began to ignite faith in my heart—faith that He would enable me to do whatever He called me to do, in spite of my personal limitations and inadequacies.

God's call in your life will probably look different than it does in mine—or in anyone else's. Regardless of the details, He asks simply that we bow the knee and say, *Yes, Lord.*

The pathway of surrender is not always an easy one. On occasion, I have found myself in some pretty turbulent waters, as a result of saying *Yes* to God. There have been points when it seemed like my little boat was going to capsize. But I have learned that there really is no safer place to be than in His will. And in the midst of the storms, I have found *joy*—indescribable joy. And blessings more than I can number—blessings to be enjoyed here and now and the anticipation of eternal blessings that I cannot begin to fathom now. It really is true that "there's no other way to be happy in Jesus, but to trust and obey."[2]

"Annie, It's Complete Surrender"

In the 1924 Paris Olympics, a twenty-two-year-old Scottish athlete made headlines when he determined to say *No* to self and *Yes* to God. Eric Liddell made a decision that would have been unthinkable for most—to drop out of his best event, the hundred-yard dash, because the qualifying heats were being held on a Sunday. While his competitors were participating in the heats, Liddell was preaching a sermon at a nearby church.

Subsequently, Liddell entered himself in the 400-yard dash, a race for which he had not trained. He ran the race, finishing five yards ahead of his nearest competitor and setting a new world record. However, that Olympic gold medal, earned under such extraordinary circumstances, was far from Eric Liddell's greatest accomplishment.

His obedience to God in Paris was just one of a lifelong series of surrenders that earned Eric the applause of heaven. After his Olympic triumph, he returned to China where he had been raised, to serve as a missionary. In 1943, he was interned in a Japanese concentration camp in China, where he continued to serve God and joyfully ministered to his fellow prisoners. While still in the camp, Liddell suffered a brain tumor that ravaged his body and left him partially paralyzed.

On February 21, 1945, Eric lay on a hospital bed, struggling to breathe and moving in and out of consciousness. Finally, he went into a convulsion; the nurse who had been by his side took him into her arms as he managed to breathe his final words: "Annie," he said, his voice barely audible, *"it's complete surrender."*

Eric Liddell slipped into a coma and then into eternity, where the bondservant bowed the knee before the Master he loved so dearly and for whom he had labored so faithfully.

MAKING IT PERSONAL . . .

My friend, *it's all about complete surrender.* Whatever the issue may be for you, however trivial or daunting that issue may seem, whatever the price, whatever your fears, however foolish you may feel or look, wherever that surrender may lead you . . . right here, right now, will you bow the knee? Relinquish control. Let Him have His way. Say simply, *Yes, Lord; I surrender all.*

Notes

1. Dick Bohrer, *Bill Borden: The Finished Course—the Unfinished Task* (Chicago: Moody, 1984), 41–42.
2. John H. Sammis, "Trust and Obey."

SURRENDER
DISCUSSION GUIDE

As You Begin

The whole idea of surrendering to someone else's control runs counter to the prevailing mind-set of our culture—we don't want anyone telling us what to do—we want to be in control of our own lives! But paradoxically, we are never truly free until we have fully surrendered ourselves to the Word and will of God.

The thought of delving into this topic may cause some apprehension in your heart, but as you engage in this study, you will encounter a wise, loving, merciful Lord who can be trusted.

The more fully you relinquish yourself to Him, the more you will discover that He has your best interests at heart and that His will truly is "good, acceptable, and perfect" (see Romans 12:2).

May your deepest heart's desire become that of the Savior who lifted His eyes heavenward, even as He faced the cross, and said, *"I delight to do Your will, My God."*

Tips for Group Leaders

Open and close each meeting by praying together. Ask the Holy Spirit to guide you through the Word, to help you be real with one another, and to bring about any needed change in each heart.

Seek to lead by example. You can serve your group best by modeling a surrendered heart—by being quick to say, *Yes, Lord,* and encouraging others to do the same.

Some of the questions in this discussion guide call for a level of transparency and openness that many people are not accustomed to. Encourage the members of your group to respect each other's privacy by not discussing others' contributions outside of this group. Remind them that God is patient and gracious with us as He conforms us to the image of His Son, and that we need to extend the same patience and grace toward each other.

This discussion guide is designed to be used in a variety of contexts—from small groups to Sunday school classes. Feel free to direct the discussion based on the size of your group and the allotted time. Avoid rabbit trails into secondary or unrelated issues. However, don't feel pressured to get through all the questions each time you meet.

Depending on your available time and the size and openness of your group, you may end up only discussing two or three questions. The goal is to grow together in your understanding of God and His ways and to experience individually and as a group the reality of the message of this book.

Encourage each member to read the chapter and to complete the "Making It Personal" section found at the end of most chapters, prior to your group meeting. If possible, they should also preview and be prepared to discuss the questions found in this discussion guide.

Keep your group centered on the truth of the gospel: We are *all* sinners in need of a Savior. Help your members steer clear of self-righteous responses to the confessions of others in the group and from condemnation about their own performance by pointing them to the One who is both the author and perfecter of their faith (Hebrews 12:2 NIV).

INTRODUCTION

Opening Prayer

Turn to the prayer from *The Valley of Vision*, found at the beginning of *Surrender*. Start your time together by reading this wonderful expression of trust in the will of God. You may choose to read as a group in unison or have one or more read aloud while others listen.

Getting Started

Sometimes we dig our heels in about things that appear foolish in hindsight. Describe a situation where you held out for something that you realized in retrospect was misguided or didn't make sense. What finally convinced you to "surrender" your position?

Going Deeper

1. The introduction distinguishes between our *initial* surrender to Christ as our Lord and Savior (or conversion), and a *lifetime* of surrender (or consecration), as we learn to live out the implications of that initial surrender. Briefly describe the setting and circumstances of your conversion—your initial surrender to Christ.

2. *"The fully surrendered life is intended to be—and can be—the norm for every one of God's children"* (p. 146). Do you agree with this statement? From your perspective, is the "fully surrendered life" the "norm" for most of the believers you know?

3. Review and discuss the four reasons suggested in this chapter for why professing Christians may have areas of their life that are "unsurrendered" to God (pp. 144–45). Which of those four scenarios do you think are most common among "believers" whom you have observed? Have several in the group share an illustration out of their own lives of one of those scenarios.

4. *"Do you fear what a lifestyle of full surrender might cost you?"* (p. 146). What fears might people have about fully surrendering every aspect of their lives to God? What fears have you experienced at one point or another in relation to full surrender?

5. *"The truth is that resistance is far more costly than surrender"* (p. 147). What might we stand to lose by holding out on God?

6. Share out of your personal experience either the cost of resisting God on some particular point or the blessing you have experienced through relinquishing control of some area of your life to the Lord.

7. In many ways, surrender is an act of trust. You drop your defenses and trust your opponent will honor the terms of your surrender. The pardon given by President Marcos of the Philippines to Hiroo Onoda is a picture of the pardon we are given by God when we repent. What do you know about the heart and ways of God that should make it easier to trust Him and relinquish control to Him?

A Word of Encouragement

As you read the introduction and considered your own spiritual condition, your heart may have been pricked with the thought that perhaps you have never been truly regenerated (born again). You may have made a profession of faith; others may think of you as a "good Christian." But you have never "waved the white flag" and surrendered your life to Christ.

Don't try to talk yourself out of (or let anyone else talk you out of!) any conviction that God may be bringing to your heart. Seek out your pastor or another mature Christian for care and counsel. It may be that the tug of conviction you are experiencing is the doorway to the great joy of true salvation!

This could be a God-designed moment for you to repent of your sins and receive His forgiveness—please don't delay this important conversation!

For Next Time

"Could it be that there are some issues on which you are reserving the right to control your own life?" (p. 144). As you read and discussed the introduction to *Surrender*, God may have brought to mind specific areas in your life that are not fully surrendered to His control. Record these areas in a personal journal. Ask God to help you see these issues as He does and express your desire for every area of your life to be under His control.

Grace Note

In the life of a believer, the Holy Spirit brings conviction, not condemnation. Conviction is sweet because it is accompanied by the promise of grace to change. Condemnation brings on guilt (usually heaped on by the Enemy) that we will never measure up to God's demands. Without being born again and trusting in God's power to change us, that would be true. Don't let condemnation rob you of the joy of this journey toward change!

Remember: *"Our God abounds in mercy and grace; He is willing to offer a full and complete pardon to those who lay down their weapons"* (p. 147).

Chapter One:
THE BATTLE
FOR CONTROL

Getting Started

Has anyone in your group ever served in combat or had a friend or relative who did? Describe your experience of being in battle (or what you have heard from your loved one). What did you learn about how to wage and win a battle?

Going Deeper

1. What evidences do you see of nature being "surrendered" to God's control? Why do you think God gives human beings the freedom to submit to or to resist His control? What limitations has He placed on that freedom, both here and now, as well as ultimately?

2. Did you relate to any of the fictitious scenarios at the beginning of this chapter (pp. 149–50)? What is one example of a recurring battle you have experienced in your Christian life? How could that struggle actually be a battle for control?

3. *"Count on it—the very points on which you refuse to surrender will become 'enemies' that rule over you"* (p. 156). What are some practical examples of how this principle could take place in someone's life?

4. What is one area of your life that has ended up ruling you as a "tyrant" (either in the past or in the present) because of a lack of surrender to God?

5. Lynda's testimony (pp. 155–57) illustrates the truth of Romans 6:16—"Do you not know that to whom you present yourselves slaves to obey, you are that one's slaves whom you obey, whether of sin leading to death, or of obedience leading to righteousness?"

Share one particular area of your life where you have experienced (or currently experience) a sense of being *enslaved* to sin or ungodly desires. How could surrender to God set you free from that slavery?

6. Take time to pray for each other in relation to any specific battles for control or surrender issues that have been shared.

For Next Time

With regard to any "unsurrendered" areas you have identified in your life, reflect on the effects of being enslaved to these areas. List the bad fruits of being submitted to these desires, so you can see more clearly the cost of your lack of surrender.

Grace Note

Surrender brings peace and a foretaste of the "paradise restored" that every believer will enjoy one day in heaven. You can begin to enjoy those benefits now by saying yes to God. As the familiar song says, "There's no other way to be happy in Jesus, but to *trust and obey*."

Chapter Two:
THE TERMS OF CHRISTIAN SURRENDER

Getting Started

Has anyone in your group ever visited Appomattox? If so, what did you learn during your visit? What struck you about the illustration in this chapter of Robert E. Lee's surrender at Appomattox (pp. 161–63)? What parallels did you see to Christian surrender?

Lee's surrender was a "decisive moment" that changed the course of the Civil War and assured its ultimate outcome. What does that illustrate about the importance of a "decisive moment" of surrender in our relationship with God?

Going Deeper

1. *"The person who has never acknowledged Christ's right to rule over his life has no basis for assurance of salvation. . . . Surrender to the will of God is a mark of the truly converted"* (p. 164).

What part does surrender have in true Christian conversion? What concerns does this raise about our message and methods as we seek to share the gospel with unbelievers?

2. How would you define or describe *unconditional* surrender? What does that mean for a believer? What might *conditional* surrender look like? Why is it unacceptable for a child of God?

3. How would you distinguish between an *initial point* of surrender to Christ, and an ongoing, *lifelong process* of surrender in a believer's life? What is the connection between the two? Why are both important? How can an initial, unconditional surrender to the lordship of Christ simplify subsequent points of surrender along the way? (Think of the illustration of the dieter on pp. 166–67!)

4. Share a situation you have faced recently that required you to freshly affirm and live out your surrender to the will of God. It may have been a choice to obey God's Word or the prompting of His Spirit on a simple, everday matter, or it may have been a more major point of surrender.

5. Why might some consider John and Betty Stam's surrender and sacrifice to be a net loss? How would you evaluate their surrender from an eternal perspective?

6. Why might the concept of "signing a blank contract" for your life and letting God fill in the details seem risky or frightening to some? Why is it really not risky at all? What do we stand to lose by unconditional surrender to God? What do we stand to gain?

7. Discuss any reservations or fears you have about signing your life over to God, or share what you have learned or experienced that has relieved your fears of that kind of surrender.

For Next Time

If you haven't already done so, write out a prayer expressing your heart's intent to be wholly surrendered to Christ. Then date and sign your "contract" with the Lord.

Grace Note

There are three wonderful prayers from saints of old included in this chapter (pp. 168–69). If time permits, read these aloud in your group. If not, read them aloud during your personal time with the Lord over the next week.

Chapter Three:
A HOLE
IN THE EAR

Getting Started

Has anyone in your group traveled abroad or spent time ministering internationally? If so, did you observe anything in the lives of the believers in that part of the world that particularly impressed you or struck you as different than American Christianity?

Going Deeper

1. Discuss the difference between *commitment* and *surrender* as Josef Tson explains it (p. 174). Which term do you think better characterizes contemporary Christianity in the West? What are the implications of adopting one perspective or the other?

2. Discuss the difference (as Josef Tson and Webster's dictionary explain it) between a servant and a slave. Which term would the majority of believers in our culture be more comfortable using to describe our relationships to Christ? Why?

3. What are the implications of the fact in the Greek Bible that one never *serves* God but rather one *slaves* to God (pp. 174–75)?

4. How does the ceremony of joyful slavery found in Exodus 21 illustrate a believer's relationship to God? How was this Old Testament picture fulfilled in Christ?

5. What are some of the "requirements" of being Christ's bondslave that you have found difficult at one time or another?

6. What are some of the privileges, joys, and blessings you have experienced as a result of being His bondslave?

7. Close your time by reading the words of David Livingstone (p. 172) and Mary of Nazareth (p. 180). Then pray together and express your desire to make these words your own.

For Next Time

A man or a woman with "a hole in the ear" is easily identifiable to others. Are there any relationships or circumstances in which you are tempted to, in effect, "cover up" that hole? Prayerfully consider those situations, and ask the Holy Spirit to show you the motivations and cravings of your heart that compel such a reaction—and then after asking His forgiveness, ask for the grace to change.

Grace Note

As you consider this idea of being a slave to Christ, meditate on the truths found in Psalm 40. Jesus fulfilled this prophetic statement through His atoning death; He is the first and foremost bondslave to God. He fulfilled the prophetic picture of Exodus 21 in His joyful submission to a gracious and loving Master!

Chapter Four:
THE WHOLE
OF OUR LIVES

Getting Started
Probably few if any in your group can identify with the passion for Communism described at the beginning of this chapter. But you have probably seen that kind of fanatical devotion to some cause or endeavor (other than the kingdom of God). What have you observed and what were the results?

Going Deeper
1. How did the young Communist's letter to his fiancée impress you? How does his level of devotion to the Communist cause compare to the average Christian's devotion to Christ and His kingdom? How does it compare to your own values and priorities?

2. What were the characteristics of a burnt offering in the Jewish worship system? How did Christ fulfill that Old Testament picture? How does that picture help us understand what it means to be a true follower of Jesus Christ? How is the sacrifice of our lives *different* than the Old Testament burnt offerings?

3. How does marriage illustrate the twofold aspect of surrender (an initial point, followed by an ongoing, lifetime process)?

4. Between the different members of your group, share some specific sacrifices you can recall God asking you to make—ranging from "twenty-five-cent pieces" to perhaps much larger sacrifices. Would you agree that, regardless of their size, *"the sacrifices God asks of us are never pointless"* (p. 189)?

5. Have you ever felt that something God was asking of you seemed unreasonable? What perspective does Romans 12:1 give to those sacrifices? Why do you think Paul used the Greek word *logikos* to

describe the offering up of ourselves to God as a living sacrifice? How does Christ's sacrifice for us affect the way we view our sacrifices for Him?

6. What might it mean for you this week to offer yourself as a "living sacrifice" to God?

For Next Time
Reread Helen Roseveare's description of what it means to be a living sacrifice (pp. 189–90). Then try writing your own description of what it means to be a living sacrifice.

Grace Note
Don't forget the accent and emphasis of Romans 12:1 . . . "in view of God's mercy" (NIV). That's where the Holy Spirit started as He inspired the apostle Paul to write, and that is where we are to start. If you are wrestling with discouragement or fear, remember that surrender is always done "in view of God's mercy."

Chapter Five:
FACING
OUR FEARS

Getting Started

This chapter describes the "going but not knowing" aspect of surrender in Abraham's life. Some in your group have also probably undertaken such a "journey"—stepping out in faith without knowing precisely what lay ahead. Have one or more individuals share their story.

Going Deeper

1. Review the four fears addressed in this chapter in relation to surrendering everything to God. Is it wrong to have those fears?

2. Share an instance in which you experienced one of these fears in relation something God was asking you to do. Discuss as a group what promise(s) of God could have counteracted your fear in that situation.

3. What is the role of faith in helping us face our natural fears regarding the will of God? How can we grow in our faith? Why is it so important that we know the promises and the character of God if we're going to trust Him?

4. In addition to "going but not knowing," there's also the test of "waiting but not receiving." Abraham experienced both. *"For more than twenty-five years, [Abraham] didn't have a shred of visible evidence that God's promises would be fulfilled"* (p. 198).

Is there some matter on which you have been waiting on the Lord for what seems like a very long time? What has helped you to continue trusting God? What additional encouragement can others in the group offer from God's Word?

5. The word *Hebrew* means "stranger" or "alien." In what sense is every child of God a "Hebrew"? Can you think of a verse or passage

in the New Testament that supports that concept?

6. "Trust or tyranny. *That is the option.* Trust *the promises of God—which will free you to live joyfully under His loving Lordship—or live under the tyranny of that which you will not surrender*" (p. 201).

Encourage one or more in your group to share how failing to trust the promises of God caused them to resist surrender on a specific matter and resulted in living under the tyranny of that very thing.

7. *"Isn't that the heart of the matter for every child of God?* Can you trust Me?" (p. 205). Close your meeting with a time of prayer. Thank God for His character and His promises; express your trust in Him; ask Him to give you grace to face your fears and to fully surrender to Him any areas of life where you may have been afraid to say, *"Yes, Lord."*

For Next Time

Look for several verses that address the fear(s) you most related to in this chapter. You may want to post a visible reminder of these verses in your kitchen, on your bathroom mirror, on your dashboard, or your screen saver—wherever you are likely to encounter this truth consistently in your daily life.

Grace Note

Our loving God is not unmindful of our fears, tests, and trials. The loving reassurance He extended to Abram echoes throughout time to us today: "Do not be afraid, Abram. I am your shield, your exceedingly great reward" (Genesis 15:1). Whatever we surrender is *more* than matched by the exceedingly great reward of knowing God!

Chapter Six:
LIVING THE
SURRENDERED LIFE

Getting Started

"It's one thing to have an emotional experience at a Christian gathering where you are inspired and challenged to surrender control of everything to God. It's another matter to live out that surrender once the emotion of the moment has passed—when the bus gets home from the conference . . . when you lose your job and the bills keep coming . . . when you find out you're expecting your fifth child in seven years . . . when your mate is diagnosed with a terminal illness" (p. 208). Describe such an occasion or experience in your life.

Going Deeper

Talk through each of the ten categories in this chapter (based on Frances Havergal's hymn "Take My Life and Let It Be"). (If time does not permit you to go through all of them, as a group select several to review.) What does it mean for each of these areas of our lives to be consecrated to God? Share any specific questions you found particularly challenging or convicting as you read this chapter.

1. My Life
2. My Time
3. My Body
4. My Tongue
5. My Possessions
6. My Mind
7. My Will
8. My Affections
9. My Relationships
10. Myself

For Next Time

Select one category from this chapter that you feel prompted to focus on between now and your next meeting. Each day, review the questions in that category that will help remind you of areas where you need a deeper surrender to the Lord.

If you haven't walked through the exercise recommended on p. 216, take time to do that this week.

Grace Note

Meditate on Frances Havergal's quote at the beginning of this chapter: *"Full consecration may be in one sense the act of a moment and in another the work of a lifetime. It must be complete to be real, and yet—if real—it is always incomplete. Consecration is a point of rest and yet a perpetual progression."* This thought should both motivate and encourage us to press on in the matter of full surrender to God.

Chapter Seven:
THE PATTERN

Getting Started

Does anyone in your group enjoy reading Christian biographies? If so, whose life story has been especially meaningful to you? What inspired you about that person's life?

Going Deeper

1. How is Jesus the perfect pattern of what it means to live a fully surrendered life:

- In His pre-incarnate existence (i.e., prior to coming to earth in human form)?
- In His incarnation (coming to earth)?
- In His wilderness temptation?
- In His earthly ministry?
- In Gethsemane?
- In His crucifixion?
- Throughout eternity?

2. For Jesus, surrender to God's will meant suffering at times. Why do you think Jesus was able, not only to *do* His Father's will, but to *delight* in doing the will of God? How can we learn to *delight* to obey God?

3. Describe a recent occasion when your natural desires were contrary to the will of God, and you chose to *bow the head* in surrender to the will of God.

4. What is an issue you are currently facing in which you need to *bow your head*? Pray for each other in relation to those needed points of surrender.

For Next Time

Throughout the week ahead, ask God to make you alert to opportunities to bow your head in submission to His will.

Grace Note

Jesus' surrender to His Father's will spans from eternity past, through His earthly life and ministry, and continues all the way to Calvary and beyond for all eternity. Though we as redeemed sinners will fail many tests on this earth, we have a Savior who stands at the right hand of the Father interceding for us at this moment and every time we are tempted to resist the will of God. Put your trust in His triumphs on your behalf as you bow your head in glad surrender to His loving control.

Chapter Eight:
YES, LORD!

Getting Started

Can you think of a time when you surrendered to God by faith, contrary to your feelings, and some time later, God allowed you to see the positive results of that choice—either in your life or someone else's life?

Giving Thanks!

Undoubtedly you have some specific testimonies of the Holy Spirit's work among the members of your group as a result of this study—beyond what may already have been shared in previous meetings. Provide an opportunity for each individual to express gratitude for what God has done during your time together. You may want to share about:

- A change in your thinking about—or your heart attitude toward— the will of God

- An area of your life where you were resisting God but have now surrendered to His control

- One or more areas of your life where you have been challenged to say, *Yes, Lord!*

- A specific passage of Scripture God has used to bring you to a place of greater surrender

- The ways the bad fruit of tyranny has been replaced by the good fruit of trust

- The prayer you wrote out as a "contract" with the Lord

- Any new insights into the character, heart, and ways of God

A Final Project

Think of one or more individuals whose walk with God has inspired you to a life of greater surrender. Write a note to one or more of those people. Share what you have observed in their lives and how their surrender to God has influenced your life. Remember the encouragement from Proverbs 11:25: "The generous soul will be made rich, and he who waters will also be watered himself."

HOLINESS
The Heart God Purifies

Editor: Cheryl Dunlop
Interior Design: BlueFrog Design
Cover Design: Smartt Guys
Cover Photo: David Mendelsohn/Masterfile

Library of Congress Cataloging-in-Publication Data

DeMoss, Nancy Leigh.
    Holiness : the heart God purifies / Nancy Leigh DeMoss.
        p. cm. — (Revive our hearts series)
    Includes bibliographical references and index.
    ISBN-13: 978-0-8024-1279-9
    ISBN-10: 0-8024-1279-3
    1. Holiness—Christianity. 2. Christian life. I. Title. II. Series.

BT767.D412 2004
234'.8—dc22
2004005168

Lord God Almighty,

Holy is thy wisdom, power, mercy, ways, works.
How can I stand before thee
    with my numberless and aggravated offences?
I have often loved darkness,
    observed lying vanities,
    forsaken thy given mercies,
    trampled underfoot thy beloved Son,
    mocked thy providences,
    flattered thee with my lips,
    broken thy covenant.
It is of thy compassion that I am not consumed.
Lead me to repentance, and save me from despair;
Let me come to thee renouncing, condemning,
        loathing myself,
    but hoping in the grace that flows
        even to the chief of sinners.
At the cross may I contemplate the evil of sin,
        and abhor it,
    look on him whom I pierced,
        as one slain for me, and by me. . . .
Thus may my soul rest in thee, O immortal
        and transcendent one,
    revealed as thou art in the Person and work
        of thy Son,
    the Friend of sinners.

—From *The Valley of Vision: A Collection
of Puritan Prayers and Devotions*

CONTENTS

FOREWORD

SEVERAL YEARS AGO, my daughter Karina—whose judgment I deeply respect—read Nancy Leigh DeMoss's *Lies Women Believe* and recommended it to me as a great book. Since then I've come to know Nancy as a precious sister. When I've read her books, and spent time with her doing her radio program or talking on the phone, I've been drawn to Jesus.

Readers can rest assured that *Holiness: The Heart God Purifies* comes out of a life that has firsthand experience with the subject matter. The holiness I've seen in Nancy doesn't scream "Look at me—I want you to be impressed with my holiness." It's not the check-off-the-boxes legalism perfected by the Pharisees and paraded by a thousand Christian groups since. It flows from a heart humbly submitted to Christ's lordship. Nancy's holiness is saturated with grace.

"Be holy for I am holy." God is the reason we should be holy. But He's also the empowerment for our holiness. Many of us are convinced we should be more holy, but we've gone about it wrong. To be holy in our strength, and for our glory, is to be distinctly unholy. To be holy in

Christ's strength and for His glory . . . that's our calling, and our joy.

Like Jesus, this book is full of grace and truth —challenging yet winsome, convicting yet inviting. True holiness isn't cold and deadening— it's warm and inviting. It's irresistible. Those who think otherwise have never seen it, but only its caricatures. In this book Nancy strips "holiness" of its baggage, so we see it as it is. And, contrary to popular belief, it's something beautiful.

Yes, there is the carry-your-cross demand. But there's also Christ's assurance, "Come to me, all you who are weary and burdened, and I will give you rest. . . . For my yoke is easy and my burden is light" (Matthew 11:28, 30 NIV).

Holiness is the only path to happiness. Every time I've been unholy it has made me unhappy. Every time I've been holy it has made me happy. Holiness sometimes hurts in the short run, but an hour or day or month or year or lifetime from now, holiness *always* brings happiness. Jesus promised it would: "Happy are the pure in heart, for they shall see God."

Nancy says, "No amount of striving or self-effort can make us holy. Only Christ can do that." Gladly, I want to shout, "That's true!"

She says, "Somehow, the evangelical world has managed to redefine sin; we have come to view it as normal, acceptable behavior—something perhaps to be tamed or controlled, but not to be eradicated and put to death. We have sunk to such lows that we can not only sin thoughtlessly, but astonishingly, we can even laugh at sin and be entertained by it."

Sadly, this time, I say, "That's true."

Each day the God in whose presence the seraphim cry "Holy, Holy, Holy" examines every secret corner of our lives. He's the Audience of One. What really matters is whether *He* is pleased with our lives.

May we humbly acknowledge that when it comes to holiness—with all its sacrifices and rewards and pleasures—apart from Christ we can do nothing. But by His grace and empowerment, we really *can* live so that we may one day hear Him say those amazing, thrilling words: "Well done, My good and faithful servant!"

The moment we hear those words, from the mouth of our Lion and Lamb, we'll know that in comparison, nothing else matters.

RANDY ALCORN

ACKNOWLEDGMENTS

THIS BOOK HAS BEEN far from a solo undertaking. Many dear friends and colleagues have labored with me through a lengthy birthing process. I owe special gratitude to:

+ The Moody Publishers team—particularly *Greg Thornton, Bill Thrasher,* and *Elsa Mazon*—apart from whose vision, partnership, and perseverance there would not have been a *Revive Our Hearts* trilogy.

+ *Dr. Bruce Ware* for your theological review and *Bob Lepine* for your iron-sharpening input and insights throughout the process. Your biblical oversight and "guardianship" of this message have meant so much!

+ *Del Fehsenfeld III, Steve and Carter Rhoads, Lela Gilbert, Mary Ann Lepine, Elisabeth DeMoss, Betsey Newenhuyse,* and *Josef Tson,* among others, who interacted with me about this vast, grand subject, supplied helpful resources, read the manuscript in part or in whole at various stages, and offered valuable suggestions.

✦ *Dawn Wilson* for your research assistance, *Cheryl Dunlop* for your careful copyediting, and Carolyn McCulley for your creative input on the discussion guide.

✦ *Mike Neises* for countless hours of invaluable behind-the-scenes administrative efforts—you are truly a faithful servant of Christ.

✦ The entire *Revive Our Hearts* team that has so graciously and effectively carried on with the ministry through my extended periods of hibernation, all the while praying and cheering me on—you are an extraordinary group, and I am honored and humbled to be your fellow "under-rower."

✦ I don't know that I have ever had—or needed—more earnest prayer support than that which has undergirded this project from start to finish. Many precious *Praying Friends* have paid a price to see this book born. May God reward your labors, and may He soon grant the revival of holiness for which our hearts long.

Oh for holiness!

Oh for more of God in my soul!

Oh this pleasing pain!

It makes my soul press after God.

DAVID BRAINERD[1]

INTRODUCTION

NOTHING COULD HAVE prepared me for the call I received early one morning about a year ago. A brokenhearted pastor was calling to ask me to pray and to be prepared to reach out to a mutual friend whose husband was about to confess to her that he had been committing adultery with a young woman in their church for the past six months.

I gasped in disbelief. This couple has been among my dearest friends for most of my adult life. From all appearances, they both had a deep, genuine love for the Lord, as well as an unusually strong marriage and family.

Now, this husband had flagrantly broken his covenant with his God and his wife; worse, his heart had become hard and cold. This man who had often been known to weep over his sin was now dry-eyed and unrepentant.

I don't believe it was a coincidence that this call came just as I was getting ready to start writing this book. Or that in the prior three weeks I had learned of several other believers whose "private" sin had become public and created no small eruption.

My passion for the message of holiness has been fueled by these and far too many other real-life stories I have heard and witnessed in the course of working on this book.

The burden on my heart has intensified as I have received letters and e-mails from people who are troubled about what they see going on around them in the church. The following excerpt represents the concern of this remnant of believers:

> The leadership in our church doesn't seem to have the same fire for purity that we want to have. They don't share our sense of right-from-wrong when it comes to things like movie/TV watching, modest dress, and drinking. They seem to think the best way to witness to the lost is to be like them.
>
> My own accountability partner does not have a problem with watching R-rated movies or TV shows that promote fornication, adultery, and blatant sin. Our youth pastor has told me that watching R-rated movies is all right since that's how he keeps in touch with what the youth of today are exposed to.
>
> We don't want to be divisive or to come across as self-righteous or "legalistic." It's just that the more we learn about purity and godliness, the more we see the dilution of the Christian life around us, and we're at a loss to know what to do about it. My wife and I have wasted too much time "playing church," and we don't want our kids to think that God is a God of compromise. We're not wrong . . . are we??

Holiness and sin both matter— more than we can imagine.

Are they wrong? Are they unnecessarily uptight or narrow-minded? Do these issues really matter? Or are they simply a matter of personal conscience? Do they change with the culture? These are questions I've wrestled with and tried to examine in the light of Scripture.

Something else has haunted me as I've worked on this book. It's the matter of my own heart.

Early in the yearlong process of birthing this book, I began to pray this prayer:

Oh, God,
show me more of Your holiness.
Show me more of my sinfulness.
Help me to hate sin and to love righteousness as You do.
Grant me a deeper conviction of sin
and a more thorough spirit of repentance.
And make me holy as You are holy.

The result is that as I have worked on this book, the Spirit of God has worked on me. As I have grieved over the subtle (and not-so-subtle) ravages of sin among professing believers and the extent to which the church has adopted the world's values, I've had to face the fact that I am often more bothered by others' failures than by my own shortcomings. I tend to minimize or rationalize in my life certain offenses that disturb me when I see them in others.

As I have wrestled with how to communicate the message of holiness, God has gently and graciously exposed unholiness in my own heart—things like lack of self-control in relation to my tongue, my reactions, and my eating and spending habits. I've had to admit that I love myself more than I love others, that I care too much about the impression I make on others and too little about pleasing God, and that I have set up idols (substitutes for God) in my heart.

As I have pondered both what I've heard and seen in others over these months, as well as my own battle with indwelling sin, the message that has reverberated in my heart is that *holiness and sin both matter—*more than we can imagine. They matter to God, and the more we comprehend their true nature, the more they will matter to us.

The message of repentance and holiness needs to be proclaimed, heard, and heeded among God's people in every generation. It must become more than a theological tenet that we politely nod agreement to; it needs to transform the way we think and the way we live.

My goal in writing this book is not to offer a theological treatise on holiness.[2] Rather, my heart is to issue an earnest appeal to God's people—those He calls *saints* or *holy ones*—to pursue holiness.

Believe me when I say that I feel even more unqualified to write a book on holiness now than when I began a year ago (unless being a sinner desperately in need of God's mercy qualifies someone to address this subject). But through this process, my heart has become more tender and my conscience more sensitive; I have been given a clearer vision of Calvary and of the incredible, sanctifying grace of God. I echo the words of the hymn writer:

> *From my smitten heart with tears two wonders I confess:*
> *The wonders of redeeming love and my unworthiness.*[3]

I invite you to join me in a pursuit of radical holiness. You can start right now. Before reading on, would you turn back to that prayer on page 275 and make it your own? One phrase at a time, express to the Lord your desire to have a pure heart.

Then I want to encourage you to pray this prayer at least once a day for the next thirty days. As you make these requests to the Lord from your heart, expect Him to hear and to answer!

True holiness is the pathway to fullness of life and joy. To be holy is to be wholly satisfied with Christ. Above all, it is to reflect the beauty and the splendor of our holy Lord in this dark world. In pursuing holiness, you will fulfill and experience all that God had in mind when He created you.

> *Now may the God of peace himself sanctify you completely, and may your whole spirit and soul and body be kept blameless at the coming of our Lord Jesus Christ. He who calls you is faithful; he will surely do it.*
>
> —1 Thessalonians 5:23–24

Notes

1. *The Life of David Brainerd*, ed. Norman Pettit, *The Works of Jonathan Edwards*, vol. 7 (New Haven, Conn.: Yale Univ. Press, 1985), 186.

2. Many excellent books on holiness have already been written. Those I have found most helpful include: Jerry Bridges' *The Pursuit of Holiness* (NavPress, 1996), J. I. Packer's *Rediscovering Holiness* (Vine Books, 2000), R. C. Sproul's *The Holiness of God* (Tyndale, 2000), and J. C. Ryle's *Holiness* (Evangelical Press, 1985). I urge you to read these and other such books as part of your personal pursuit of holiness.
3. "Beneath the Cross of Jesus," Elizabeth Clephane, 1872.

How little people know who
think that holiness is dull.
When one meets the
real thing . . . it is irresistible.

C. S. Lewis[1]

THE SPLENDOR
of HOLINESS

HOLINESS ISN'T EXACTLY an easy subject to "sell." It's not one of the top ten topics people look for in a Christian bookstore; there aren't a lot of hit songs about holiness; and I can count on two hands the number of messages I recall hearing on the theme.

"Holiness" is discussed in theology classes, but rarely in dinner table conversations. "Holy" is an adjective we apply to "Bible," "Communion," and "the night Christ was born." But how many contemporary Christians are really interested in devoting serious thought or discussion to holiness?

We don't mind talking about holiness as an abstract concept. But if that concept gets too personal or starts to interfere with our lifestyle, we can quickly become uncomfortable.

Part of the problem may be that the word *holiness* has picked up some baggage that most people—understandably—don't find particularly desirable. Does "holiness" conjure up any of these images in your mind?

+ Somber, straitlaced people with outdated hair and clothing styles

+ An austere, joyless lifestyle based on a long list of rules and regulations

+ A monklike existence—"holy" people talk in hushed tones, spend hours a day in prayer, always have their nose in the Bible or a spiritual book, fast frequently, hum hymns under their breath, and have no interest in "normal" life activities

+ People with a judgmental attitude toward those who don't accept their standards

+ An unattainable ideal that has more to do with the sweet by-and-by than the real world, which is right here, right now

Holiness. When you put it that way . . . who wants it?! Sounds about as appealing as drinking saltwater.

Holiness may not be at the top of our list of things to talk about, but let me remind you that those in heaven never stop talking about it! I believe we need to "reclaim" true holiness—to see it in all its beauty, as it is revealed in the Word of God.

"Holiness" is discussed in theology classes, but rarely in dinner table conversations.

I was blessed to grow up in a home where holiness was emphasized and taken seriously, while being presented as something wonderfully desirable and attractive. From earliest childhood, I remember thinking that holiness and joy were inseparably bound to each other.

My dad longed to be "as pure as the driven snow" and challenged us to aspire to the same standard. He was deeply disturbed by sin—whether his own, ours, or others'. At the same time, my dad was a happy man; he actually *enjoyed* his life in Christ.

Prior to his conversion in his midtwenties, he had been a freewheeling gambler in mad pursuit of happiness and thrills. When God reached down and redeemed him, his lifestyle changed dramatically—he no longer desired the earthly "treasures" with which he had been trying to fill the empty places of his heart. Now he had found "the pearl of great price" he had been lacking for so many years. He loved God's law and never considered holiness burdensome—he knew that sin was the real burden, and he never got over the wonder that God had mercifully relieved him of that burden through Christ.

The eighteenth-century theologian Jonathan Edwards was compelled by a similar vision of holiness. In his memoirs, written at the age of thirty-five, he spoke of the fascination and attractiveness that thoughts of holiness held for him.

> It appeared to me, that there was nothing in it but what was ravishingly lovely; the highest beauty and amiableness—a *divine* beauty; far purer than any thing here upon earth; and that every thing else was like mire and defilement in comparison of it.[2]

Likewise, A. W. Tozer saw the need to challenge the misconceptions often associated with holiness.

> What does this word *holiness* really mean? Is it a negative kind of piety from which so many people have shied away?
>
> No, of course not! Holiness in the Bible means moral wholeness—a positive quality which actually includes kindness, mercy, purity, moral blamelessness and godliness. It is always to be thought of in a positive, white intensity of degree.[3]

The beauty of holiness, as it shines forth in the Scripture, is seen in two related but distinct facets.

Set Apart

The word *holy* comes from a root that means "to cut, to separate." It means "to be set apart, to be distinct, to be different."

Throughout the Scripture, we find that God set apart certain things and places and people for Himself; they were consecrated for His use. They were not to be used for common, ordinary, everyday purposes; they were *holy*. For example,

✦ God set apart one day out of the week and called it "a *holy Sab-bath* to the Lord" (Exodus 16:23).

✦ The Israelites were required to set apart the first portion of their income as a *holy tithe* (Leviticus 27:30).

✦ God set apart a particular room where He would meet with His people; He called it "the *holy place*" (Exodus 26:33).

The biblical concept of holiness carries with it a sense of belonging to God.

In the Old Testament, the nation of Israel was set apart by God to be a "holy nation" (Exodus 19:6). That didn't mean their *conduct* was holy or that they were inherently more upright than others who were not set apart. God called them "holy" because He had set them apart from other nations, and with that distinction and privilege came the obligation to live holy lives.

Not only were the Israelites set apart *by* God—they were also set apart *for* God. "I the Lord am holy and have separated you from the peoples, *that you should be mine*," God told His people (Leviticus 20:26). The biblical concept of holiness carries with it a sense of belonging to God, much as a mother might claim, "These children are *mine*."

In the New Testament, God set apart a new body comprised of both Jews and Gentiles. He called it the *church*. The Greek term *ekklesia* means "a called-out assembly." The church is not a building or merely an institution; it is a body of believers who have been called out of this world and set apart for God's holy purposes.

I remember first discovering as a child something of what it meant to be "set apart" for and by God. Based on their understanding of the heart and ways of God, my parents established what they felt to be wise practices and limitations for our family. At times, we would complain, *"But everybody else . . . !"* My parents' response was along these lines: "You don't belong to 'everybody else'—you belong to God!" They convinced us there was something really special about being set apart for

God rather than being squeezed into the world's mold.

I learned early on that to be "set apart" is not a punishment; it is not an attempt on God's part to deprive us or to condemn us to a cheerless, joyless lifestyle. It is a priceless privilege—it is a call

> *God is holy, and holiness is not a option for those who belong to Him.*

✦ to belong, to be cherished, to enter into an intimate love relationship with God Himself, much as a groom declares his intent to set his bride apart from all other women to be his beloved wife

✦ to fit into the grand, eternal plan of our redeeming God for this universe

✦ to experience the exquisite joys and purposes for which we were created

✦ to be freed from all that destroys our true happiness

Morally Clean

The second facet of holiness has to do with being pure, clean, free from sin. In this sense, to be holy is to reflect the moral character of a holy God.

If you've ever tried to wade through the book of Leviticus, you may have found yourself wondering, *Why did God bother to give all those detailed instructions about cleansing and ceremonial purity?*

God intended those regulations to be an object lesson to the children of Israel—and to us. He wants us to understand that He is holy, and that holiness is not an option for those who belong to Him. He wants us to know that He is concerned with every detail and dimension of our lives. He wants us to understand the blessings of holiness and the consequences of unholy living.

When we come to the New Testament, we find that God's standard has not changed. Over and over again, Jesus and the New Testament authors call us to a life of absolute purity:

"You therefore must be perfect, as your heavenly Father is perfect." (Matthew 5:48).

Keep yourself pure. (1 Timothy 5:22)

Awake to righteousness, and do not sin. (1 Corinthians 15:34 NKJV)

Let everyone who names the name of the Lord depart from iniquity. (2 Timothy 2:19)

Abhor what is evil; hold fast to what is good. (Romans 12:9)

Holiness is not just for some select few spiritual giants; it is not just for pious people who sit around all day with nothing to do but "be holy." Holiness is for moms who battle a sense of uselessness and dis-couragement and who are tempted to escape into self-pity, romance novels, or the arms of an attentive man. It is for students who are constantly bombarded with pressure to conform to the world and to indulge in ungodly forms of entertainment. It is for lonely widows, divorceés, and singles who are struggling to stay sexually abstinent. It is for husbands and wives who wrestle with bitterness toward mates who have abused or abandoned them. It is for men who are tempted to cheat on their expense reports or their wives or to abdicate their spiritual leadership in the home.

Grace gives us the desire and the power to be holy.

"*Everyone* who names the name of the Lord" is called to live a holy life!

We're going to explore *how* we can be holy, but it's important to realize that God would not command us to do anything without also enabling us to do it. He knows we cannot possibly be holy apart from Him. That's why He has made provision for us to overcome sin through the cross of Christ. That's why He has sent His Spirit to live in our hearts. And that's why He has given every believer a supernatural resource called *grace* that gives us the *desire* and the *power* to be holy.

The Fruit of Relationship

True holiness is cultivated in the context of a relationship with God. His love for us moves us to reject all lesser loves and all the fleeting delights sin can offer.

As our love for Him grows, we are motivated to aspire to holiness. The fact that He is our Father and we are His beloved children makes us long to be close to Him and compels us to avoid anything that could cause a breach in the relationship.

Yes, holiness involves adherence to a standard, but the obedience God asks of us is not cold, rigid, and dutiful. It is a warm, joyous, loving response to the God who loves us and created us to enjoy intimate fellowship with Him. It is the overflow of a heart that is deeply grateful to have been redeemed by God from sin. It is not something we manufacture by sheer grit, determination, and willpower. It is motivated and enabled by the Holy Spirit who lives within us to make us holy.

Extreme Holiness

The congregation of the Gustaf Adolph Evangelical Lutheran Church, located in a small town in northern Maine, learned just how dangerous a little bit of impurity can be. On Sunday, April 27, 2003, the church council gathered after services to discuss the installation of a new heater. Several in the group stopped by the kitchen to grab a cup of coffee on the way into the meeting. Within hours more than a dozen people were gravely ill, and within days one man had died.

Investigators discovered that a man with a vendetta had dropped a handful of powdered arsenic in the church's coffee urn. No one had noticed the small amount of poison—until its consequences became apparent. Like the bit of leaven that leavens a whole lump of dough, tolerating "just a little sin" in our lives can be deadly.

The makers of Ivory soap pride themselves on their product being "$99\frac{44}{100}$% pure." When it comes to holiness, however, if it's only $99\frac{44}{100}$% pure, it's not pure.

A commitment to be holy is a commitment to be clean through and through—to have no unholy part. True holiness starts on the inside—with our thoughts, attitudes, values, and motives—those innermost parts of our hearts that only God can see. It also affects our outward and visible behavior: "Be holy in *all your conduct*" (1 Peter 1:15).

This passion for purity is what I saw in my dad's example that made holiness so compelling to me as a young person. Of course, he often failed (and was willing to admit it when he did); but he sought to live a life that was morally upright and completely above reproach: in the way he ran his business, used his time, conducted himself with members of the opposite sex, treated family members and employees, talked about other people, responded to his critics, spent his money, and honored the Lord's Day; in his work habits, leisure activities, and entertainment choices—what he read and listened to and watched. He so loved God that he wanted holiness to characterize every area of his life.

He believed, as did Helen Roseveare, a missionary surgeon in (then) Congo, that "there must be nothing, absolutely nothing, in my daily conduct that, copied by another, could lead that one into unholiness."[4]

I have a friend whose ninety- and ninety-two-year-old parents recently moved out of the house where they had lived for fifty years. My friend spent an entire month sorting through a lifetime of their accumulated "stuff"—correspondence, financial data, clippings, photos, and on and on. "It was a complete record of their lives," my friend reflected.

How would you fare if someone were to go through the record of your life?

After poring through the massive collection of memorabilia and paperwork, this son observed with a sense of wonder, *"There was not one single thing in my parents' belongings that was inconsistent with their profession of their relationship with Christ!"*

How would you fare if someone were to go through the record of your life—all your possessions, the books and magazines you've read, your CD and DVD collections, checkbooks, tax returns, journals, daily planners, phone bills, correspondence, past e-mails, a record of all your Internet activity?

What if the person could also review a photographic replay of the choices you've made when you thought no one was watching? Add to that a script of your thought life . . . your attitudes . . . your secret motives.

Does the thought of such "extreme holiness" seem burdensome to you? If so, you may never have considered that *holiness* and *joy* are inseparable companions.

The Joy of Holiness

What words do you associate with "holiness"?

Would *gladness* be one of those words?

Think about it the other way around. When you think of things that make you *glad*, do you think of *holiness*?

Surprising as it may seem, *holiness* and *gladness* really do go hand in hand.

In both the Old and New Testaments we find a wonderful description of the Lord Jesus that makes this connection:

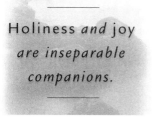

Holiness *and* joy *are inseparable companions.*

> *You have loved righteousness and hated wickedness; therefore God, your God, has anointed you with the oil of gladness beyond your companions.*
>
> —Hebrews 1:9; see Psalm 45:7

We might picture someone who has a passionate love for holiness and an intense hatred for sin as being joyless, uptight, and rigid.

In fact, nothing could be further from the truth. The result of Jesus' holy life was overflowing gladness—gladness surpassing that of anyone else around Him. It was true of Jesus. And it will be true of anyone who, like Jesus, loves righteousness and hates evil.

I remember the first time I heard Calvin Hunt share his story. For years, this young man lived an irresponsible, destructive lifestyle as a crack cocaine addict. Then he encountered the irresistible, transforming grace of Christ. To this day, Calvin exudes irrepressible joy as he testifies of the purifying work of God in his life and then lifts up his powerful tenor voice and sings what has become his trademark song, *"I'm clean! I'm clean! I'm clean!"*

Why do we make holiness out to be some austere obligation or burden to be borne, when the fact is that to be holy is to be clean, to be free from the weight and the burden of sin? Why would we cling to our sin any more than a leper would refuse to part with his oozing sores, given the opportunity to be cleansed of his leprosy?

To pursue holiness is to move toward joy—joy infinitely greater than any earthly delights can offer.

> To be holy is to be clean, to be free from the weight and the burden of sin.

To resist holiness or to be halfhearted about its pursuit is to forfeit true joy and to settle for something less than that God-intoxication for which we were created.

Sooner or later, sin will strip and rob you of everything that is truly beautiful and desirable. If you are a child of God, you were redeemed to enjoy the sweet fruit of holiness—to walk in oneness with your heavenly Father, to relish His presence, to rejoice in His mercy, to know the joy of having clean hands, a pure heart, and a clear conscience, and, one day, to stand before Him unashamed.

Why settle for anything less?

Notes

1. C. S. Lewis, *Letters to an American Lady,* ed. Clyde S. Kilby (Grand Rapids: Eerdmans, 1967), 19.
2. *Memoirs of Jonathan Edwards,* Works of Jonathan Edwards, vol. 1 (Edinburgh: Banner of Truth Trust, rept. 1974), xiv.
3. A. W. Tozer, *I Call It Heresy* (Harrisburg, Pa.: Christian Publications, 1974), 63.
4. Helen Roseveare, *Living Holiness* (Minneapolis: Bethany House, 1986), 173.

The serene beauty of a holy life is the most powerful influence in the world next to the power of God.

———

BLAISE PASCAL[1]

THE MOTIVATION
for HOLINESS

IN SPITE OF ALL THAT I know and believe about the "splendor of holiness," there are moments when I think, *It's so hard to have to "be holy"
all the time! Why can't I just relax and take it easy sometimes?*

Yes, I understand that holiness isn't about sheer human effort and
self-striving. I know it's about depending on God's enabling grace and
letting Jesus live His holy life in and through us.

But be honest—don't you find that it often seems a lot easier to go
with the flow of your natural, fleshly desires than to deny your flesh and
choose the pathway of holiness?

So why swim upstream against the current of your flesh and the culture? Why pay the price to be intentional and vigilant in pursuing holiness—every moment of every day for the rest of your life? Why make the
tough, daily choices that holiness requires:

✦ To get out of bed in the morning and wash your heart in the water
of God's Word before you jump into your "to-do" list?

✦ To turn off that suggestive or crude TV program or to put down that magazine that promotes selfish, worldly values, or that novel that glamorizes sensuality?

✦ To admit you have sinned and seek forgiveness for speaking roughly to that family member or lying to your boss or being critical of that fellow church member?

✦ To say no to every hint of sexual impurity?

✦ To eat and sleep and dress and go to work and play and give and pray and go to church—all for the glory of God?

In this chapter I want to explore seven powerful biblical motivations for holy living—incentives that have been helpful in my personal pursuit of holiness. Above all other reasons, we are to be holy . . .

Because God Is Holy

As a photograph is an image of an object, so our lives are intended to portray the image of God. People are supposed to be able to look at Christians and see what God is like!

My house sits on a hill overlooking a river. This morning, as the sun shone brightly on the trees across the river, the likeness of those trees with their gorgeous fall foliage was magnificently reflected on the still waters below. The mirror image caused me to pause and pray, "Lord, may others see Your likeness reflected in me; may my life reveal to the world how lovely and pure You are!"

This is the motivation for holiness that is stated in the Scripture more frequently and explicitly than any other reason:

> But as he who called you is holy,
> you also be holy in all your conduct,
> since it is written, "You shall be holy, for I am holy."
> —1 Peter 1:15–16

In our everyday life and conduct, we are to reflect what God is like and what it means to belong to Him and to be His redeemed, "set apart" people. Our lives are to *make God believable* to our world. As they see His image in us, they will be moved to worship and glorify Him (Matthew 5:16).

What does your life reflect to those around you? Do your attitudes, words, and behavior give others an accurate picture of God? Or do you sometimes profane His holiness—perhaps by a complaining or controlling spirit, by harsh or angry words, by participating in coarse conversation, or laughing at off-color humor? It saddens me to think of how often I have given others a distorted perception of God through my ungodlike choices and responses.

> *He is the standard for your holiness, and* He is the source *of your holiness.*

Because God is holy, we must be holy. And here's the good news—because God is holy, we *can* be holy. If you are a child of God, the Holy God lives in you. He is the standard for your holiness, and He is the *source* of your holiness— *He* is your righteousness. He can wash your unholy heart with the blood of Jesus and make you clean—so the world will know what He is like.

To be holy as He is holy—what an awesome responsibility. But more than that, what an astounding privilege—that the Holy One should choose us, earthbound, frail, and flawed as we are, that He should cleanse us from our sins, fill us with His Holy Spirit, and then use us to reflect the splendor of His holiness in this dark world.

Here's another motivation to pursue holiness:

Because Holiness Is God's Stated Goal for Every Believer

God's goal in saving you was not just to make your few years on planet Earth easier or more enjoyable. He had an eternal end in view. His intent was to make you holy, as He is holy, that you might perfectly glorify Him, that you might bring Him pleasure, and that you might enjoy intimate fellowship with Him for all eternity.

The apostle Paul reminds us that God "chose us in [Christ] before the foundation of the world, that we should be holy and blameless before Him" (Ephesians 1:4).

Your holiness is not secondary to whatever other goals you may have for your life—it is God's supreme purpose for your life. It is something He desired, planned, and made provision for before He even created the world.

Your holiness is God's supreme purpose for your life.

Not only is it our individual calling to be holy but also it is our collective calling, as the body of Christ. The church is a living organism, indwelt by the Holy Spirit of God and being prepared to be a bride for the Lord Jesus. And the stated intent of our Bridegroom for His bride is that "he might present the church to himself in splendor, without spot or wrinkle or any such thing, that she might be holy and without blemish" (Ephesians 5:27).

As an earthly groom eagerly anticipates the moment when his bride walks down the aisle to meet him, beautifully arrayed in a spotless, white wedding dress, so the Lord Jesus anticipates the day when we will appear before Him, free from all defilement, clothed in His righteousness, to be His holy bride forever.

And as an engaged woman eagerly, lovingly prepares for her wedding, desirous to be her most beautiful for her groom, so the thought of being wedded to our holy Groom should motivate us to spend our lives here on earth in pursuit of the holiness that we know is our ultimate end and His great desire for His bride.

To be holy is our created purpose. It is our destiny. And it will be the outcome for every true child of God and for the entire body of Christ, according to that wonderful promise in 1 John 3:2—"We know that when he appears *we shall be like him,* because we shall see him as he is."

So what is our response to that certainty? "Everyone who has this hope in him purifies himself, just as he is pure" (1 John 3:3 NIV).

When I consider my created purpose and my ultimate destiny—when I remember that I am a splendid, pure bride-in-the-making—I am inspired to be intentional about pursuing holiness, in anticipation of that glorious day when I will finally be holy through and through.

Do you share His goal for your life? What are you living for? From the time you put your feet on the floor in the morning till you pillow your head at night, are you consciously cooperating with Him and pursuing His eternal purpose to make you holy?

Because Jesus *Died* to Deliver Us from Sin

To secure our salvation was no small matter to God. It was (and is) a work of infinite, matchless wonder, sacrifice, and grace. You and I were rebels who spurned God and rejected His right to rule over us. We despised righteousness and cherished our sin. We loved what God hated and hated what He loved. We were sinners—enemies of God and objects of His righteous wrath.

The penalty for our sin was death. Our redemption was costly—it required that a sinless substitute suffer and die in our place. And that is exactly what Jesus did. He took on Himself the full force of the wrath of God, dying in the sinner's place. Why? The Scripture is clear: "Jesus Christ, who gave himself *for our sins* to deliver us from the present evil age" (Galatians 1:3b–4).

In his classic book titled simply *Holiness*, J. C. Ryle writes,

> Surely that man must be in an unhealthy state of soul who can think of all that Jesus suffered, and yet cling to those sins for which that suffering was undergone. It was sin that wove the crown of thorns; it was sin that pierced our Lord's hands and feet and side; it was sin that brought Him to Gethsemane and Calvary, to the cross and to the grave. Cold must our hearts be if we do not hate sin and labour to get rid of it, though we may have to cut off the right hand and pluck out the right eye in doing it.[2]

When we tolerate our sin and refuse to be parted from it, we spurn the love and the grace of Christ; we trample His cross and count His sacrificial death of no value.

Jesus didn't shed His blood so you and I could have a passport to happiness and heaven, while continuing to indulge our lust, anger, and jealousy; our addictions and critical, competitive spirits; our selfishness and pride. His death provides the motivation and the power to say *no* to sin and *yes* to holiness in every area of our lives.

Jesus *died* to make us holy, to deliver us from sin. How, then, can we carelessly or casually continue to sin against such a Savior?

Because We Are Saints

We sometimes hear the word *saint* used to describe someone who is unusually pious or virtuous. Some religious traditions venerate particular individuals who have been officially recognized as "saints."

Yet when the apostle Paul wrote to the New Testament churches, he often began by addressing *all* the believers as "saints" (literally, "holy ones" or "set apart ones").

Are you living like a saint?

Ironically, many of the people to whom Paul was writing were acting like anything *but* saints. They were guilty of many of the same sins we find among believers today—divisiveness, bitterness, immorality, selfishness, a love affair with the world.

So why did Paul call these early believers "saints"? Because that's what they were! Their sinful hearts had been washed by the blood of Jesus. Paul wanted them to see how incongruous their behavior was with their true nature. He was saying to them (and to us) in effect, "Because you *are* saints, *live* as saints!"

When an unbeliever sins, he is doing what comes naturally. He sins because it is his nature to sin—he is a sinner. But when a sinner becomes a child of God, he is born anew; he is set apart from Satan and the world to belong wholly to God—he becomes a saint. He is given a new heart, and the Holy Spirit within him begins the process of transforming him into the very likeness of Christ.

As a "new creation" (2 Corinthians 5:17), he desires fundamentally to please God. When he sins, he denies his new identity and acts contrary to the nature into which he is being transformed.

Therefore, Paul tells the Ephesians,

Among you there must not be even a hint of sexual immorality, or of any kind of impurity, or of greed, because these are improper for God's holy people [saints].

—Ephesians 5:3 NIV

Are you a saint? If you are a child of God, the answer is *yes*. You have been chosen and set apart as one of His holy people.

Are you living like a saint? If you are truly a child of God, the answer will be, *Yes—not perfectly, but that is my heart's desire, and by His grace, I am actively pursuing holiness and growing to be more like the One who has saved me.*

Because Our Intimacy with God Depends on It

Ever since I was born again as a young girl, I have longed to experience a more intimate relationship with God and to enjoy the reality of His presence. The psalmist expressed the same desire when he asked, "Who shall ascend the hill of the Lord? And who shall stand in his holy place?" (Psalm 24:3). His answer ("he who has clean hands and a pure heart"— verse 4) reminds us that only those who have holy hearts and lives can draw near to God.

"Blessed are the pure in heart," Jesus said, "for they shall see God" (Matthew 5:8). Unholy people cannot fellowship with a holy God. I cannot cling to my impatience, gluttony, slothfulness, and moodiness, and have fellowship with God at the same time.

Only those who have holy hearts and lives can draw near to God.

> For what fellowship has righteousness with lawlessness? And what communion has light with darkness?
>
> —2 Corinthians 6:14 NKJV

A teenager who willfully violates his parents' instructions is going to have a hard time looking them in the eye when he gets home that night. A wife who lies to her husband about why she exceeded their credit card limit is not likely to enjoy marital intimacy when the lights are turned out at night.

So sin destroys our fellowship with God. "For you are not a God who delights in wickedness; evil may not dwell with you" (Psalm 5:4).

We can sing praise choruses loudly enough to be heard in the next county, we can join sell-out crowds in cheering for God at concerts and conferences, we can applaud speakers who stir our emotions, we can have mystical spiritual experiences; but none of that will get us one iota closer to God if we are ignoring or cherishing sin in our hearts.

"Who among us can dwell with the consuming fire?" the prophet asked. "He who walks righteously" (Isaiah 33:14–15). Intimacy with God is reserved for those who are holy: "For the Lord is righteous; he loves righteous deeds; the upright shall behold his face" (Psalm 11:7).

Because We Are Going to Live Eternally in a Holy City

If you were moving to another part of the world, you would give careful thought to how you packed for the move. You wouldn't want to be burdened with snowsuits, mittens, and winter boots if you were planning on spending the rest of your life in a tropical paradise.

Our ministry is in the process of relocating to a brand-new headquarters building. In anticipation of the move, our staff members are in the midst of a massive effort to "sort and eliminate." Unnecessary files, obsolete equipment, worn-out furniture, accent pieces that won't fit with the new décor—anything and everything that won't be needed in the new facility is being disposed of.

How much attention and effort are you devoting to preparing for the move to your eternal home?

The fact is, you and I will soon be moving to our eternal home. How much thought have you given to your ultimate destination and to what you need to do to get ready for the move?

Three times in the last two chapters of the Bible, our heavenly home is referred to as "the holy city" (Revelation 21:2, 10; 22:19). The city is holy because it is where our holy God lives and rules. Heaven is a place of indescribable joy and beauty, a place where there will be no sickness or sadness or sorrow. That is because there will be *no sin* in heaven. None. "Nothing unclean will ever enter it" (Revelation 21:27).

How then can we hold on to our sin and think we are ready to go to heaven?

Charles Spurgeon warns,

Dost thou think to go [to heaven] with thine unholiness? God smote an angel down from heaven for sin, and will he let man in with sin in his right hand? God would sooner extinguish heaven than see sin despoil it.[3]

And, as J. C. Ryle points out, those who don't have a heart for holiness can hardly expect to feel comfortable in heaven:

Without holiness on earth we shall never be prepared to enjoy heaven. Heaven is a holy place. The Lord of heaven is a holy Being. The angels are holy creatures. Holiness is written on everything in heaven. . . . How shall we ever be at home and happy in heaven if we die unholy?[4]

In light of the new, holy home God is preparing for us, the apostle Peter says, "Since you are waiting for these, be diligent to be found by him without spot or blemish" (2 Peter 3:14). This world is just a dressing room—a staging area—for eternity. How much attention and effort are you devoting to preparing for the move to your eternal home?

Because the Well-Being of Others Depends on It

Robert Murray McCheyne, the nineteenth-century Scottish preacher, said, "The greatest need of my people is my personal holiness." That applies to more than preachers. The greatest need of your mate, your children, your friends, and fellow workers is not your friendship or your acts of service; it is not your abilities or your financial provision; their greatest need is not even your verbal witness of your faith.

What others most need is to see in you a reflection of what God is like.

What they most need is to see in you a reflection of what God is like and of the transforming power of the gospel. Your life can create hunger and thirst for

God in others' lives and can be a powerful instrument in the hand of the Holy Spirit to draw their hearts to Christ.

On the other hand, your life can cause irreparable damage to others. Adam could not have fathomed how the effects of his sinful choice would reverberate through all of human history: "Many died *through one man's trespass*" (Romans 5:15). So you cannot calculate all the lives that may be turned astray and devastated through what you might consider inconsequential acts of disobedience.

By contrast to Adam's disobedience, the obedience of the Lord Jesus to the will of His Father brought untold blessing to the human race: "*Through one Man's righteous act* the free gift came to all men, resulting in justification of life" (Romans 5:18b NKJV).

Jesus said in His high-priestly prayer, "For their sake I consecrate myself, that they also may be sanctified in truth" (John 17:19).

This verse has often been a source of motivation and challenge to me as I have wrestled with issues of obedience. When I am tempted to secretly indulge my flesh with excessive food or sleep or by watching a video that condones immorality (even if it is an old "black-and-white classic"), to be slack in my work, to be harsh with my words, or to yield to self-centered emotions, it helps me to stop and think about the impact of my life on those who look to me as an example.

It's bad enough for me to make choices that hurt my own relationship with God. How much more serious is it to be the cause of someone else deciding to sin? Not only must I choose the pathway of holiness for God's sake and for my own sake; I must also do it for the sake of others.

Other believers are affected by our choices. And, to a significant degree, *the lost world* determines its view of God based on the lives of those who profess to know Him. A friend once said to me about another believer, "If I was ever to decide not to be a Christian—and I almost did—it would be because of that man." I wonder how many people have been dissuaded from believing in Christ because of something they have seen or experienced from those of us who bear the name of Christ.

Perhaps far more than you imagine, *your children's* personal and spiritual well-being is affected by your obedience to God.

Be careful to obey all these words that I command you, that it may go well with you and with your children after you.
—Deuteronomy 12:28

Parents seldom realize until it's too late how determinative their example is in the lives of their children. Your children see you being warm and gracious with people at church while being rude or irritable with those in your own home. They see you using a radar detector so you can break the law without getting caught. They hear you call in sick to work when they know you're going shopping with a friend. They hear you use language at home that you'd never use in public. They know how you belittle your mate. And they know the only time they ever see you open your Bible at home is when you're preparing your Sunday school lesson.

They know what your moral standards are—not what you've *told* them your standards are, but what they really are. How? Because they know the kinds of videos you rent and what you laugh at on TV and the kinds of books and magazines you bring into your home.

If those kids grow up loving the world and having no hunger for spiritual things, will that be any great surprise? And will you be prepared to give an account for the way your life influenced their choices? In a very real sense, your heart for holiness—or the lack thereof—is shaping the heart and character of the next generation.

It is your created purpose and your ultimate destiny to be holy.

Do you love your sin so much that you are unwilling to relinquish it for the sake of others? Do you care more about indulging your fleshly appetites than about the eternal well-being of those who are following behind you?

Why care about being holy? Why be willing to say *no* to your flesh and *yes* to God, day in and day out? Because the world desperately needs to see what God is like. Because it is your created purpose and your ultimate destiny to be holy. Because of the price Jesus paid to make you holy. Because you are a saint. Because holy people get to see and know God. Because you're getting ready to move to a place where there is no

301

sin. And because your example may inspire someone who is watching you to choose or reject the pathway of holiness.

NOTES

1. Blaise Pascal, quoted in *New Encyclopedia of Christian Quotations*, compiled by Mark Water (Grand Rapids: Baker, 2000), 477.
2. J. C. Ryle, *Holiness: Its Nature, Hindrances, Difficulties, and Roots* (Welwyn, Hertfordshire, England: Evangelical Press, 1985 rept.), 40.
3. *Spurgeon's Expository Encyclopedia: Sermons by Charles H. Spurgeon:* "Holiness Demanded" (Grand Rapids: Baker, 1978), vol. VIII, 465.
4. Ryle, *Holiness,* 42.

Gonna get the Good Lord to forgive a little sin
Get the slate cleaned so he can dirty it again

"God I'm only human, got no other reason . . ."
Sin for a season . . .

STEVE TAYLOR[1]

THE ENEMY
of HOLINESS

FOR MORE THAN a dozen summers, Timothy Treadwell, an avid outdoorsman and "bear specialist," lived peacefully and without weapons among Alaskan grizzlies, living alone with and videotaping the bears. He was known for his confident attitude toward the animals, naming them, and often getting close enough to touch them.

In an appearance on the David Letterman show, Treadwell described the bears as mostly harmless "party animals." Two years later, on October 6, 2003, Treadwell and his girlfriend's bodies were discovered after they were fatally mauled in a bear attack in Katmai National Park on the Alaska Peninsula.

The lesson was all too obvious—wild animals can't be "reformed." Regardless of how comfortable or trusting you may become around them, sooner or later they will act according to their nature. To assume otherwise is to flirt with disaster.

A healthy fear and respect keeps most people from getting cozy with wild beasts. So what makes us think we can get close to a far more deadly beast called *sin*—and survive? Subconsciously perhaps, we tend to think of certain sins as "mostly harmless"—especially if we've played with them for years and never been seriously bitten.

What makes all sin so heinous and grievous is that it is against God.

I'm reminded of a story a friend told me about a church service he attended recently in which a lay leader stood before the congregation and confessed, "I've become comfortable with a certain level of sin in my life."

This church member hadn't committed adultery or embezzled money from the church. He had simply done what most of us have done—he had become desensitized to the sinfulness of sin and had come to accept its presence in his life in "tolerable" doses.

I believe our perspective on sin will be changed as we take a serious look at its nature and its consequences.

What Is Sin?

If you grew up in the church as I did, you probably learned early on that the essence of sin is breaking God's law. One systematic theology textbook, for example, says: "Sin is any failure to conform to the moral law of God in act, attitude, or nature."[2]

The primary Hebrew word used for "sin" in the Old Testament means "to miss the mark." Other words used to describe sin indicate man's failure to measure up to a divine standard or expectation.

This legal or judicial definition of sin is important and helpful. However, in recent years, I've been struck by the realization that sin is not merely an objective "missing of the mark" or "lack of conformity" to an impersonal standard. Sin is also intensely personal and has profound relational implications. What makes all sin so heinous and grievous is that it is *against God*.

Yes, sin harms others, and yes, there are consequences for those who sin. But above all, sin is against God, for it violates His holy law and character.

Joseph refused to fall prey to the advances of his boss's wife, because he recognized that if he yielded, he would not merely be wronging the woman and her husband; he would not just violate his own conscience and tarnish his own reputation. He was restrained by the knowledge that his sin would be against God: "How then can I do this great wickedness and sin against God?" (Genesis 39:9). That is what makes adultery—and every other sin—"great wickedness."

You and I will never experience appropriate grief and brokenness over our sin until we come to see that our sin is against God.

Spiritual Adultery

The reason adultery is so devastating to a marriage is that it is a breach of a covenant; it is a violation of a relationship; it rips apart what God has joined together.

In Scripture, when God wants to communicate the nature and the seriousness of sin, He often chooses imagery related to marital unfaithfulness and sexual sin—strong words like adultery, prostitution, lewdness, harlotry, and whoredom.

> You have played the whore with many lovers;
> and would you return to me?
> declares the Lord. . . .
>
> You have polluted the land
> with your vile whoredom . . .
> yet . . . you refuse to be ashamed.
> —Jeremiah 3:1–3

Throughout Scripture, God is seen as a faithful, devoted Husband who is intensely jealous for an exclusive relationship with His wife. When His bride is unfaithful, God is pictured as a rejected Lover who has been grievously wronged; He is provoked to righteous anger and grief when a rival lover enters the relationship.

The next time you sin, picture your husband locked in a passionate embrace with a woman he met over the Internet. Think of your father leaving your mother after thirty-five years of marriage and sleeping with a co-worker. Imagine your son-in-law, who you thought loved your daughter, secretly sleeping with prostitutes while away on business trips.

Try to feel the intensity of the shock, the rejection, the pain, the anger that would well up from the innermost part of your being upon discovering the truth.

Then realize that what you would experience would be just a minuscule glimpse of the way God feels about our sin.

Now, imagine your mate walking in the door and saying in a casual tone of voice, "By the way, honey, I've been carrying on a little affair with that gal who works down the hall from me. Nothing serious, really —just a fling. OK, I'll admit we've slept together—but probably not more than six or seven times. I want you to know that I still love you, and I really hope you'll stay with me and keep meeting my needs."

Worse yet, imagine how you would feel if your mate refused to break off the illicit relationship, but continued to sleep with his girlfriend once or twice a week, month after month, year after year, all the while insisting that he really loved you and wanted to keep living with you when he wasn't with her.

How long would it take for you to say, "No! You can't have her and me! You've got to make a choice."

As heartbreaking and revolting as such scenarios are for those who have experienced them, they give us an inkling of what we are doing to our heavenly Husband when we persist in "sleeping" with our sin, while claiming to be committed to our relationship with Him.

Some time ago, I found myself with a deeply distraught friend who had recently learned that her husband had been unfaithful to her. At one point, she collapsed on the floor next to my feet and began to sob uncontrollably. As I knelt beside her and began to weep with her, she said, with deep emotion, "I never imagined I could ever hurt so deeply or feel so rejected!"

To say yes to sin is to fall into the embrace of a paramour.

For perhaps twenty minutes, this devastated woman just cried and cried and cried, grieving over the breach in the intimate, exclusive relationship she had once shared with her husband.

As I held my friend in my arms, I had a whole new sense of what our sin and unfaithfulness does to God. I hope never to forget that picture.

Somehow, the evangelical world has managed to redefine sin; we have come to view it as normal, acceptable behavior—something perhaps to be tamed or controlled, but not to be eradicated and put to death.

We have sunk to such lows that we can not only sin thoughtlessly, but, astonishingly, we can even laugh at sin and be entertained by it. I have heard virtually every conceivable kind of sin rationalized by professing Christians, including some in full-time Christian service.

I wonder if we could be so cavalier about sin if we had any comprehension of how God views it. Our sin breaks the heart of our Lover-God who created us and redeemed us for Himself. To say yes to sin is to fall into the embrace of a paramour. It is to bring a rival into a sacred love relationship.

What Are the Effects of Sin?

Beyond how sin affects a holy God and how it affects others, it also exacts a price from those who sin. As surely as the wild animals Timothy Treadwell had come to trust rose up to attack him, so sin will make a prey of those who indulge it. *Before* you yield to temptation the next time, try reminding yourself of these consequences:

Sin will disappoint you. Sin never pays what it promises. Without a doubt, sin does yield pleasure, but—and here's what we need to remember in the flush of temptation—those "joys" are "fleeting pleasures" (Hebrews 11:25).

> *The more ground you concede to sin, the more you dull your capacity for truth.*

We've all known what it is to sinfully indulge our flesh in the hopes of feeling better, finding relief, getting an emotional thrill, or satisfying some inner longing. But do you look back now and say, "WOW! That was sure worth it!" Doubtful. If you're honest, you'd probably have to say, "Whatever gain I derived from that choice was short-lived. And it sure wasn't worth the price I paid to get it."

Sinful pleasures just don't last. Once the initial "rush" wears off, the enjoyment inevitably turns to emptiness, misery, and shame.

Sin will deceive you. The more ground you concede to sin, the more you dull your capacity for truth. As your conscience is violated, you gradually lose your moral compass—your ability to discern right from wrong. You start to think black is white and down is up. You become blind to the seriousness and extent of your sin.

When others try to point out those blind spots, rather than humbling yourself and admitting your fault, you defend yourself or insist you've been misjudged. You begin to think you can get by with sinning, that somehow you can be an exception to the rule, and that you will escape sin's consequences.

Sin will lead you step-by-step through incremental compromises, all the while convincing you that you can handle this, that you're not so bad. *Sin will dominate you.* Sin lures us with the illusion that it is the doorway to freedom. The truth is that those who dance with sin ultimately become sin's slaves.

> *The iniquities of the wicked ensnare him,*
> *and he is held fast in the cords of his sin.*
> —Proverbs 5:22

Peter speaks of ungodly, false teachers (masquerading as just the opposite) who entice their hearers to sin: "They promise them freedom, but they themselves are slaves of corruption. For whatever overcomes a person, to that he is enslaved" (2 Peter 2:19).

What kind of freedom is it to be under the control of sinful cravings? To feel compelled to yield every time your fleshly appetites demand to be fed? To come running every time the urge to indulge your flesh rings your bell?

Every unconfessed sin is a seed that will produce a multiplied harvest.

Our culture has promoted a "double the pleasure, none of the guilt" sort of lifestyle. And what's the result? We have become a compulsive, highly addicted society. We are *slaves*—slaves to sex, lust, food, entertainment, games, recreation, work, toys, noise, activity, alcohol, drugs, busyness, therapy, and on and on. We have become dominated by the very "pleasures" we thought would liberate us.

Sin will destroy you. In October 2003, raging fires devastated massive portions of southern California, consuming more than 750,000 acres, destroying more than 3,600 homes, and claiming twenty-two lives.

Ken Hale, a state Forestry Department division chief, was one of many heroic firefighters who labored tirelessly to control the fires. After being on the fire line for fifty-five hours, Hale spoke of how his perspective changed when he saw the killer-nature of the fires: "As soon as I found out people had died, it changes the entire outlook on the fire. It goes from being an adversary, a worthy adversary, to something that's very deadly, a monster."[3]

Most of us have become so familiar with sin that we no longer see it as a deadly monster. Sin is more dangerous than wild bears, more deadly than blazing forest fires. Ask Nebuchadnezzar, who lost his mind because he refused to deal with his pride. Ask Samson, who was reduced to a pathetic shred of a man because he never got control over the lusts of his flesh. Ask Achan and Ananias and Sapphira, who all lost their lives over "small," secret sins.

It's not just the "serious sins" your neighbor or your co-worker commits that are deadly; your "subtle sins" can be just as destructive. You may never get in bed with someone else's mate; but your heart for God may be just as easily destroyed by allowing the fires of jealousy, anger, self-pity, worry, or gluttony to go unchecked in your life.

J. C. Ryle cautions against being naive about sin's influence, and urges us to see sin for the destructive monster it really is.

I fear we do not sufficiently realize the extreme subtlety of our soul's disease. We are too apt to forget that temptation to sin will rarely present itself to us in its true colours, saying, "I am your deadly enemy and I want to ruin you for ever in hell." Oh, no! Sin comes to us, like Judas, with a kiss, and like Joab, with an outstretched hand and flattering words. The forbidden fruit seemed good and desirable to Eve, yet it cast her out of Eden. The walking idly on his palace roof seemed harmless enough to David, yet it ended in adultery and murder. Sin rarely seems sin at its first beginnings. . . . We may give wickedness smooth names, but we cannot alter its nature and character in the sight of God.[4]

Are you content to maintain a "certain level of sin" in your life, as long as you can tame and manage it? Mark it down: *There is no such thing as a small sin.* Every unconfessed sin is a seed that will produce a multiplied harvest. As Charles Spurgeon warned, "Those who tolerate sin in what they think to be little things, will soon indulge it in greater matters."[5]

The moral or spiritual landslides that take us by surprise most often occur because we have paid little or no attention to the cracks and fissures in our walk with God and our moral conduct. Seemingly small, "harmless" compromises snowball and set the stage for tragic consequences.

Sexual sin is the tip of the iceberg that emerges after a host of under-the-surface sins (lust and lying, for example) have been excused or over-looked—both by the guilty party *and*, far too often, by other believers who shy away from confronting sinful practices they observe, for fear of seeming judgmental or intolerant.

I recall a meeting some friends and I had with a man who had been in the throes of an adulterous relationship for some time. As we asked questions and appealed to him to return to God and his family, it be-came apparent that this man hadn't awakened one morning and decided to devastate his wife and children and lose his job by having an affair. The fact was, for years he had allowed sins such as bitterness, anger, and pride to fester in his spirit. Then, to medicate his "wounded heart," he justified "small" moral compromises, which led to greater compromises and more justification and deceit. Ultimately, he ended up in the vise-like grip of a powerful sexual addiction.

As we listened to him talk, I could hardly believe the toll sin had taken in the life of this man who had once been a faithful, loving hus-band and dad. He had become hard, bitter, and disoriented—a poster child for the consequences of sin.

He was miserable—sin had not brought him the happiness it prom-ised. His thinking was profoundly twisted and deceived; he was hopelessly trapped (apart from the grace of God, which he was unwilling to appropriate at that point), and he was in the process of self-destructing. Yet he was so attached to his sin that he was willing to live with its consequences rather than reject the sin.

When he initiated the affair, he had no idea where it would lead him. He said, "I figured when I got caught, I'd dump the relationship and go back to my family." Then he said, "What I didn't count on was that I wouldn't be *able* to get out of it." Satan threw out the bait; this man swallowed it, thinking he'd enjoy it for a while, only to discover that he was ensnared.

As I listened to his story, I found myself thinking, *It's just not worth it! It's not worth it to cling to one single sin. Oh, Lord, please don't let me ever bring reproach to Your name by failing to take sin seriously.*

Facing Our Own Sinfulness

Most people reading a book like this are not in the midst of an affair (though some, no doubt, are playing with fire). But "good" people who have never committed adultery may have a harder time recognizing their own sinfulness. Growing up as I did in the evangelical world, trained to "live right," and immersed in Bible study, church, and Christian friends and activities, one of my greatest personal struggles has been to see myself as a *sinner* and to see *my* sin as truly detestable.

I can attest that when we cease to sense the seriousness of our sin, we also cease to be moved by the wonder of Christ's sacrifice on the cross for sin. Our hearts get dry and crusty—we know that, we've heard that, ho-hum, same-old, so what? We'd never say those words, of course—but truth be told, I know all too well what it's like to hear one more sermon about God's amazing grace, sing one more song about the wondrous cross, go through one more Communion service, sit through one more Passion play—and be strangely unstirred by the whole thing.

As I have worked on this book, the Lord has graciously given me a greater sense of the sinfulness of my sin. I recall one particular evening when I was struck with the image of my sin as spiritual adultery against God; I was overcome with what it cost Him to forgive sins I had committed so casually and hadn't seen to be a "big deal." In the light of His holy presence, sins I had minimized or thought I could "manage" seemed monstrous. I was faced with my depraved heart in a way I had not seen it for far too long.

In that moment, God granted me the gift of brokenness and repentance; I began to sob, feeling myself to be a sinner desperately in need of God's mercy, and crying out to be freshly washed with the blood of Jesus.

As I reflected on that tender time of contrition and confession, I had an overwhelming sense of gratitude and wonder—I could hardly believe that He would be so merciful to *me*. I also had to admit that, though I could think of occasions when I had wept over the sins of others, I could not remember the last time I had wept over *my* sin.

I'm not suggesting that God intends for His children to live under the weight of sin that has been confessed, or that we should seek gut-wrenching, emotional experiences. But I am convinced that periodically every believer needs to be given a fresh glimpse of the corruption of indwelling sin, apart from which the mercy, the grace, and the cross of Christ cease to be precious in our eyes.

Returning and Restoration

The prophet Hosea knew firsthand the rejection of being betrayed by an adulterous mate. His painful experience became an object lesson to show God's people how He viewed their sin. In the final chapter, Hosea pleads with the people to acknowledge their sin and to choose the pathway of repentance:

> *Return, O Israel, to the Lord your God.*
> *Your sins have been your downfall!*
> *Take words with you*
> *and return to the Lord.*
> *Say to him:*
> *"Forgive all our sins*
> *and receive us graciously."*
> —Hosea 14:1–2 NIV

Do you need to return to God? Have you become comfortable with "a certain level of sin" in your life? Is God opening your eyes to see the seriousness of your sin before Him? Perhaps you hardly dare to believe that He would receive you. Perhaps you feel you just can't face what you've done.

God's response to His people infuses us with hope. It reveals Him to be a God of amazing, infinite mercy and forgiveness—a Redeemer and Restorer who is willing and able to make all things new for those who truly repent:

> *I will heal their waywardness*
> *and love them freely,*
> *for my anger has turned away from them.*
> *I will be like the dew to Israel;*
> *he will blossom like a lily. . . .*
> *His splendor will be like an olive tree,*
> *his fragrance like a cedar of Lebanon.*
> *Men will dwell again in his shade.*
> *He will flourish like the grain.*
> —Hosea 14:4–7 NIV

Dear friend, believe it, repent, and be restored!

NOTES

1. Steve Taylor, "Sin for a Season." © Birdwing Music/BMG Songs/ C.A. Music. All rights reserved. Used by permission.
2. Wayne Grudem, *Systematic Theology* (Grand Rapids: Zondervan, 1994), 490.
3. Seth Hettena, "Two Huge California Fires Threaten to Merge," Yahoo.com news story, 28 October 2003.
4. J. C. Ryle, *Holiness: Its Nature, Hindrances, Difficulties, and Roots* (Welwyn, Hertfordshire, England: Evangelical Press, 1985 rept.), 7.
5. Charles H. Spurgeon, *1000 Devotional Thoughts* (Grand Rapids: Baker, 1976), nos. 404, 204.

*The more my heart is
taken up with Christ,
the more do I enjoy practical
deliverance from sin's power.*

———————

H. A. IRONSIDE[1]

THE FACE
of HOLINESS

IF YOU'VE BEEN A CHRISTIAN for any length of time, you have probably struggled with thoughts like those expressed by this discouraged believer:

> I hated myself; I hated my sin. . . . I felt that there was nothing I so much desired in this world [as holiness], nothing I so much needed. But so far from in any measure attaining it, the more I pursued and strove after it, the more it eluded my grasp; till hope itself almost died out. . . .
>
> I cannot tell you how I am buffeted sometimes by temptation. I never knew how bad a heart I had. . . . Often I am tempted to think that one so full of sin cannot be a child of God at all.[2]

Would it surprise you to learn that these anguished words flowed from the pen of one of the most revered heroes in the history of the Christian church?

J. Hudson Taylor, nineteenth-century pioneer missionary to China, was renowned as a man of extraordinary faith, sacrifice, prayer, and devotion. When he wrote these words, Taylor was the leader of a thriving mission enterprise.

For several months, he had carried a burden for greater holiness in the mission and in his own life. He later wrote of that period:

> I prayed, agonised, fasted, strove, made resolutions, read the Word more diligently . . . but all was without effect. Every day, almost every hour, the consciousness of sin oppressed me.[3]

In the fall of 1869, Hudson Taylor found himself at a crisis point. The pressure of circumstances had been building up for months. He had experienced a bout with serious illness, the unbearably hot climate, the stresses associated with overseeing a large and growing ministry, endless demands on his time, and extensive travel under primitive conditions in the interior of China. He found himself with frayed nerves, irritable, prone to harshness, and unable to live the life of holiness he so longed to exhibit.

From start to finish, the pathway of holiness is a life of faith.

From his tormented heart, he asked a question you may have asked on occasion, as have I: *"Is there no rescue? Must it be thus to the end—constant conflict and, instead of victory, too often defeat?"*[4]

Still in turmoil, he returned home from a trip to find a letter from a fellow missionary named John McCarthy, who had recently encountered Christ in a new way. His testimony included a quote from a book called *Christ Is All:* "The Lord Jesus received is holiness begun; the Lord Jesus cherished is holiness advancing; the Lord Jesus *counted upon as never absent* would be holiness complete."[5]

McCarthy went on to describe the radical difference this message was making in his life:

> Abiding, not striving nor struggling; looking off unto Him; trusting Him for present power; trusting Him to subdue all inward

corruption; resting in the love of an almighty Saviour; . . . this is not new, and yet 'tis *new to me*. I feel as though the first dawning of a glorious day had risen upon me.[6]

As Taylor read McCarthy's letter, he was given a new look at Christ. That look proved to be transformational.

Six weeks later, Taylor received a letter from his sister in England. She poured out her heart about the pressures she was undergoing as a mother with a growing family and the frustration she was experiencing in her own walk with God. In his reply, Taylor eagerly shared with his troubled sister what God had so freshly done in his life:

As I read [McCarthy's letter] I saw it all! . . . I looked to Jesus and saw (and when I saw, oh, how joy flowed!) that He had said, "*I* will never leave *you*." "Ah, *there* is rest!" I thought. . . .

I saw not only that Jesus would never leave me, but that I was a member of His body, of His flesh and of His bones. . . . Oh, the joy of seeing this truth! . . . It is a wonderful thing to be really one with a risen and exalted Saviour; to be a member of Christ! Think what it involves. Can Christ be rich and I poor? Can your right hand be rich and the left poor? or your head be well fed while your body starves? . . .

All this springs from the believer's oneness with Christ. And since Christ has thus dwelt in my heart by faith, how happy I have been![7]

Practice the Look That Transforms

From start to finish, the pathway of holiness is a life of faith—faith in the person, the work, and the gospel of Christ. We were justified—declared righteous—by faith in the atoning work of Christ on our behalf. And we are sanctified—progressively made righteous in our practice—not by our own efforts, but through faith in His sanctifying grace.

In looking to Jesus, Hudson Taylor discovered the power to live a holy life. He wrote to his sister, "I am as capable of sinning as ever, but

Christ is realised as present as never before. He cannot sin; and He can keep me from sinning."[8]

Jesus can keep you and me from sinning. And when we do sin, it is He who will cleanse and pardon us. Through the cross of Christ, God has made provision for every sin we could possibly commit. His grace is infinitely more powerful than any sinful bondage.

> *As we look upon Him, we are changed into His image.*

As Charles Spurgeon says so eloquently, such a Savior is a sinner's only hope:

Though you have struggled in vain against your evil habits, though you have wrestled with them sternly, and resolved, and re-resolved, only to be defeated by your giant sins and your terrible passions, there is One who can conquer all your sins for you. There is One who is stronger than Hercules, who can strangle the hydra of your lust, kill the lion of your passions, and cleanse the Augean stable of your evil nature by turning the great rivers of blood and water of his atoning sacrifice right through your soul. He can make and keep you pure within. Oh, look to him![9]

There is something powerful about fixing our eyes on Jesus as we seek to be holy. The apostle Paul put it this way:

We all, with unveiled face, beholding the glory of the Lord, are being transformed into the same image from one degree of glory to another. For this comes from the Lord who is the Spirit.
—2 Corinthians 3:18

As we look upon Him, we are changed into His image. At the moment, our ability to behold the Savior is limited, because we are in these finite bodies and still have to contend with our corrupt flesh. But one day, totally freed from sin, we will be able to see Christ clearly, as He is. Seeing Him, we will adore Him fully and will be drawn to become like Him. In that moment, our transformation into His likeness will be complete.

*Beloved, we are God's children now, and what we will be has not
yet appeared; but we know that when [Christ] appears we shall be
like him, because we shall see him as he is.*

—1 John 3:2

The longing of my heart—and the longing of every follower of
Christ—is to be like Him. That transformation is not something we can
produce on our own, apart from the power of His indwelling Holy Spirit.
Like Hudson Taylor, you may have been striving and struggling to be
more holy. The Lord Jesus invites you to cease your striving, to come to
Him, and to find rest for your soul. As you meditate on His magnificence and follow in His footsteps, He will bring about in you a marvelous transformation that will be completed when you finally see Him
face-to-face.

Keep Your Eyes on the Picture

I enjoy working on jigsaw puzzles. When I first open the box, however,
it's hard to believe there's actually a picture in all those odd-shaped
pieces. As I assemble the puzzle, I keep looking at the picture on the
box. It shows me what the puzzle is supposed to look like when it's finished. Without that picture, I'd be lost.

As we look at the jumbled pieces of our lives, sometimes it's hard to
fathom that they could ever form anything attractive. God has given us
a picture that shows what we will look like when He has finished His
sanctifying, transforming work in our lives. It's a picture of Jesus. In
Christ we see a perfect reflection of our holy God, for "he is the radi-
ance of the glory of God and the exact imprint of his nature" (Hebrews
1:3). He is the pattern for our lives.

We need to be constantly reminded what the finished product is
supposed to look like. That's why it's vital that we keep looking at the
picture throughout the assembly process.

Jesus is holiness with a face. To be holy is to be like Him. Let's take a
closer look at this portrait of holiness in human flesh. As we do, ask yourself how your life compares to Jesus in each of these traits. The answer
will help you identify where you are in the process of becoming holy.

Look at Jesus—
Portrait of Holiness

HIS RELATIONSHIP WITH HIS FATHER

✦ He lived a life of total dependence on His Father. He looked to God to supply His needs, to provide direction for His life and ministry, and to enable Him to fulfill His purpose on earth.

✦ He was fully surrendered to the will of His Father. He loved the law of God and obeyed it continually.

✦ He lived to please God rather than men. He was willing to forfeit the approval of men in order to be pleasing to God.

HIS VALUES AND PRIORITIES

✦ His supreme motivation was to glorify God. He came to earth with no agenda of His own but to fulfill God's purposes and will on the earth.

✦ He exalted the eternal over the temporal. For example, doing the will of God was more important to Him than eating (John 4:31–34).

HIS RELATIONSHIP WITH OTHERS

✦ He was selfless and put others ahead of Himself. He had a servant's heart and continually gave of Himself to meet the needs of others.

✦ He was available to those who needed Him, even when they interrupted Him at inconvenient times—e.g., when He was tired (John 4:6–7), late at night (John 3:2), when He had planned a "retreat" with His friends (Mark 6:31–34), or during His quiet time (Mark 1:35–39).

✦ He was submissive to human authorities. As a young man He placed Himself under the authority of His mother and Joseph; He taught and practiced respect and submission to civil authorities.

✦ He was merciful and extended forgiveness to those who wronged Him.

HIS WORDS

✦ He spoke only the words His Father told Him to speak. As a result, His words came across with authority and impact.

✦ He always spoke the truth.

✦ He spoke gracious words that ministered to the needs of the hearers.

HIS CHARACTER

✦ He lived a life of praise and thankfulness.

✦ He was bold when people needed to be confronted with wrongdoing; He was courageous when the will of God required Him to do something difficult.

✦ He was not competitive or jealous. He rejoiced when God blessed others or chose to use other instruments (e.g., John the Baptist).

✦ He was filled with the Holy Spirit and manifested the fruit of the Spirit at all times:

⇨ *Love.* He loved God with all His heart. He loved others selflessly and sacrificially, to the point of being willing to lay down His life for His enemies. He demonstrated all the qualities of love found in 1 Corinthians 13:4–8.

⇨ *Joy.* He was full of joy in the Lord. His joy was independent of circumstances, because He trusted God's sovereign control in all things.

⇨ *Peace.* He was calm and peaceful in the midst of storms, in the press of the crowd, and when facing the cross (John 14:27). He had an inner quiet that surpassed human understanding.

⇨ *Patience.* He was long-suffering; He willingly endured adverse circumstances as well as injuries inflicted by others.

⇨ *Kindness.* He demonstrated genuine concern for others. He was particularly attentive to people who had been rejected by others. He was thoughtful, considerate, and alert to the needs of others.

⇨ *Goodness.* His inner moral excellence manifested itself in active good works toward others. "He went about doing good" (Acts 10:38).

⇨ *Faithfulness.* He was utterly trustworthy and always true to the will of God. He obeyed, served, and loved God faithfully, all the way to the cross.

⇨ *Meekness.* He endured misunderstanding and abuse without retaliating. He responded meekly to provocation; He was not defensive, but entrusted Himself and His case to God. He was humble—He refused to promote Himself or to seek His own glory.

⇨ *Self-control.* He was temperate; His natural passions and appetites were always under the control of the Holy Spirit.

The call to holiness is a call to follow Christ. A pursuit of holiness that is not Christ-centered will soon be reduced to moralism, pharisaical self-righteousness, and futile self-effort. Such pseudo-holiness leads to bondage, rather than liberty; it is unattractive to the world and unacceptable to God. Only by fixing our eyes and our hope on Christ can we experience that authentic, warm, inviting holiness that He alone can produce in us.

To be holy is to appropriate His holiness as our own. As Oswald Chambers reminds us,

The one marvellous secret of a holy life lies not in imitating Jesus, but in letting the perfections of Jesus manifest themselves in my mortal flesh. Sanctification is "Christ in you." . . . Sanctification is not drawing from Jesus the power to be holy; it is drawing from Jesus the holiness that was manifested in Him, and He manifests it in me.[10]

No amount of striving or self-effort can make us holy. Only Christ can do that. As we turn our eyes upon Him, we will find Him to be our "priceless treasure, source of purest pleasure."[11] We will begin to desire Him—His beauty, His righteousness—more than we desire the sparkling enticements this world has to offer. And we will be transformed into His likeness.

NOTES

1. H. A. Ironside, *Holiness: The False and the True* (Neptune, N.J.: Loizeaux Brothers, 1980), 33.
2. Dr. and Mrs. Howard Taylor, *Hudson Taylor and the China Inland Mission* (Edinburgh: R & R Clark, 1918), 174, 166–67.
3. Ibid., 174.
4. Ibid.
5. Ibid., 168.
6. Ibid., 169.
7. Ibid., 175–76.
8. Ibid., 177.
9. *Spurgeon at His Best*, compiled by Tom Carter (Grand Rapids: Baker, 1988), 101.
10. Oswald Chambers, *My Utmost for His Highest,* July 23.
11. "Jesus, Priceless Treasure," words by Johann Franck, translated from German into English by Catherine Winkworth.

*Be killing sin or
it will be killing you.*

———————

J O H N   O W E N [1]

The Pathway to Holiness:
"PUT OFF"—SAY "NO"
to CORRUPTION

IN PATRICIA ST. JOHN'S NOVEL *Star of Light,* a British missionary nurse reaches out to an eleven-year-old Moroccan beggar named Hamid. Night after night, she welcomes him and other beggar children into her home for dinner and a warm place by the fire. One evening after dinner, Hamid impulsively steals two eggs from the kind woman's kitchen, just before he and the nurse go out into the cold, rainy night to visit another needy child. The woman takes a torch to light their way on the dark street. However,

> To the nurse's surprise Hamid did not wish to walk in the light. He seemed to be taking great care to keep out of the beam, slinking along the gutters, shuffling against the wall. It was very dark and very muddy, and once or twice he slipped a little, clutching his precious eggs tightly in both hands. . . .
>
> He was not enjoying himself at all. He was so afraid of that broad beam of light, and the eggs somehow did not seem worth

it. He wished he could get rid of them, and yet at the same time
he wanted to hold on to them.[2]

As is so often the case with us, Hamid was torn between his desire
to do what was right and his desire to hold onto his sin, even though it
was making him miserable.

A letter I received from a disheartened woman illustrates the struggle every Christian experiences at times between fleshly desires and the
indwelling Spirit of God.

> I've been a Christian for thirty years and am actively involved in
> my church and Bible study. I keep wondering why my sin nature
> is the "path of least resistance." A sinful mind-set (worry, anger,
> doubt) seems to be my "default" mode—unless I'm making an
> effort, it's where my thoughts seem to go. It seems like as a new
> creation in Christ, it wouldn't be such a struggle.

I think deep down we'd like to find a pathway to sanctification that
is instant and effortless—no long process, no hard battle. The fact is,
there is no such thing.

According to Hebrews 12:14, the pathway of holiness requires intensity and intentionality. Various translations help us understand the
force of this exhortation.

> *"Make every effort . . . to be holy"* (NIV).
> *"Strive for . . . holiness"* (ESV).
> *"Pursue . . . holiness"* (NKJV).

**Holiness requires
intensity and
intentionality.**

Or, as Kenneth Wuest translates it: *Constantly
be eagerly seeking after . . . holiness.*[3]

In other words, we must make it our constant,
conscious ambition and aim to be holy. We have
to work at it, concentrate on it, as an athlete sets
his sights on winning an Olympic gold medal: He
focuses on his objective, he trains and strains to

achieve his goal, he sacrifices for it, he endures pain for it, and he puts aside other pursuits for the sake of a higher pursuit.

Weed Control

When it comes to our responsibility in the matter of sanctification, Scripture describes a twofold process that involves "putting off" and "putting on." As children of God in pursuit of holiness, we must "put off" our old, corrupt, sinful way of life and everything that might fuel its growth. And we must consciously "put on" the holy life that is ours through Christ.

These two sides of the coin of holiness often appear within the same passage:

> *Flee* [put off] *youthful passions and pursue* [put on] *righteousness, faith, love, and peace.*
>
> —2 Timothy 2:22

> *Put away* [put off] *all filthiness and rampant wickedness and receive with meekness* [put on] *the implanted word, which is able to save your souls.*
>
> —James 1:21

Another word for "putting off" is *mortification*. It comes from a Latin word that means "to kill" or "to put to death." In a spiritual sense, it relates to how we deal with sin. It indicates that there is a struggle—a battle—involved in dealing with sin and that determined, decisive action is required. It speaks of putting the ax to the root of our sinful inclinations and desires. It implies intolerance for anything in our lives that is contrary to the holiness of God.

Every gardener knows what a constant challenge it is to contend with weeds that keep poking their way through the soil. Those weeds have to be "mortified"—put to death, pulled out by the roots.

Holiness and sin cannot both thrive in our lives. One or the other must die. If we allow weeds of sin to grow up unchecked in our hearts and minds and behavior, the holy life of Christ within us will be choked out.

Mortification involves more than getting rid of things that are inherently sinful. It also suggests the willingness to eliminate influences that may not be sinful in and of themselves, but that could fuel unholy thoughts or behavior and thereby lead us into sin. It means cutting off every possible means to sin.

Some years ago, I discovered that the television had become a weed that was choking out holiness in my life. It was dulling my spiritual sensitivity and diminishing my love and longing for God. Slowly, subtly, the world was stealing my affection, altering my appetites, and seeping into the pores of my being. I found myself being entertained by behavior, speech, attitudes, and philosophies that the world (and many Christians!) would consider acceptable, but that I knew were unholy.

The longer I held on to and justified my viewing habits, the less motivated I was to change. In my heart, I knew that my spiritual life would be better off without the TV. But for many months, though the Spirit was tugging at my heart, I resisted doing anything about it.

One day I finally said, *"Yes, Lord."* I agreed to mortify my flesh—to take decisive action against that which was competing with righteousness in my life. For me, that meant making a commitment not to watch TV anytime I am alone. Almost immediately, my love for God was rekindled, my desire for holiness was renewed, and my spirit began to flourish once again.

Why are we so prone to defend choices that take us right to the edge of sin?

It's a decision I've never regretted. On a handful of occasions since, when I have made exceptions to that commitment—for example, to watch news coverage of a major disaster or crisis—I've discovered that it's just too easy for me to drift into making greater allowances and to slip back into old patterns. This is one activity that, for me, needs to stay "mortified" if I am going to keep pursuing holiness!

That approach will sound extreme to some—the word *legalistic* will probably surface in such a discussion. We do need to guard against making absolutes out of personal standards that are not specified in Scripture, or assuming that others are sinning if they don't adopt our standards about issues that may not be traps for them. But why are we so prone to defend choices that take us right to the edge of sin, and so reluctant to make radical choices to protect our hearts and minds from sin?

In the Sermon on the Mount, Jesus exhorted His hearers to be ruthless in cutting off every avenue and enticement to sin.

If your right hand causes you to sin, cut it off and throw it away. For it is better that you lose one of your members than that your whole body go into hell.
—Matthew 5:30

The apostle Paul put it this way:

Put on the Lord Jesus Christ, and make no provision for the flesh, *to gratify its desires.*
—Romans 13:14 (emphasis added)

Let me pause and address something I believe is a huge issue among believers today. It's no big surprise to me to see how many professing Christians struggle with lust and sexual sin and "fall" into immoral relationships, when I learn about their entertainment choices—the books and magazines they read, the music they listen to, and the movies they watch.

A woman whose diet includes mostly romance novels or popular women's magazines is setting herself up for moral temptation, if not failure. Anyone who imbibes the sensual culture through movies and other forms of entertainment that feature sexual innuendos, suggestive and immoral scenes, and provocatively dressed women is going to struggle morally—count on it!

I'm going to be blunt here. I have no doubt that I could get drawn into committing emotional, if not physical, adultery, if I do not continually guard my heart. I am not (and never will be) so "spiritual" as to be immune to sexual sin.

Because I want to glorify God and be faithful to Him all the way to the finish line, I have embarked on an intentional pursuit of holiness. I don't want to displease the Lord or bring reproach to His name. Nor do I want to suffer the awful consequences and the destructive effects of immorality. So, as part of my "battle plan," I have resolved not to expose myself to entertainment or other influences that put immorality in a favorable light or could fuel unholy desires.

Further, I have determined, by God's grace, not to allow myself to be in situations where I could be tempted to sin morally—whether emotionally, mentally, or physically. For me, that means no meetings alone behind closed doors with married men and no traveling or meals alone with married men; it means that e-mail exchanges of a personal nature with men get copied to their wives; it means not cultivating personal friendships with married men, apart from the presence and participation of their wives.

> Only His cross has the power to strike the deathblow to our sinful selves.

Far from being a burden, these "guardrails" have been a huge protection and blessing in my life; they have spared me from many temptations that might easily have drawn my heart away from the Lord.

In today's world, such measures seem unrealistic or excessive, even to many Christians. The problem is that most people in today's world aren't in pursuit of holiness; therefore, they think nothing of sin. Behavior that was once considered unacceptable—even by unbelievers—is now considered normal.

But you and I are different—remember, we're *saints!*

That's why we must be serious about *mortifying*—putting to death—our sinful flesh and anything and everything that feeds our flesh.

The Power of the Cross

Ultimately, mortification takes us back to the cross. It is at the cross that Jesus died *for* sin and died to sin so we could be free *from* sin. Only His cross has the power to strike the deathblow to our sinful selves. Through reckoning ourselves to have been crucified with Him, our flesh, with its sinful desires, is put to death. According to the apostle Paul, this "death" is a past-tense, accomplished reality for every believer:

Our old self was crucified with him in order that the body of sin might be brought to nothing, so that we would no longer be enslaved to sin. For one who has died has been set free from sin.

—Romans 6:6–7

However, we must also make a daily, determined choice to reject sin's rule in our lives:

Let not sin therefore reign in your mortal bodies, to make you obey their passions.

—Romans 6:12

So how do we live in light of the good news that we are "no longer enslaved to sin"? Use that freedom to say *yes* to righteousness and *no* to sin.

When faced with circumstances or opportunities to indulge your flesh, don't stand around and think about it. Don't fool yourself into thinking you can handle it. Instead, do what Joseph did when Potiphar's wife tried to seduce him: "He would not listen to her." When she physically threw herself on him one day, he didn't hang around to discuss the situation with her; he acted instantly and decisively—he "fled and got out of the house" (Genesis 39:10–12). He refused to indulge himself, even for a moment, in whatever pleasures an illicit relationship might have offered.

Putting the Flesh to Death

Some of the areas where you need to practice mortification may be different from those for other believers. Overeating (the biblical term is gluttony) has been a lifelong besetting sin for me, and I continually have to mortify my flesh in relation to my physical appetite for food. If you can't control your eating habits, ask a friend or family member to hold you accountable for what you eat and when. Deny your flesh by fasting periodically.

Drunkenness isn't a temptation I struggle with—but if that's an area where you are vulnerable, mortify those desires by staying away from bars; don't allow yourself to hang out with people who drink; cut off every opportunity and occasion to abuse alcohol; purpose to stay away from it. Don't think you can handle "just one drink."

If computer games are constantly calling your name, consuming your time, and causing you to lose your hunger and thirst for righteousness, ask a godly friend to hold you accountable for how much time you spend playing games. Or you may find you need to give them up altogether in order to rekindle your love and desire for God.

If you're being enticed by pornography or lured into unwholesome relationships over the Internet, establish parameters for your computer use that will make it difficult for you to continue sinning. Put your computer in the family room where everyone can see the screen; establish restrictions against using it when you are alone or late at night. If necessary, get rid of your Internet service . . . or your satellite or cable service. Do whatever you have to do to mortify the sinful appetites and lusts of your flesh.

How serious are you about wanting to be pure?

If romantic movies make you discontent with your singleness or dissatisfied with your mate, or if they fuel sexual fantasies in your mind, don't watch them!

If certain magazines or books plant less-than-holy thoughts, desires, or images in your mind, drop your subscription, toss the books.

If you're tempted to become physically intimate with the person you're dating, don't single date. If necessary, take your sister or a friend or your mother with you! If you've already violated biblical standards of purity in the relationship, you probably need to break it off completely. Tough? Yes. The question is, how serious are you about wanting to be pure? If holiness matters to you, you'll be willing to do whatever you have to do to guard your heart and protect yourself—and the other person—from sinning against God.

If you're being drawn into an illegitimate relationship with a co-worker—or a counselor you're seeing (yes, it happens)—get out! Request a transfer, quit your job, cancel your next appointment, find a biblical counselor of the same sex, or ask a married couple to counsel with you. Don't make provision for your flesh!

One woman wrote our ministry and shared that because of her desire to be holy, she actually had to change pediatricians, as she had found herself becoming attracted to her children's doctor and looking forward to appointments so she could be with him.

I'm dead serious about this. And you need to be as well. What did Jesus mean when He said, "If your right hand causes you to sin, cut it off and throw it away" (Matthew 5:30), if He wasn't talking about the willingness to take extreme measures to avoid sinning?

To continue fueling sin or to hold on to anything that is your means to sin is like pouring fertilizer on weeds and then getting frustrated because you can't get rid of the weeds!

Given my battle with gluttony, there are some types of restaurants I have to stay away from, unless I have strong accountability in place, if I want to glorify God in what I eat.

I have a friend who gave up naps because, she said, "they make me sin"! In the past, when she tried to nap, she would inevitably find herself irritated with her children when they disturbed her rest, so she said, "I decided I couldn't take naps, because I was setting myself up to sin."

Now you and I know that restaurants and naps cannot *make* us sin—we *choose* to sin. But I'm talking about being purposeful and intentional in this battle against sin and removing yourself from anything that might fuel your appetite for sin or provide an inducement or occasion to sin. I'm talking about putting away anything that dulls your spiritual sensitivity or your love for holiness.

Death Brings Life

At first hearing, mortification may sound like a difficult, distasteful chore. At times we enjoy our sin too much to want to let it go. We think we'll be miserable if we give it up. But the truth is that those fleshly desires and deeds to which we cling will *keep* us from enjoying the life for which we were created. They will place us in bondage and misery, even as the beggar boy in Patricia St. John's story stumbled miserably down the dark, muddy street, clutching the stolen eggs.

As the story unfolds, Hamid slips and falls in the darkness, badly scraping and bruising his knees and shattering the eggs. When the nurse turns the light of her torch on him, he is covered with mud, blood, and egg yolk. He bursts into tears, terrified at the thought of what she might do, having discovered his theft. Will she call the police or have him beaten or put in jail? He knows he has forfeited the right to her kindness and is certain he will never again be allowed to enjoy the warmth or light of her home.

Instead, to his amazement, the nurse picks him up and takes him back to her home, where she washes him from head to toe, bandages his wounds, and replaces his tattered rags with fresh, clean clothes. She assures him of her forgiveness and explains his need to be forgiven by the Lord and to walk in His light.

Hamid looked down at his clean clothes and his spotless bandage, and understood. His eggs that had seemed so precious were gone, but he did not want them any more. He had been forgiven and washed and made clean. He had been brought back into the warmth and shelter of the nurse's home.

They were going out again in the dark to find Abd-el-Khader's house, but it would be quite different now. He would get under the nurse's big, warm coat and walk close beside her, sheltered from the rain; he would not stumble, and he would not be afraid of the light any longer, because he no longer had anything to hide. They would walk guided by its bright, steady beam. It would be a treat.[4]

Not until we mortify—put to death—our sinful flesh can we experience the freedom, forgiveness, and fullness for which our hearts long. Once we have been cleansed and have experienced the joys and satisfaction of His mercy and grace, we will find we no longer want those things we once craved and felt we couldn't live without. To walk in the light with Him will be our greatest treat.

NOTES

1. John Owen, *Of the Mortification of Sin in Believers*, in *The Works of John Owen* (Edinburgh: Banner of Truth Trust, 1995 rept.), 6:9.
2. Patricia St. John, *Star of Light* (Chicago: Moody, 2002), 113–14.
3. Kenneth S. Wuest, *Wuest's Word Studies from the Greek New Testament: For the English Reader*, vol. 2, Hebrews 12:14 (Grand Rapids: Eerdmans, 1973).
4. St. John, *Star of Light*, 116–17.

*Holiness means something more than the
sweeping away of the old leaves of sin;
it means the life of Jesus developed in us.*

LILIAS TROTTER[1]

THE PATHWAY TO HOLINESS: "PUT ON"—SAY "YES" *to* GRACE

NOT LONG AGO, a family in my community began experiencing severe respiratory problems. Investigation led to the discovery that their sickness was being caused by toxic black mold that had spread in their house. Thus ensued a long, arduous process to remove the poisonous substance.

As it turned out, the problem was so pervasive that it could not be solved by a simple cleanup effort; not even a major renovation would suffice. There was only one way to deal with the contamination. They were forced to tear down the entire house—piece by piece, brick by brick—all the way down to the foundation. In its place they erected a completely new, mold-free house.

Virtually all the contents of the original house had to be destroyed. The owners didn't want to risk bringing any residual mold into the new house.

Sin is a toxin that contaminates to the core of the human soul. When God saved us, it was with the intent of cleansing us from every vestige of sin. He does so through the lifelong process called sanctification. As we have seen, that process—the pursuit of holiness—requires something far more radical than simple reform or renovation. It requires that we put to death—mortify or "put off"—the "old house," that is, the corrupt deeds and desires of our flesh.

However, that's just the beginning. God—the Master Architect and Builder—has drawn up plans to rebuild new, holy lives as we "put on" the Lord Jesus and His righteousness. To put off without putting on is like tearing down a condemned house and thinking your work is complete before the rebuilding is ever begun. Putting off sinful practices isn't sufficient to make us holy. We must also put on righteousness.

Sin is a toxin that contaminates to the core of the human soul.

For example, in Colossians 3 we are exhorted to "put to death" unholy appetites, attitudes, and actions (e.g., sexual immorality, covetousness, anger, slander, obscene talk, and lying—verses 5–9). The old, contaminated house must be eliminated. In its place, God wants to build a new house as we "put on" the qualities we see in Christ—compassion, kindness, humility, meekness, patience, forgiveness, love, peace, and thankfulness (verses 12–17).

As with putting off sin, putting on the heart of Christ doesn't just happen. We have to be intentional about cultivating new patterns of godliness. This can take place only by the power of the Holy Spirit and the grace of God.

God has provided many different means of grace to help us in the process of putting on holiness. These activities and provisions are not an end in themselves—they are simply means through which we can draw near to God to receive and experience His transforming grace in our lives.

I want to highlight six "means of grace" that have been particularly significant in my personal process of sanctification and spiritual transformation.

The Word

The Word of God is one of the most vital agents of sanctification in the life of a believer. Jesus prayed, "Sanctify them by Your truth. Your word is truth" (John 17:17 NKJV).

God's Word has the power to protect us from sin and to purify us when we do sin. David understood the necessity and value of the Scripture in his pursuit of godliness.

> *How can a young man keep his way pure?*
> *By guarding it according to your word. . . .*
>
> *I have stored up your word in my heart,*
> *that I might not sin against you.*
> —Psalm 119:9, 11

As I read Scripture, I often pray that the Lord will wash me with His Word (Ephesians 5:26)—that He will use Scripture to purify my mind, my desires, and my will.

In addition to its cleansing properties, the Word has the power to renew our minds, to transform us into the image of Christ, and to infuse us with Christian graces. When the apostle Paul said farewell to the leaders of the church of Ephesus, he commended them "to God and to *the word of his grace,* which is able to build you up and to give you the inheritance among all those who are sanctified" (Acts 20:32).

Your progress in holiness will never exceed your relationship with the Word of God.

Reading, studying, memorizing, and meditating on Scripture—these disciplines provide weed control and fertilizer for the garden of my heart, guarding and purifying me from sin and stimulating growth in grace.

No believer can withstand the assault of temptation and the encroachment of the world apart from a steady intake of the Word of God. (Nor can we feed on a diet of unholy reading material and entertainment and expect to have pure hearts or to grow spiritually.) Mark it down— your progress in holiness will never exceed your relationship with the Word of God.

Confession

Though we don't hear a lot about this gracious provision in most of our churches, confession—humbly, honestly acknowledging our sin to God and to others—is an essential ingredient for anyone who wants to live a holy life.

We cannot sin and just move on as if nothing had happened, without our spiritual growth being stymied. In fact, Scripture makes it clear that:

> *Whoever conceals his transgressions will not prosper,*
> *but he who confesses and forsakes them will obtain mercy.*
> —Proverbs 28:13

We may not be consciously concealing our sin, but if we do not consciously confess it, we cannot prosper spiritually.

David knew from painful experience what it was like to live under the weight of unconfessed sin—a burden that affected even his physical body and emotional well-being.

> *When I kept silent* [about my sin], *my bones wasted*
>   *away through my groaning all day long.*
> *For day and night your hand was heavy upon me;*
>   *my strength was dried up as by the heat of summer.*
> —Psalm 32:3–4

Not until he was willing to step into the light and uncover his sin did David experience the joy and the freedom of being forgiven and clean once again.

> *I acknowledged my sin to you,*
>   *and I did not cover my iniquity;*
> *I said, "I will confess my transgressions to the Lord,"*
>   *and you forgave the iniquity of my sin.*
> —Psalm 32:5

Many Christians are bowed down under the heavy load of a guilty conscience, with its physical, emotional, mental, and spiritual consequences—all because they do not regularly confess their sin to God.

Biblical confession is first and foremost vertical—toward God. However, it also has a horizontal dimension. When our sin is against others, in addition to confessing our sin to God, we must also acknowledge our wrongdoing and, where possible, make restitution to those we have offended.

> *Confessing our sin to other believers can be a powerful means of receiving God's grace.*

Further, confessing our sin to other believers as an expression of humility can be a powerful means of receiving God's grace: "Confess your sins to each other and pray for each other so that you may be healed" (James 5:16 NIV). A couple shared with me recently that one of the key factors in dealing with sinful patterns in their lives has been learning to humble themselves and walk in the light by confessing their spiritual struggles, failures, and needs—not only to God, but to each other.

What a wonderful provision God has made for us to apply the cleansing blood of Jesus to our defiled consciences and to be sanctified through the act of confession.

Communion

The Lord's Supper is (or ought to be) one of the most vital and sacred practices (hence the name *sacrament*, as it is known by some) in the life of the church and in every believer's life. It is intended to be a time of corporate remembrance and proclamation of the Lord's death, which we are to observe "until he comes" (1 Corinthians 11:26).

Scripture cautions us against partaking of the bread and the cup "in an unworthy manner"; those who do so are "guilty of profaning the body and blood of the Lord" (verse 27). In order to avoid such serious offense, we are warned, "Let a person [first] examine himself" (verse 28). The consequences of failing to do so can be serious, or even fatal: "That is why many of you are weak and ill, and some have died" (verse 30).

I can't help but wonder how many of the physical weaknesses and illnesses experienced by believers are the direct result of God's discipline. Even more sobering is the thought of how many individuals have actually had their lives cut short because their hearts were not pure before God. Only God knows.

The point is that the Communion service should provide a regular opportunity and a powerful incentive for self-examination—making sure our conscience is clear before God and others, and "judging ourselves" so we will not have to come under the chastening hand of God (verses 29–32).

The observance of the Lord's Supper has often been an occasion for needed introspection, confession, and cleansing in my own life. I remember arriving at church one Sunday morning several years ago and realizing that we would be celebrating Communion in the service. As I took my seat, the Lord brought to mind a situation that had taken place months earlier, involving one of the senior members of our church. I had handled a "small issue" in a way that could easily have wounded the spirit of this older man. We had never discussed the matter, but ever since, I had felt awkward whenever I was around him.

As we began to sing the opening songs in the Communion service, I knew that before I could partake of that sacred ordinance, I had to be sure my conscience was clear with that brother. I slipped out of my seat, crossed over to the other side of the sanctuary where he was sitting, and knelt by his side. I expressed my sorrow over what I had done, as well as my desire to be right with him. He graciously forgave me, and I was then free to partake of the Lord's Supper with no known barriers between me and the Lord or any other believer in that place.

The Body of Christ

As a woman, knowing my physical limitations, it would be foolish for me to go out walking alone, late at night, in a dangerous part of town. However, it would be an entirely different matter if I were to go out in the company of several strong men who were looking out for me and were prepared to protect me.

As Christians, we have not been left alone to deal with our sin. God has graciously put us into a body of believers who are called to look out for one another and to stand together against the enemies that would threaten our holiness. This family—the body of Christ—is a vital provision God has given to help us in our pursuit of holiness.

This is why it is essential for every believer to be in a committed relationship to a Christ-centered local church. Many believers today think nothing of jumping from one church to another every time they find something not to their liking. In fact, a growing number of Christians don't see the need of plugging into a local church at all. Some are disillusioned with their local church experience. They think they can have an independent relationship with God or that their spiritual needs can be met simply by plugging into the Internet.

Being disconnected from the local church, for whatever reason, is a dangerous way to live. Not only do these "lone rangers" miss out on the blessings of functioning within the context of the body of Christ, but like lone sheep away from the safety of the flock and the watchful care of the shepherd, they are vulnerable to predators of every sort.

Each of us is accountable to God for our personal holiness. At the same time, God never intended that we should battle sin single-handedly. I frequently ask those in my circle of Christian brothers and sisters for prayer or accountability in areas where I know I am vulnerable to temptation or sin. Is that a sign of weakness? Yes, it is! The fact is, I *am* weak. And so are you. I need the body of Christ. And so do you.

> *No believer can afford to be without consistent, day in, day out accountability to other believers.*

Is it sometimes hard to confess my need and ask for help? Absolutely! It requires that I humble myself and acknowledge that I don't have it all together.

The very pride that keeps you from taking off your mask and getting real is the same pride that will cause you to fall into sin. Humbling yourself by letting others into your life and allowing them to help you and hold you accountable will release the sanctifying, transforming grace of God in your life.

We also have a responsibility to provide that kind of accountability and help to our Christian brothers and sisters. We cannot stand by on the sidelines when we see fellow believers who are trapped in sinful practices. Scripture requires that we get involved—that we become instruments of grace in their lives, that we actively encourage and help them in the pursuit of holiness.

> *Brothers, if anyone is caught in any transgression, you who are spiritual should restore him in a spirit of gentleness.*
> —Galatians 6:1

This kind of mutual encouragement and exhortation must take place on a *daily* basis. Why? Because *it takes less than twenty-four hours* for our hearts to become hardened or deceived by sin (Hebrews 3:13). It can happen to me; it can happen to you. No believer is immune to sin's lure. No believer can afford to be without consistent, day in, day out accountability to other believers.

Church Discipline

This means of grace is actually a function of "the body of Christ." But Scripture has so much to say about the purifying, restorative effect of addressing sin corporately that it merits being singled out.

Whenever a believer refuses to deal with his sin privately, his sin becomes a public matter that requires the involvement and intervention of others in the body.

One of the fullest treatments of this subject in the New Testament is found in 1 Corinthians 5, where Paul instructed the church on how to deal with one of its members who had committed immorality and was unrepentant. In a public setting, the church was to totally cut off all fellowship and normal social interaction with this man and to "deliver [him] to Satan for the destruction of the flesh" (verse 5).

By being excluded from the fellowship of believers, the man was symbolically removed from God's protection and was left vulnerable to Satan, who could actually destroy his physical life.

The apostle Paul explained that such extreme measures were for the good of the man himself ("that his spirit may be saved in the day of the

Lord"—verse 5). Further, they were absolutely necessary to keep impurity from spreading like gangrene throughout the church: "Do you not know that a little leaven leavens the whole lump?" (verse 6).

This passage describes the most extreme step of church discipline, which is to be taken only after all other routes have been exhausted and rejected. Matthew 18 provides further explanation of that process, in which the offender is repeatedly urged and given opportunity to repent. Seen from this perspective, church discipline is "a severe mercy." It is a gracious provision—not only for the offender, but also for the body.

> *Our heavenly Father loves us and disciplines us in order to purge us from sin.*

I attended a church recently that was exercising the final stages of church discipline with two members of the congregation. As the situation was addressed from the pulpit that Sunday, I was reminded of the seriousness and the consequences of sin. I experienced a fresh sense of the fear of the Lord and a renewed longing for God to guard my heart from sin and make me holy. That church's willingness to exercise biblical discipline on unrepentant members had a sanctifying effect in my life and in that entire congregation.

The fact that so few churches today practice the process of church discipline has made it possible for immorality and ungodliness to flourish within the four walls of most of our churches. How we need to reinstate this means of grace—for our own sakes, for the sake of fallen believers, and for the purity of the whole body.

Suffering

No one wants to sign up for the school of suffering. But suffering can be a powerful means of growing in holiness. In fact, the pathway to holiness always involves suffering. There are no exceptions, and there are no shortcuts.

When our lives are all roses with no thorns or all sun with no clouds, we tend to become spiritually complacent and careless and to neglect serious self-examination and confession. Affliction has a way of stripping away the stubborn deposits of selfishness, worldliness, and sin that build up in the course of everyday life.

The psalmist experienced this sanctifying effect of suffering in his life:

> *Before I was afflicted I went astray,*
> *but now I keep your word.*
> —Psalm 119:67

Our suffering may be our heavenly Father's loving response to our sin—sometimes called *chastening* (Hebrews 12:5–11). Suffering may also come in the form of *pruning*, as God cuts away unnecessary or unproductive "twigs and branches" in our lives so we can bear more fruit (John 15:2). We may be required to endure pain for the sake of the gospel, or on behalf of others (2 Corinthians 1:6; 4:11–15). Or our sufferings may simply be the unavoidable pain associated with living in a fallen world that awaits final deliverance from the curse of sin (Romans 8:18–23).

Regardless of its cause, affliction is a gracious gift from the hand of our heavenly Father who loves us and disciplines us in order to purge us from sin and sanctify us. "He disciplines us for our good, *that we may share his holiness*" (Hebrews 12:10).

In Peter's first epistle, the Lord Jesus is set forth as an example of enduring suffering with submission and meekness, so we could be delivered from our sin. The fourth chapter begins with an exhortation that sets forth a powerful principle regarding the sanctifying effect of suffering in the life of a believer.

> *Since therefore Christ suffered in the flesh, arm yourselves with the same way of thinking, for* whoever has suffered in the flesh has ceased from sin.
> —1 Peter 4:1 (emphasis added)

Peter urges believers to adopt the same submissive attitude Christ demonstrated when the will of God required Him to suffer. As you suffer, he says, you will be freed from the power of sin.

MAKING IT PERSONAL . . .

What are you doing to cultivate a heart for holiness and to put on the character of Christ? The following exercise will help you assess which of the means of grace we have considered in this chapter you are actively using in your pursuit of holiness, and which ones you may be neglecting.

Don't just skim through these questions—set aside some time to respond prayerfully and thoughtfully, perhaps journaling your answers. If you really want to be challenged, discuss your answers with your mate or with one or more close friends of the same sex who can help hold you accountable to be more intentional in pursuing holiness.

1. THE WORD

✦ Are you getting a steady, sufficient intake of the Word into your life?

✦ How has the Word protected you from sin in the past month?

✦ What passage(s) of Scripture have you meditated on in the past week?

✦ Are you getting more input from worldly sources or from the Word of God?

2. CONFESSION

✦ When is the last time you consciously confessed your sin to God?

✦ Have you committed any sins that you have not confessed to God?

✦ Is there anyone you have sinned against to whom you need to confess your offense and whose forgiveness you need to seek?

✦ Is there any sin you need to confess to other believers to humble yourself, and so they can pray for you?

3. COMMUNION

✦ Do you take the Lord's Supper as a matter of routine? Do you adequately realize the seriousness of this ordinance?

✦ Before partaking of the Lord's Supper, do you examine your heart for unconfessed sin?

✦ Have you been partaking of the Lord's Supper "in an unworthy manner"?

4. THE BODY OF CHRIST

✦ Are you a committed, faithful member of a local church?

✦ When is the last time you asked another believer to pray for you regarding a specific sin or temptation in your life?

✦ To whom are you spiritually accountable in matters of personal and moral purity?

✦ Are you consistently receiving exhortation from other believers regarding your spiritual life?

✦ Do you know another believer who is trapped in some sinful pattern and needs to be spiritually restored? What part does God want you to play in that process?

5. CHURCH DISCIPLINE

✦ Are you under the spiritual authority of a local church?

✦ Does the spiritual leadership of your church know that you welcome accountability for your personal holiness? Would they feel the freedom to confront you over any questionable or sinful practices in your life?

✦ Is there any practice in your life that, if your church knew, would be reason for the process of church discipline to be initiated?

✦ Is there another believer whose sin you have justified or covered, rather than being willing to confront the issue or to allow others to confront it as needed?

6. SUFFERING

✦ How has God used suffering as an instrument of sanctification in your life?

✦ Is there any area of suffering that you are resisting rather than embracing?

✦ Is there any area where you may currently be experiencing the chastening hand of God for your sin? How have you responded to God's discipline?

SUMMARY

✦ Name one or two of these six means of grace that you need to be more intentional about using in your pursuit of holiness.

✦ List two or three steps you will take to allow God to use these means more fully in your life.

✦ Share your response with another believer who will encourage you to follow through on your commitment.

NOTE

1. Cited in *Draper's Book of Quotations for the Christian World,* ed. Edythe Draper (Wheaton: Tyndale, 1992), nos. 5748, 312.

Our lives must be such that observers may peep within doors and may see nothing for which to blame us.

C. H. SPURGEON[1]

THE HEART
of HOLINESS

A FAMILY I KNOW has been trying to sell their house for more than a year. They lead busy, active lives and currently have six children living at home. Sometimes they'll go for weeks without anyone wanting to see the house. Then all of a sudden, the real estate agent will call and say, "Can we show your house in thirty minutes?" You can imagine the mad dash that ensues to get the house presentable!

In those frantic "crisis" moments, my friends have become adept at transforming a "lived-in" home with normal clutter into a showcase in record time. The mom grins as she explains how she has learned to stash laundry, dirty dishes, and other assorted household items in places that prospective buyers are unlikely to look—like the clothes dryer . . . and the back of the family Suburban in the garage.

By the time the agent arrives, the residents are nowhere to be seen and the house is in tip-top shape—at least that's how it appears. They just hope no one looks too closely!

How would *you* feel if the doorbell rang right now, and you went to the door to discover you had a surprise visit from distant relatives who were planning to stay for a week and were eager to take a tour of your house? Would you have to scramble to avoid embarrassment?

If you're like me, there are probably some closets and drawers you wouldn't want them to open. Unless you've just finished your spring-cleaning, chances are you'd be hoping your guests didn't look closely enough to see the accumulated dust, the sun streaming through streaked windows, or the cobwebs in the corners.

As Christians, we are called to maintain lives that can be "toured" by outsiders at any time, without embarrassment. A commitment to holiness means having a life that is always "ready for company" and open for inspection—a life that can stand up to scrutiny—not just in the obvious things, but in the hidden places where most might not think to look.

Matching Inside and Outside

Most Christians know how to do a quick pickup in their lives, whenever others come around to take a look. They've learned how to keep up a holy appearance. They know how to look and act "clean" when they're at church or want to leave a good impression on a friend.

Is what's on the outside the same as what's on the inside?

But here's the real test: What would others discover if they took a closer look at your life? What would they find if they started opening the closets and drawers of your life?

This is one of the primary issues Jesus had with the Pharisees of His day. They were consumed with keeping up appearances, while content to live with and overlook the mess beneath the surface, where it counted most. The problem wasn't with their outward behavior—their lust for human praise made them star performers. But Jesus could see what the people they were trying so hard to impress couldn't see—their hearts. And that's where the trouble was.

As Jesus pointed out, it's not that what's on the outside is unimportant. It's that it's meaningless to present a polished, immaculate image while masking the underlying scum. Such hypocrisy evoked a response from the Lord that was far from mild.

Woe to you, scribes and Pharisees, hypocrites! For you are like white-washed tombs, which outwardly appear beautiful, but within are full of dead people's bones and all uncleanness. So you also outwardly appear righteous to others, but within you are full of hypocrisy and lawlessness.

—Matthew 23:27–28

No wonder no one wants to be known as a "Pharisee" today! However, like the Pharisees, we have an amazing capacity to feel good about ourselves because we don't commit certain kinds of sins, while brushing off as insignificant the interior pollution of our hearts. So we've never committed physical adultery . . . but we entertain lustful thoughts about someone else's mate. We don't commit acts of physical violence . . . but we harbor hatred toward those who have wronged us and mentally assassinate them or emotionally cut them off.

Does Jesus' description of the Pharisees in any way apply to you?

✦ Is there any hypocrisy in your life? Is what's on the outside the same as what's on the inside? Do you appear outwardly to be godly, while inwardly harboring unholy attitudes, thoughts, or values?

✦ Are you as concerned about the inward reality of your life—that which only God can see—as you are about how you appear to others?

✦ If people could see your inner thoughts and desires, would they conclude that you are a holy person?

MAKING IT PERSONAL . . .

The New Testament authors challenge believers to recognize their position in Christ—justified, redeemed, chosen by God, set apart for His purposes. Then we are exhorted to live a life—inside and out—that is consistent with our position.

The rest of this chapter is not designed to be read in the same way as the rest of the book. I'd encourage you to set this portion aside and make it a part of your personal devotional time over the next few days. Take time to look up each of the following passages from Paul's epistles that describes some aspect of what it means to live a holy life. Then prayerfully consider the application questions.

As with the questions in previous chapters, consider recording your responses in a journal. Then get together with one or more other believers to discuss what God has been saying to you about the condition of your heart and your walk before Him.

Put on the new self (Ephesians 4:17–24)

✦ Are you a new creature in Christ (2 Corinthians 5:17)?

✦ Is your lifestyle obviously different from those who do not know the Lord?

✦ Could it be that you are struggling and striving to be holy, but finding it impossible, because you have never been made right with God through faith in Christ?

✦ Do you have a spiritually sensitive and responsive heart, or has your heart become hard and cold toward God?

✦ Do you have an underlying desire to be holy and to please God in all you do?

Speak the truth (Colossians 3:9–10; Ephesians 4:25)

✦ Are you an honest person? (Be honest!)

✦ Are you deceiving anyone about anything—in your home? In your workplace? In your church?

✦ Are you pretending to be something that you're not, trying to leave a better impression of yourself than is honestly true?

✦ Are you more concerned about what others think of you than about what God knows to be true?

Put away anger (Ephesians 4:31)

✦ Are you holding anger in your heart toward anyone?

✦ Do you have a hot temper? Do you fly off the handle easily?

✦ Are you easily irritated? Prone to impatience?

Don't steal—give! (Ephesians 4:28)

✦ Have you taken things that don't belong to you? Borrowed things you've never returned?

✦ Are you a hard worker, or are you sometimes slothful or undisciplined in your work? Do you give your boss a full day's work for a full day's pay?

✦ Are you honest in completing expense reports? Tax returns? Taking exams and writing papers for school?

✦ Have you stolen the affections of someone else's mate? Have you defrauded someone of the opposite sex by creating expectations you can't righteously fulfill? Have you robbed anyone of his or her sexual purity?

✦ Are you sensitive to the needs of others and quick to respond to those needs in practical ways?

✦ Are you robbing God by spending on yourself money that belongs to Him?

Watch your tongue (Ephesians 4:29; 5:4)

✦ Do you speak words that are true, pure, good, and kind?

✦ Does profanity, unholy talk, or coarse jesting come out of your lips?

✦ Do you gossip? Slander others with your tongue?

✦ Do you tease others in ways that could be hurtful?

✦ Do you have a critical tongue, perhaps under the guise of being helpful?

✦ Do you speak words that are useless or toxic to those who hear them?

✦ Do your words encourage and build others up? Do your words minister grace to those who hear them?

✦ Do you express thankfulness verbally—to God and to others?

Be sensitive to the Spirit (Ephesians 4:30)

✦ Are you sensitive to the things that grieve the Holy Spirit, or can you sin and not be grieved about it?

✦ Is there anything in your heart attitudes or outward behavior that you know is not pleasing to the Lord?

✦ Are you quick to obey the promptings of the Spirit through His Word and in your heart?

✦ Are you quick to respond to the conviction of God's Spirit when you have sinned?

Put on forgiveness and love (Colossians 3:12–13)

✦ Are you holding a grudge or harboring bitterness in your heart toward anyone?

✦ Is there anyone who has hurt or wronged you that you have not fully forgiven?

✦ Is your life marked by love?

Let His peace rule (Colossians 3:15)

✦ Does the peace of Christ control your life, or do you often fret and worry about circumstances beyond your control?

✦ Do you trust the sovereign wisdom and love of God to order your steps?

Be filled with His Word (Colossians 3:16–17)

✦ Do you seek to fill your mind and heart with the Word of God?

✦ Do your conversations with other believers center on the Word and the ways of God?

✦ Is the whole of your life lived in the name and for the sake of the Lord Jesus?

✦ Are you a grateful person? Do you frequently express gratitude to God and to others?

Embrace your God-designed role in the home (Colossians 3:18–21)

✦ Are your family relationships ordered according to the plan God has revealed in His Word?

✦ Wives: Are you submitting to the authority and leadership of your husband? Do you show reverence and respect in your attitude toward him and in the way you talk to him and about him to others?

✦ Husbands: Do you love your wife in the selfless, sacrificial way Christ loves His church? Do you treat her gently and kindly?

✦ Sons and daughters: Are you obedient to your parents' authority?

✦ Parents: Are you giving godly direction to your children?

✦ Fathers: Are you leading your children spiritually in a way that encourages and motivates them to follow Christ?

Holiness in the workplace (Colossians 3:22–23; 4:1)

✦ In your workplace (whether in or out of your home), do you labor as unto the Lord?

✦ Are you diligent in your work? Do you do what you're assigned to do?

✦ Why do you do what you do? Do you have a hidden desire for fame, recognition, or human praise? Are you trying to impress your boss and your fellow workers, or are you trying to please the Lord?

✦ Do you deal fairly with your employees?

✦ Do you treat those you serve, and those who serve you, in a way that is consistent with the way God treats you?

Exhibit godly character (Ephesians 5:1)
✦ Is there anything in your life that does not bear a "family resemblance" to God?

✦ Is there any pattern or practice in your life that, if others followed it, would lead them away from God?

✦ Is your conduct blameless and above reproach in every area of your life—not by the world's standards, but by the standard of God's Word and His holiness?

Be morally pure (Ephesians 5:3)
✦ Are you walking in moral purity and freedom? Is your thought life pure?

✦ Do you guard your heart and your eyes from influences that might tempt you to sin morally?

✦ Are you chaste and discreet in your relationships with members of the opposite sex?

✦ Do you secretly fantasize about a relationship with another man's wife or another woman's husband?

✦ What about the things you read and watch and listen to when you are alone—are they pure, are they lovely, are they holy?

✦ Do you have any secret or private moral habits that are impure?

Avoid the darkness (Ephesians 5:8, 11)
✦ Do you have an appetite for activities you know to be sinful?

✦ Do you enjoy talking with others (or even laughing) about shameful things?

✦ Does your life paint a contrast to the darkness of the world around you and draw people to His light?

Walk in the light (Ephesians 5:8–10)

✦ Do you consciously seek to know and to do what will please the Lord?

✦ Is there any area of your life that could not withstand the scrutiny of His holy light? Any area in which you are not walking as a child of light?

✦ Does your lifestyle mark you as a child of God?

NOTE

1. C. H. Spurgeon, *Twelve Sermons on Holiness* (Swengel, Pa.: Reiner Publications, n.d.); "Holiness, the Law of God's House," 71.

Conspicuous holiness ought to be the mark of the church of God. . . . Would God that whenever they speak of you or me they may have no evil thing to say of us unless they lie.

C. H. SPURGEON[1]

THE PASSION
for HOLINESS

FOR MORE THAN TWENTY YEARS, the people of Romania suffered under the iron-fisted, Communist rule of Nicolae Ceausescu—one of the most repressive and corrupt dictators of the twentieth century. Christians were especially targeted by the regime and were subjected to intense intimidation and relentless harassment. Evangelical believers were ridiculed and were referred to in derision as "repenters."

In 1969, the government revoked the preaching license of a pastor in Timisoara. After struggling to find work, the pastor finally ended up gluing paper shopping bags to support his family. For four years, as he did this work, he prayed for revival. In 1973, his license was miraculously reinstated and he was assigned to the Second Baptist Church in Oradea.

From the outset, his ministry in Oradea was characterized by an emphasis on prayer. Church members were encouraged to pray for the salvation of their unbelieving friends, relatives, and colleagues.

However, this pastor's burden was not simply for those outside the church. He was convinced that the revival for which he had been longing and praying all these years must begin in the church. He explained to his people that unbelievers weren't the only ones who needed to repent. Unapologetically, he stressed the need for the "repenters" to repent.

Not content to deal in generalities, he was straightforward in pointing out what he viewed as habitual sins among the "repenters"—issues he believed were hindering the church from experiencing true revival.

In our age of moral ambiguity that asserts every person's right to determine what is right for himself, many will struggle with the stance this pastor took in his church.

For example, he confronted his people about stealing from the state. The government had confiscated and collectivized the farms and factories, forcing the people to turn over to the government the fruit of their labors. The people had felt justified in keeping back from their "own" farms and factories a share of what they believed rightly belonged to them. The pastor preached that this was wrong and led them to take a vow not to "steal" from the government.

Another issue related to the use of alcoholic beverages. Oradea is in an area with many vineyards, and drinking was an accepted part of the culture, even among believers. The pastor believed that drinking alcohol led to sin, and he challenged the believers to take a vow of total abstinence.

Many contemporary evangelicals would be uncomfortable categorizing these particular practices as "sin." While there may be room for discussion, the point is that the "repenters" repented—they began to take holiness seriously; they turned from everything they believed was displeasing to God.

When they did, God sent revival. After six months of preaching, praying, and repenting, the fruits of the cleansing began to manifest themselves. One of the most obvious results was the conversion of great numbers of unbelievers. Before the revival began, this church of five hundred members had baptized about ten new believers each year. From June to December 1974, the church in Oradea baptized some 250 new converts! Approximately four hundred new believers were baptized over the following two years—in a country where a public profession of faith in Christ required a readiness to be martyred for Christ.

The revival could not be contained within a single church. It spread throughout the surrounding area, and its impact was experienced in evangelical churches throughout the entire country. The revived believers were infused with courage and began to stand up for what they believed. Many believe that this fire in the hearts of God's people was one of the elements that ultimately led to the overthrow of the Ceausescu regime fifteen years later.

In many of our churches, we're knocking ourselves out trying to be "relevant" so we can attract new members. We don't want to appear to be different, extreme, or too spiritual, for fear of turning off unbelievers. By contrast, once the church in Oradea was willing to be different from the world, the very unbelievers who had once ridiculed them were irresistibly drawn to Christ.

> *The world is not impressed with a religious version of itself.*

We have accommodated to the world rather than calling the world to accommodate to Christ. When will we realize that the world is not impressed with a religious version of itself? Our greatest effectiveness is not to be found in being like the world; it is to be found in being distinct from the world, in being like Jesus.

The absence of revival in evangelicalism today certainly does not reflect a lack of activity and opportunities. We have more Christian concerts, conferences, programs, strategies, media events, books, tapes, magazines, and radio/TV ministries than any generation in history. In fact, we have more prayer gatherings and more events and resources geared toward "spiritual awakening" than ever. But something is missing.

I remember discussing this matter with a ministry leader who observed, "Lots of people are praying, and lots of people are repenting, but so few are changing their lifestyle." A light went on in my mind when I heard that statement. The fact is, *if people are not changing their lifestyle, they're not repenting.* And if we're not repenting, then all our singing and praising and praying and producing are useless—perhaps worse than useless, because all the noise and activity may deceive us into thinking that we're OK and that we are actually experiencing revival.

Taking Holiness Seriously

How important is holiness to you? How much thought, attention, and effort do you devote to the pursuit of holiness? Are you intentional about putting away everything that is displeasing to God and living a holy life? Is it your priority—your mission—to be holy?

How important is your children's holiness to you? Do you care more about their grade point average, their batting average, and their earning capacity, or about their purity of heart and life? Are you consciously training them to be godly? Does their sin drive you to your knees? Does it cause you to plead with God to give your children a heart for righteousness and to plead with them to repent?

How concerned are you about the holiness of the body of Christ? Does it grieve you:

✦ when Christians are unloving and unforgiving,

✦ when they are gossips and gluttons,

✦ when they have more interest in possessions and pleasure than in spiritual riches and pleasing God,

✦ when they dishonor their parents and divorce their mates,

✦ when they are self-absorbed and self-promoting,

✦ when they are cantankerous and contentious,

✦ when they use profanity and pornography,

✦ when they can sin glibly and without blushing?

What would happen in our day if the "repenters" were to repent? What if believers were to get honest about their sin and serious about pursuing holiness? Might we not once again experience the manifest presence of God in our churches? Might we not see God supernaturally convert multitudes of lost sinners to faith in Christ?

C. H. Spurgeon put it this way: "In proportion as a church is holy, in that proportion will its testimony for Christ be powerful."[2]

Could we honestly say that most of our churches have a powerful testimony for Christ? If not, what does that say about the condition of the church? And how exercised should we be about all this?

Sewage in the Church?

If plumbing or septic problems caused raw sewage to overflow into the hallways and aisles of your church, one thing is for sure: The problem would not be ignored. Everyone would be horrified. The health hazard would prompt immediate action. Business would not continue as usual. Services would be relocated and crews would work overtime if necessary, until the problem was resolved.

The fact is that something far more serious than raw sewage is running through the lives of countless professing Christians and most of our evangelical churches. And by and large, we are oblivious to the threat.

The floodgates of unholiness—including willful, presumptuous, blatant sin—have opened within the church. Adultery, drunkenness, abuse, profanity, outbursts of temper, divorce, pornography, immodest dress— such sins among professing believers, often members in good standing of respected local churches, are no longer rare exceptions.

Sadly, the church has become a safe place to sin.

And then there are the more "respectable" forms of sewage that are often overlooked and tolerated among believers—things such as overspending, unpaid debts, gluttony, gossip, greed, covetousness, bitterness, pride, critical spirits, backbiting, temporal values, self-centeredness, and broken relationships. Sadly, the church—the place that is intended to showcase the glory and holiness of God—has become a safe place to sin.

A Missing Message

Why are we experiencing such an epidemic of open—and not-so-open—sin in the church today? High on the list of reasons would have to be the fact that for more than a generation, the evangelical church, by and large, has abandoned preaching on sin and holiness.

Whenever I have spoken on the subject of holiness in recent years, the resounding response has been, *"Thank you! . . . Why aren't we hearing this message today?"*

We have tiptoed around Old and New Testament passages that proclaim the holiness of God, His hatred of sin, and His wrath and judgment against unrepentant sinners, preferring to consider only references to His mercy, grace, and love.

We have promoted a "gospel" that says it is possible to be a Christian while stubbornly refusing to address practices or behaviors we know are sinful. We have accepted the philosophy that it's OK for Christians to look, think, act, and talk like the world.

We have made it an offense to admonish people about their sin, either privately or, when necessary, publicly. (If only we were as loath to commit sin as we are to confront it!)

Church Marries World

Lest you think I'm overstating the case, let me share several recent illustrations.

I received a letter from a woman expressing deep concern about the lack of a commitment to holiness on the part of so many "believers." She wrote:

> Worldly entertainment and coarse talk are rampant in our churches. Just this week at a women's luncheon, the conversation was about how aggravating it is to go to an R-rated movie and see people bringing their children in with them. I listened for a couple of minutes; then I couldn't keep silent any longer. As graciously as I could, I said, "Ladies, we are Christians! I can't believe we're even talking about attending R-rated movies!"

I know a man who has been involved in the Christian entertainment industry for many years. I was grieved to learn that he has adopted an "alternate" sexual lifestyle. I asked the mutual friend who gave me the report, "Is the [Christian] company where he works aware of this?" The response was hard to fathom: "It probably would not be a concern if they knew."

THE PASSION FOR HOLINESS

A friend told me about a Christian dad who, upon learning that his teenage son had been involved in a ring of kids who were drinking and passing around pornography at school, shrugged off the behavior with, "Kids will be kids! Anyway, soft-core porn isn't the same as hard porn."

Some friends lead a weekly Bible study for kids in their daughter's Christian high school. These students would be considered "the cream of the cream"—some of their parents are on the staff of a large parachurch ministry. Recently, my friends distributed a set of lyrics to several popular songs and asked the kids to discuss whether

Have we been lulled to sleep by a watered-down, compromised version of "Christianity"?

they agreed or disagreed with the message of each song and the behavior it advocated. Three of the songs had lyrics that were blatantly offensive—for example, a song by rap star Eminem who sings in graphic terms about murdering his mother, accompanied by an endless stream of profanity.

After analyzing the words, the kids were asked if they would continue to listen to a song even if they disagreed with its message. With two exceptions, the consensus of those teens was yes, they would continue to listen to music with these kinds of degrading messages.

Knowing I was working on this book, my friends wrote to me about their experience. They concluded:

> Our hearts are breaking. This is one lost generation. We adults and the church have failed to pass the baton of holiness on to the next generation. Frankly, we don't blame these teens. How can they aspire to a life of holiness when they haven't been presented with a standard of holiness in the home or from the pulpit?

Speaking of which . . . a friend told me recently about a Christian woman she knows who was elated that her daughter had just been hired as a salesclerk at Abercrombie & Fitch, a clothing manufacturer that is defiant in its blatant promotion of immorality and has been widely boycotted for sexual exploitation of children in its catalogs. My friend continued, "When most of the Christians you know (many of whom also happen to be leading Bible studies) are forever following the latest fad or talking about the latest movie they've just been to see, you can start to feel like you're from a different planet!"

As I was writing this chapter, I received an e-mail from a friend who had just been listening to an influential Christian radio station in one of the nation's largest markets. In the past ninety minutes, my friend had heard half a dozen commercials from a "really nice sounding divorce attorney" advertising his services. I can understand that the secular media would be comfortable selling advertising to a divorce attorney. But how have we come to the point that a *Christian* media outlet would promote something God says He hates?

I wonder—were the believers who were listening to that station as they drove down the freeway that day disturbed by what they heard? Did they even notice? Have they—have we—been lulled to sleep by a watered-down, compromised version of "Christianity"?

You need to understand that these examples are not rare or exceptional. That would be cause enough for concern. But the reality is that this kind of twisted thinking has become characteristic of a growing number of professing believers and is being widely defended in the evangelical world. I have heard these perspectives expressed over and over again, by individuals in many of the most respected ministries and churches in the country.

We are seeing the fulfillment of Vance Havner's prophetic words spoken decades ago: "The world and the professing church first flirted with each other, then fell in love, and now the wedding is upon us."

A Passion for God's Glory

Nehemiah was one man who refused to get sucked in by the allure of the world. He never got accustomed to sin, even when everyone around him had become desensitized. The law of God was written in his heart. And love for God compelled him to care when that law was disregarded.

Nehemiah was one of the Jewish exiles living in Persia. In 444 B.C., fourteen years after Ezra led a group of exiles back to Jerusalem to rebuild the demolished temple, Nehemiah received word that the walls of the city were still in disrepair. Nehemiah left his comfortable job and made the nine-hundred-mile journey to assist his fellow Jews in the restoration of the city. Amid fierce opposition from the determined trio of Sanballat, Tobiah, and Geshem, the walls were finally rebuilt.

Nehemiah became the governor of Judah and, along with Ezra the priest, turned his attention to rebuilding the spiritual and moral foundations that had eroded in people's hearts. Nehemiah 8–10 tells the story of the great revival that transpired when the people were challenged to repent and return to the Word of God they had neglected for so long.

As part of that revival, the people made a covenant with God. Similar to the vows taken by the Romanian "repenters," the terms of their covenant were specific and dealt with issues where God's people had been violating His commands: The people agreed not to intermarry with the unbelieving nations around them, to refrain from buying and selling on the Sabbath, and to support the needs of the temple and the Levites.

After serving in Jerusalem for twelve years, Nehemiah returned to Persia for some unknown period of time—perhaps a couple years. When he returned to Judah, he was shocked to discover that the people had failed to keep the commitments they had made to the Lord and were flagrantly disobeying His Word. They were conducting commerce on the Sabbath, they had neglected the maintenance and care of the temple, and they had married foreign wives who were not of their faith. Nehemiah was intensely distressed and boldly confronted the people over their backslidden condition.

A spirit of tolerance became exalted over a love for truth.

The most egregious offense involved Tobiah the Ammonite, the man who years earlier had done everything he could to oppose the work of God in the rebuilding of the city walls. Over the years, the Jewish people had gradually let down their guard. They had begun to socialize with their former enemy; in turn, that had led to more intimate relationships, including marriage ties between Tobiah's family and the family of Eliashib the priest. Over time, any differences between Tobiah and

God's "set apart" people had all but disappeared.

Unbelievably, by the time Nehemiah returned, this sworn enemy of God was actually living *in the temple.* This was in direct violation of God's command that no Ammonite should ever be allowed to set foot in the temple. Yet there Tobiah was, living in a room that had been given to him by the priest.

Undoubtedly, this change of affairs did not take place overnight. More likely, one compromise led to another and another. The priests and the people found ways of justifying their actions. A spirit of tolerance became exalted over a love for truth. *After all, Tobiah has turned out to be a nice man and his family fits in so well here. It doesn't seem right to tell him he can't stay, just because he's not a Jew. We don't want to be legalistic about this!*

So godless Tobiah moved into the temple, while the people carried on with "church"—not the least bit troubled over the state of affairs. But to Nehemiah, who cared deeply about holiness, this was an unthinkable situation. He was furious. And he acted decisively.

> God simply won't make Himself at home in an unholy place.

He physically hurled Tobiah and all his possessions out of the temple; then he gave orders to purify the desecrated rooms. He denounced the evil situation and called the priests and the people to repent.

Why were these offenses such a big deal to Nehemiah? Why did he feel the need to interfere in others' lives? Why wasn't he content to just obey God and leave others alone? Why? Because Nehemiah was compelled by a passion for the glory of God to be displayed in His people.

That passion is evident throughout the book that bears Nehemiah's name. It is seen in the way he worshiped and in the way he prayed, in the career choices and the personal sacrifices he made, in his tears as he confessed on behalf of the people of God, and in his tenacity as he confronted the enemies of God.

His love for holiness is seen in his commitment to personal integrity—even in the "little things" (e.g., Nehemiah 5:18). And it is seen in his boldness in dealing with the sins of others.

Nehemiah had seen God's people pay a terrible price for their sins. They had been exiled in the midst of nations that did not worship Jehovah, first in Babylon and then in Persia. Nehemiah also had seen that through repentance and obedience, once they were allowed to return to Jerusalem, the people of God had been richly blessed and had experienced great joy. He could not bear to see them lose those blessings by returning to the very sins that had caused them to end up in captivity.

His heart for holiness put him in a tiny minority, even among his fellow leaders. He didn't seem to notice or care. He wasn't trying to win a popularity contest. All that mattered to him was that the holy name of God had been profaned, and he longed for it to be hallowed once again.

Time for the "Repenters" to Repent

The parallels between the story of Nehemiah and the church in our day are striking. Lots of people who call themselves believers are churning out a lot of religious activity, but we have rewritten the law of God and we have prostituted the grace of God, turning it into a license to sin.

The spirit of tolerance has triumphed over the spirit of truth. And now, Tobiah is living in the temple. Lust, greed, materialism, anger, selfishness, pride, sensuality, divorce, deceit, ungodly entertainment, worldly philosophies—little by little, we've let down our guard, cultivated a relationship with these sworn enemies of God, welcomed them into our churches, and given them a home there.

Beyond that, we've worked so hard to make lost and backslidden people feel comfortable in our churches that there is little conviction of sin, little life transformation, and little manifestation of the presence of God, who simply won't make Himself at home in an unholy place.

I'm not suggesting that we try to alienate unbelievers in our churches or that irrelevance is a virtue. I *am* saying that sinners ought to be uncomfortable in the presence of a holy God. And that they will never be truly converted until they have experienced the conviction of God's Spirit.

In the midst of such a state, the question is, *Where are the Nehemiahs of our day?*

Where are the men and women who love God supremely and who fear nothing and no one but God? Where are the saints who live like saints—whose lives are above reproach in every matter—in their homes, their work, their speech, their habits, their attitudes, their finances, and their relationships?

The world is waiting for the church to get right with God.

Where are the believers whose eyes are filled with tears, whose hearts ache when they see an unholy church partying and entertaining herself to death, and whose knees are sore from pleading with God to grant the gift of repentance?

Where are the Christian leaders with the compassion and the courage to call the church to be clean before God? Where are the moms and dads and young people who are willing to deal thoroughly and decisively with everything that is unholy in their hearts and their homes?

The church has been waiting for the world to get right with God. When will we realize that the world is waiting for the church to get right with God?

Oh, child of God, it is time for the "repenters" to repent. We can scarcely imagine the impact that will be felt in our world when we do.

I will vindicate the holiness of my great name, which has been profaned among the nations, and which you have profaned among them. . . . I will sprinkle clean water on you, and you shall be clean from all your uncleannesses. . . . Then they will know that I am the Lord.

—Ezekiel 36:23, 25, 38

NOTES

1. C. H. Spurgeon, *Twelve Sermons on Holiness* (Swengel, Pa.: Reiner Publications, n.d.); "Holiness, the Law of God's House," 70–71.
2. Charles H. Spurgeon, *1000 Devotional Thoughts* (Grand Rapids: Baker, 1976 rept.), nos. 408, 205.

Let us rejoice and exult and give him the glory,
for the marriage of the Lamb has come,
and his Bride has made herself ready.

———————

JOHN THE APOSTLE[1]

Epilogue:
HERE COMES
the BRIDE!

IMAGINE FOR A MOMENT . . . we're seated together at a royal wedding. The invitations have been sent, all the preparations have been made, the guests have arrived, the music is playing, the flowers are spectacular—the sanctuary is decked for a king and queen. The bridegroom and his attendants take their places at the front.

The first strains of the wedding march begin to sound. We all rise.

It's hard to see from where we're standing off to the side. Finally, we're able to catch a glimpse of the bride holding the arm of her father as she begins to move down the aisle toward her bridegroom.

We crane our necks trying to take it all in. As she gets closer, we realize *something is wrong!* It can't be—but yes . . . *her veil is torn, and it's askew on her head.*

She gets closer, and we see that it's not just her veil—her hair is matted and in disarray. She looks like she just got out of bed. And her face—it's filthy; she has no makeup on.

As she walks by the row where we're standing, we get a closer look at her dress. It's unbelievable. Her gown is disheveled and wrinkled from top to bottom. It looks like it's been stuffed in a drawer for weeks. Not only that—the once-white dress is covered with an awful assortment of dark stains.

Have you ever seen such a sight? *How can this be?*

Then we see the saddest sight of all, as she approaches her bridegroom. It's the look of profound sorrow in his eyes as he realizes that his bride—the one he loves with all his heart—*didn't care enough to get ready for the wedding.*

My friend, there's a Wedding coming.

It's that Wedding toward which all earthly weddings are intended to point us. The bridegroom is a holy Bridegroom, and He must have a holy bride.

And our Savior will have a holy bride. That's why He loved the church and gave Himself up for her. That's why He took all those stains and blots on Himself.

> *. . . to make her holy*
> *. . . and to present her to himself as a radiant church,*
> *without stain or wrinkle or any other blemish,*
> *but holy and blameless.*
> —Ephesians 5:26–27 NIV

My goal in life is not that I would be free from problems or pain; it's not that I would be a best-selling author or have a successful radio ministry or get invited to speak at large conferences; it's not that I would have great relationships or be healthy and financially secure.

Are you ready for the wedding?

My deepest desire is that I would be a holy woman and that the church of Jesus Christ would be holy.

How I look forward to that day when you and I, along with all the other saints from all ages, walk together down that aisle toward our Beloved Bridegroom. I want to face Him with joy—radiant, unashamed, "dressed in His righteousness alone, faultless to stand before the throne."[2]

Are you ready for the Wedding? If not, what would you have to do to get ready? Is there a sin you need to confess and forsake? Is there a habit you need to give up—or cultivate? Is there a relationship you need to break off—or reconcile? Are there items in your possession you need to get rid of? Are there debts you need to pay? Are there people whose forgiveness you need to seek? Is there restitution you need to make?

Whatever it is, for Jesus' sake, for the world's sake, for His body's sake, for your family's sake, for your sake—*do it*. By His grace and the power of His Holy Spirit—*do it*.

Nothing, nothing, nothing could be more important. Nothing could bring Him greater glory in our world, and nothing could bring you greater joy—both now and throughout all eternity.

Having therefore these promises, dearly beloved,
let us cleanse ourselves from all filthiness of the flesh and spirit,
perfecting holiness in the fear of God.
　—2 Corinthians 7:1 KJV

NOTES
1. Revelation 19:7.
2. Edward Mote, "The Solid Rock." Circa 1834; first appeared in Mote's *Hymns of Praise*, 1836.

HOLINESS
DISCUSSION GUIDE

As You Begin

For most believers, holiness is a concept that evokes mixed emotions and, at best, seems shrouded in mystery. But no word better captures the splendor of who God is and the destination to which He has called us.

The call to pursue holiness is an invitation to experience the blessings and joys of intimacy with God, to be free from the weight and the burden of sin, and to become all He created us to be.

The study of holiness raises many challenging questions and issues. The purpose of this study is not to answer all those questions or solve all those theological dilemmas, but to encourage you to take a fresh look at our holy God and to engage in a lifelong pursuit of the holiness to which He has called us.

Getting Your Bearings

When you think you may be lost, one of the first things you try to do is get your bearings—to figure out where you are in relation to where you want to be.

Do you know where you are in relation to the matter of holiness? Here are a few questions to help you find out. Respond as honestly as possible. You'll be asked to revisit these questions at the end of this study, so you can see in what direction you're headed.

1. How important is holiness to you? How much thought, attention, and effort do you devote to the pursuit of holiness? Are you intentional about putting away everything that is displeasing to God and living a holy life?

2. [if applicable] How important is your children's holiness to you? (A good gauge—do you care more about their grade point average, their batting average, and their earning capacity, or about their purity of heart and life?) Does their sin drive you to your knees?

3. How concerned are you about the holiness of the body of Christ? Does it grieve you when you see yourself or others treating sin lightly?

An Important Reminder

Any discussion of holiness necessarily involves the discussion of sin. It's important to remember two helpful boundaries when discussing sin in a group setting:

1. Confess your own sin—not someone else's. No fair confessing your spouse's sin, your children's sin, your best friend's sin—just your own! If someone else sinned against you in a particular situation, you don't need to supply those details and cause someone else in the group to stumble by taking up an offense.

2. Speaking of details, you don't need many to be biblically accurate in your confession. Identify biblical categories of sin that apply to your situation; avoid sharing unnecessary details of the sinful action itself. It's enough for the group to know that you are convicted of gossiping about someone else—without repeating the gossip! Or that you spoke harshly to your spouse—without repeating the insult you uttered to him or her. Too much detail isn't helpful or necessary in most cases.

A good rule to remember is that unless someone has been part of the problem or is being used by God as part of the solution (e.g., an accountability partner, a pastor), repeating the details may just be gossip.

Tips for Group Leaders

Open and close each meeting by praying together. Ask the Holy Spirit to guide you through the Word, to help you be real with one another, and to bring about any needed change in each heart.

Seek to lead by example. You can serve your group best by modeling a heart for holiness—being the first to confess your own sin and the first to encourage others in God's grace at work in them.

Some of the questions in this discussion guide call for a level of transparency and openness that many people are not accustomed to. Encourage the members of your group to respect each other's privacy by not discussing others' contributions outside of this group. Remind them that God is patient and gracious with us as He conforms us to the image of His Son, and that we need to extend the same patience and grace toward each other.

This discussion guide is designed to be used in a variety of contexts—from small groups to Sunday school classes. Feel free to direct the discussion based on the size of your group and the allotted time. Avoid rabbit trails into secondary or unrelated issues. However, don't feel pressured to get through all the questions each time you meet.

Depending on your available time and the size and openness of your group, you may end up only discussing two or three questions.

The goal is to grow together in your understanding of God and His ways and to experience individually and as a group the reality of the message of this book.

Keep your group centered on the truth of the gospel: We are *all* sinners in need of a Savior. Help your members steer clear of self-righteous responses to the confessions of others in the group and from condemnation about their own performance by pointing them to the One who is both the author and perfecter of their faith (Hebrews 12:2).

INTRODUCTION

Getting Started

What motivated you to read this book and begin this study? What do you hope to get out of it?

Opening Prayer

The Valley of Vision: A Collection of Puritan Prayers and Devotions is rich food for the soul. Read aloud the prayer at the beginning of *Holiness*—either as a group in unison, or have one or more individuals read while others listen. Then discuss this prayer:

   • What words or phrases in this prayer describe our natural, sinful condition? What feeling(s) or reaction(s) do those words evoke in you?

   • What words or phrases describe God—His character, His grace, and His work on behalf of repentant sinners?

   • What words/phrases describe the sinner's appropriate response to this holy, redeeming God?

Going Deeper

1. Review the letter quoted on page 274. Briefly discuss the questions that follow: *"[Is this couple] wrong? Are they unnecessarily uptight or narrow-minded? Do these issues really matter? Or are they simply a matter of personal conscience? Do they change with the culture?"* (p. 274).

What Scriptures come to mind that could apply to the issues this couple is wrestling with? (Resist the urge to spend your whole time on this exercise or to end up in a debate about these particular issues! Just share some initial responses and move on.)

2. What have you heard, seen, or experienced recently—in your own life or in others—that highlights the need for holiness among God's

people? (Be sure not to reflect negatively on other believers by sharing specific names or private details.)

3. "Holiness and sin both matter—*more than we can imagine. They matter to God, and the more we comprehend their true nature, the more they will matter to us*" (p. 275). Do you think "holiness and sin" matter enough to most believers? If not, why not, and what could increase our sense of their importance?

4. "*I invite you to join me in a radical pursuit of holiness*" (p. 276). What do you think that kind of pursuit might look like? What might be involved in such a pursuit? Do you find this challenge a bit scary? Daunting? Appealing? Why?

5. Discuss the David Brainerd quote at the beginning of the introduction. What could give someone such an intense burden and longing for holiness and for "more of God"? What do you think Brainerd meant by "this pleasing pain"? What does it mean to "press after God"? Have you ever experienced this kind of intense desire in your own heart?

Concluding Prayer
If it expresses the desire of your hearts, one at a time, have each member of the group read aloud the prayer on page 275.

On Your Own
If you've not already done so, take the challenge to pray the prayer on page 275 at least once a day for the next thirty days. Begin to take note of how God is answering this prayer in your life.

Grace Note
Our natural flesh has no appetite for holiness, so don't be discouraged if your honest answers to the questions at the beginning of this study (page 382) reveal that you are not sufficiently concerned about holiness in your life or the lives of those around you—right now. Remember that God gives grace to the humble. You are on a journey, and God won't leave you where you are today.

Chapter One:
THE SPLENDOR
OF HOLINESS

Getting Started

"Holiness isn't exactly an easy subject to 'sell'" (p. 279). Do you agree? If so, why do you think that is the case?

Going Deeper

1. Discuss C. S. Lewis's quote at the beginning of the chapter (p. 278). Do you think most unbelievers think of "holiness" as something *dull* or as something *irresistible*? Why? What about most believers? Why?

2. Review the two facets of holiness explained in this chapter (pp. 281–84).

3. In what sense is holiness the fruit of a relationship?

4. What is the resource that gives us the desire and the power to be holy?

5. *"To resist holiness or to be halfhearted about its pursuit is to forfeit true joy"* (p. 288). Do you agree? How would you explain to someone else the connection between *holiness* and *joy*?

6. This chapter included the account of the elderly couple who moved out of their home and left nothing behind that was inconsistent with their profession of faith (p. 286). Do you think the same thing would be said if someone were to go through "the record of your life"? If not, what would you need to do for that to be true?

7. How do you respond to the concept of "extreme holiness" found in this chapter?

Pray About It

Thank God for His nature and character. Ask Him to give you a new sense of joy and delight in the concept of holiness.

On Your Own

Begin to highlight and make a list of every reference to holiness that you come across in the Scripture (include words like *holy, clean, pure, righteousness, upright,* etc.). Continue to do so throughout the course of this study.

Grace Note

At times our desires for sin feel so strong that the prospect of pursuing "extreme holiness" may seem burdensome. C. S. Lewis uses a wonderful word picture that helps put things in proper perspective:

> If we consider the unblushing promises of reward and the staggering nature of the rewards promised in the Gospels, it would seem that our Lord finds our desires not too strong but too weak. We are halfhearted creatures fooling about with drink and sex and ambition, when infinite joy is offered us, like an ignorant child who wants to go on making mudpies in a slum because he cannot imagine what is meant by the offer of a holiday at the sea. We are far too easily pleased.

Chapter Two:
THE MOTIVATION FOR HOLINESS

Getting Started

Name an individual you have known who has "made God believable" to you. What is it about his or her life that has increased your desire to know God and to become more like Him?

Going Deeper

1. "Why care about being holy? *Why be willing to say no to your flesh and yes to God, day in and day out?*" (p. 301). Review the seven biblical motivations for holy living considered in this chapter.

2. Did any of these points raise a thought you had not seriously considered before as a motivation to pursue holiness?

3. Which of these motivations do you find particularly compelling in terms of your personal pursuit of holiness?

4. Holiness is God's stated goal for every believer. What lesser, competing priorities can tend to consume our time, energy, and focus as believers?

5. How does Christ's sacrifice on the cross provide a motivation to pursue holiness?

6. Can you think of an example of an unbeliever whose view of God was negatively affected by something she saw in a so-called Christian? What about an instance in which an unbeliever was drawn to Christ because of what he saw in a believer?

7. Identify as many categories as you can of people who are watching you and who may either choose or reject the pathway of holiness based on the example of your life (e.g., your family, colleagues at work).

8. *"This world is just a dressing room—a staging area for eternity. How much attention and effort are you devoting to preparing for the move to your eternal home?"* (p. 299). What kinds of things could/should you be doing now to get ready for that move?

On Your Own

Continue compiling biblical references to holiness. As you review your list, note which of the passages might fall under one of the seven motivations for holy living.

Grace Note

On the topic of holiness, it can't be repeated too often: While we do bear personal responsibility for our choices, holiness is not anything we can work up in our own strength. It's grace in action. Remember that every small victory in changing your motivations is a reason to vigorously praise God for His divine help!

Chapter Three:
THE ENEMY OF HOLINESS

Getting Started

This chapter opens with a story of a man who underestimated the true nature of grizzly bears. Have you ever underestimated something extremely dangerous—a storm, an animal, explosives? Share your story and what you learned.

Going Deeper

1. How did this chapter influence your understanding of and your attitude toward sin?

2. *"I wonder if we could be so cavalier about sin if we had any comprehension of how God views it"* (p. 309). How does God view our sin? Why is it important to come to grips with the fact that our sin is a relational offense against God? How does the image of spiritual adultery affect your perspective on your sin?

3. *"'I've become comfortable with a certain level of sin in my life'"* (p. 306). Can you relate to that confession? If so, share an example (past or present) of how you have become desensitized and come to accept sin in your life in "tolerable" doses.

4. *"Beyond how sin affects a holy God and how it affects others, it also exacts a price from those who sin"* (p. 309). Discuss the four consequences of sin considered in this chapter (pp. 309–12). Between the members of your group, see if you can come up with a real-life illustration of each of those consequences.

5. "There is no such thing as a small sin. *Every unconfessed sin is a seed that will produce a multiplied harvest*" (p. 312). Can you think of an illustration of this principle in your own experience?

6. Does your general attitude and response toward your own sin in-

dicate that you take it seriously and that you are grieved by that which grieves God's heart?

7. In this chapter you read the sad story of a man ensnared by the sin of adultery who thought he'd be able to extricate himself, only to discover he couldn't. There may be those in your group or among your relationships who are struggling with some sinful entanglement.

Galatians 6:1–10 is a helpful passage for such situations. According to this passage . . .

- How are we to think of ourselves?
- How are we to help others?
- What principles or insights do you see in verses 6–10 that could be helpful to someone caught in a sinful snare (or to keep someone from falling into a snare)?

Pray About It

Review the J. C. Ryle quote on pages 311–12. Then take time to pray for a clearer view of the enemy of holiness—sin. Ask the Holy Spirit to convict you and others in your group of any sins that have become like "familiar grizzly bears." If time permits, you may want to break down into smaller groups of men and women for confession and prayer, as appropriate.

On Your Own

Page 311 refers to several people who grew accustomed to their sin or treated it lightly—Nebuchadnezzar, Samson, Achan, and Ananias and Sapphira. What did each of these individuals believe sin would "deliver" for him or her and how was he or she deceived?

Grace Note

Some who read this chapter may be tempted to morbid introspection and melancholy. If that is your response, remember this: Yes, sin is the enemy within and the wages of sin is death. But Christ has overcome that enemy. Be sobered by your sin, but rejoice in your Savior!

Chapter Four:
THE FACE
OF HOLINESS

Getting Started

What did you learn from the accounts of Nebuchadnezzar, Samson, Achan, and Ananias and Sapphira (from chapter 3) about the nature and consequences of sin?

Going Deeper

1. Have you ever experienced the kind of struggle, sense of defeat, or discouragement over your sin that Hudson Taylor describes?

2. How would you explain what it was that was so transformational in Taylor's walk with God?

3. *"A pursuit of holiness that is not Christ-centered will soon be reduced to moralism, pharisaical self-righteousness, and futile self-effort. Such pseudo-holiness leads to bondage, rather than liberty . . ."* (p. 324). Can you identify with this statement in your own life?

4. *"No amount of striving or self-effort can make us holy. Only Christ can do that"* (p. 325). Discuss the difference between striving or self-effort, and a Christ-centered pursuit of holiness.

5. What does 2 Corinthians 3:18 tell us about the process of being transformed into the likeness of Christ?

6. Spend some time together simply fixing your eyes on Jesus, in one or more of the following ways.

   - Read aloud one or more of the following passages that describes Him (Hebrews 1:1–3; Colossians 1:13–22; Philippians 2:5–11; Revelation 5).
   - Sing some familiar hymns or choruses that exalt Christ.
   - Praise Him for who He is and for His transforming grace and power in the lives of those He has redeemed.

On Your Own

Read several chapters in one of the four Gospels this week. Meditate on what "holiness in human flesh" looks like.

Grace Note

Are you frequently aware of how you fall short of the glory of God? Does it disturb you that certain sin patterns in your life require such great vigilance and constant battle? When you're tempted to give up, meditate upon the only One who was perfect holiness in human flesh.

As you ponder the Gospels, you will see frequent occasions where the disciples failed as we all do, but you will also discover a Savior who walked in perfect obedience and who has died and been raised again so that we may experience the reality of "Christ in [us], the hope of glory"!

Chapter Five:
THE PATHWAY
TO HOLINESS
("Put Off")

Getting Started

Have you ever wished for a quick and painless path to godliness? Why do you think God didn't design the Christian life to work that way?

Going Deeper

1. Read 2 Peter 1:3–7. What does this passage tell us about *God's* part in our sanctification? What does it tell us about *our* responsibility?

2. The apostle Paul exhorts us to "Put on the Lord Jesus Christ, and make no provision for the flesh, to gratify its desires" (Romans 13:14).

What does it mean to "make provision for the flesh"? What are some ways you have made provision for your flesh at times? What have been the results? What does it mean to "put on the Lord Jesus Christ"? What are some ways we can do that?

3. This chapter introduces the concept of the mortification of sin—the "putting off" of our old, corrupt way of life. Colossians 3:1–17 offers helpful insights into what we are to put off, as well as what we are to put on in its place. Read through this passage together, one paragraph at a time, considering the following questions:

- *Verses 1–3.* What is the theme and significance of this opening paragraph? (Think about the chapter of this book you discussed in the previous lesson.)
- *Verses 5–11.* What are we to "put to death"? Why should these things no longer be a part of the Christian's life?

- *Verses 12–17.* What are we to put on? Why? How do these qualities compare and contrast with the things we are to put off?
- How are Christians described in this passage? How should that description spur us on to pursue holiness?

Giving Thanks

Did you notice the three references to "giving thanks" in Colossians 3:15–17? Why do you think this passage ends with an emphasis on thankfulness? Wrap up your time by offering up prayers (and songs, if you wish!) of thanksgiving for what you have seen in this passage.

On Your Own

"Be killing sin or sin will be killing you" (John Owen, p. 326). Are you consciously committed to waging war against sin in your life? If so, consider these questions:

- Are there any ways you are "making provision" for your flesh? Are you involved in any activities or practices that could increase your appetite for sin? Is there any source of temptation you are holding on to? Are you in any situation that might diminish your resistance to sin? Is there anything that is dulling your spiritual sensitivity or diminishing your love for God and your desire for holiness?

- What are the "guardrails" you need to erect to keep from swerving into sin? Pick an appropriate accountability partner, confess any specific sins you need to "put off" or areas where you have been making provision for your flesh, and share your proposed "guardrails" —then check in with that person on a regular basis to let him or her know how you are doing.

As you "put to death" that which is not pleasing to God, don't forget to also consciously "put on" your new life in Christ! Select one particular virtue from Colossians 3 that you sense a need for in your life; meditate on how that virtue is perfectly manifest in Christ, and ask God to make that quality real in your life by the power of His Holy Spirit.

BROKENNESS · SURRENDER · HOLINESS

Grace Note

No doubt we all have long lists of things we need to "put off." Remember that you aren't asked to make these changes on your own. No one wants to see us "put off" sin more than our heavenly Father! He has given us the Holy Spirit to convict us of sin and help us to change by His grace.

Chapter Six:
THE PATHWAY
TO HOLINESS
("Put On")

Getting Started

If appropriate, share something God showed you or has been doing in your life as you worked through the "On Your Own" section in the last lesson.

Going Deeper

1. *"Sin is a toxin that contaminates to the core of the human soul. When God saved us, it was with the intent of cleansing us from every vestige of sin"* (p. 339). How do these two statements differ from the way many believers actually live?

Last time, we discussed the concepts of "putting off" sin and "putting on" godliness. But sanctification isn't just about replacing one habit with another. It's about developing love for Christ and a taste for holiness and being filled with His Spirit. This chapter highlighted six ways to experience intimacy with God and to be transformed into the likeness of Christ—six "means of grace."

2. Review these "means of grace" by walking through the "Making It Personal" section on pages 349–51. Discuss how each of these areas is essential in our pursuit of holiness.

3. As you highlight these six areas, share with one another any particular points where you have recognized a lack or a need in your own life. Share any specific steps God has put on your heart for being more intentional in taking advantage of these means of grace.

Giving Thanks

It's not often that you hear Christians praise God for the grace found in things such as confession, discipline, or suffering. But they are indeed praiseworthy because of what they produce in our lives! End this meeting by doing just that.

On Your Own

Which of these "means of grace" need intentional development in your life? List two or three steps you will take to allow God to use these means more fully in your life. Share this plan with your accountability partner. (And don't forget to give an update about your "guardrails"!)

Grace Note

Did you look at the "means of grace" and see another "to-do" list? It's really not. It's a lavish menu of transforming grace. It's an arsenal of resources for change. Isn't it kind of the Lord to give us so many avenues for pursuing change?

Chapter Seven:
THE HEART
OF HOLINESS

Getting Started

"A commitment to holiness means having a life that is always 'ready for company' and open for inspection—a life that can stand up to scrutiny—not just in the obvious things, but in the hidden places where most might not think to look" (p. 354).

Does that kind of standard motivate you or discourage you? What can help us *want* to live this way? What can help us be *able* to live this way?

Going Deeper

1. What was it about the Pharisees that evoked such a strong response from the Lord Jesus?

2. How would you define hypocrisy? Why is it so abhorrent to God? Did God reveal any hypocrisy in your own life as you read this chapter? How did you respond to the questions on page 355?

3. Take time to discuss how God worked in your heart through the "Making It Personal" section in this chapter (pp. 356–61). Which points did He identify as areas of need in your life? How are you responding to His conviction?

Pray About It

Close your time by praying for one another in the specific areas of need that have been shared. Thank God for the ways His grace and His Spirit are at work in each of your lives.

Grace Note

A list of questions such as those found in this chapter can be over-whelming for some people. Remember God's not asking us to be re-formed into a better version of ourselves—He's wanting to *conform* us to the image of perfection in His Son! "He who calls you is faithful; he will surely do it" (1 Thessalonians 5:24)!

Chapter Eight:
THE PASSION
FOR HOLINESS
Epilogue: Here Comes the Bride!

Getting Started

"Conspicuous holiness ought to be the mark of the church of God" (C. H. Spurgeon, p. 362). What are some of the things our churches today are most known for? Do you think "holiness" would be high on the list of most observers?

Going Deeper

1. Review the story of how God sent revival to Romania in the 1970s. What might it look like today if "the repenters" began to repent— if God's people took holiness seriously and turned from everything they knew was not pleasing to Him? What kinds of changes would take place—in individual believers, in Christian homes, in our churches, in our communities, our nation, and our culture?

2. *"We have accommodated to the world rather than calling the world to accommodate to Christ"* (p. 365). Do you agree with that statement? If so, what evidences do you see of it being true? Why do you think it is so? What should be true instead?

3. What parallels do you see between the Jews in Nehemiah's day and the church in our day? Why do you think we are seeing such an epidemic of sin in the church (i.e., among professing believers) today? What qualities do you see in Nehemiah's life that are needed in believers today?

4. Share the highlights of this study and what fruit you've seen from reading about and discussing holiness. How has your view of God changed? What about your understanding of holiness? Of sin? How have you been growing in "putting off" and "putting on"? What about growing in the means of grace?

5. The epilogue depicted an unimaginable scene in which a bride doesn't care enough about her groom to get ready for the wedding! There's another Wedding coming soon. *"The bridegroom is a holy Bridegroom, and He must have a holy bride"* (p. 378). Are you ready for the Wedding? If not, what would you have to do to be ready? What can you do to encourage others in the Bride to get ready for the Wedding?

Pray About It

Nehemiah was compelled by a passion for the glory of God to be displayed in His people. Among the first things Nehemiah did when he became aware of the trouble in Jerusalem was to fast and pray for the people of Israel. Let us be faithful to do the same for the bride of Christ. Conclude your study by praying together for the church to take holiness seriously and to be ready to meet her Bridegroom as a radiant bride, "holy and without blemish" (Ephesians 5:27).

On Your Own

At the beginning of this study, you were asked to respond to a series of questions. How would you answer those same questions now?

1. How important is holiness to you? How much thought, attention, and effort do you devote to the pursuit of holiness? Are you intentional about putting away everything that is displeasing to God and living a holy life?

2. [if applicable] How important is your children's holiness to you? Does their sin drive you to your knees?

3. How concerned are you about the holiness of the body of Christ? Does it grieve you when you see yourself or others treating sin lightly?

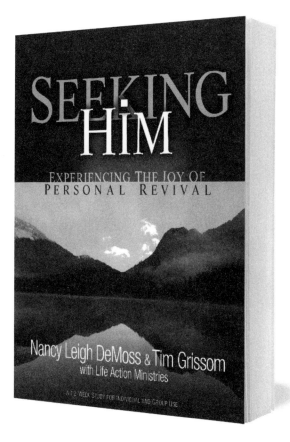

Revival is not just an emotional touch . . . but a complete transformation! It can happen . . . in your heart . . . in your home . . . in your church . . . in your world.

Seeking Him is a 12-week interactive study on personal revival. Get ready to experience the freedom and joy of an honest and humble heart, true repentance, God's amazing grace, genuine holiness, a clear conscience, radical forgiveness, sexual purity, and walking in the Spirit. Each week includes five days of individual study, questions for group discussion and interaction, testimonies of changed lives, and "Making it Personal" questions and exercises. God says that if you seek Him you will find Him. What are you waiting for?

by Nancy Leigh DeMoss and Tim Grissom
Find it now at your favorite local or online bookstore.

www.MoodyPublishers.com

Calling Women to Freedom, Fullness, and Fruitfulness in Christ

Revive Our Hearts™

.com

with Nancy Leigh DeMoss

www.ReviveOurHearts.com

OVER ONE-THIRD MILLION SOLD

LIES WOMEN BELIEVE

AND THE TRUTH THAT
SETS THEM FREE

FOREWORD BY ELISABETH ELLIOT

NANCY LEIGH DEMOSS

We are like Eve. We have all experienced defeats and failures, trouble and turmoil. We have all experienced a selfish heart, a shrewish spirit, anger, envy, and bitterness. And we ache to do things over, to have lives of harmony and peace. Nancy Leigh DeMoss exposes those areas of deception most commonly believed by Christian women. She sheds light on how we can be delivered from bondage and set free to walk in God's grace, forgiveness, and abundant life. The book offers the most effective weapon to counter and overcome Satan's deceptions—God's truth.

by Nancy Leigh DeMoss
Find it now at your favorite local or online bookstore.

www.MoodyPublishers.com

Scripture says that offenses will happen. People will let us down and we will let others down, as well. Forgiveness is left up to us to pray about and then practice. Far from minimizing the hurt of the offense, readers are called to understand that offering forgiveness and letting go of bitterness is the only way to walk in faithfulness. Drawing on biblical teaching of our call to forgive, Nancy shows the reader that forgiveness is a choice—and the only pathway to true freedom. The study guide currently found online is now included in the book. First time in paperback.

by Nancy Leigh DeMoss
Find it now at your favorite local or online bookstore.

www.MoodyPublishers.com